Dave and Jon Ferguson are two of ~~~ ~~~ ~~~ ~~~ ~~~ ~~~ n-
planters I know. Their new book, E. ~~~ ~~~ ~~~ ~~~ ~~~ s
and essential spiritual insights to plar ~~~ ~~~ ~~~ ~~~ ~~~ l.

—Craig Groeschel,
pastor of Lifechurch.tv and author of *It*

Dave and Jon Ferguson's work on reproducing leaders and catalyzing movements has the great potential to awaken the sleeping giant of the American church. It is a timely word for our generation of church leaders.

—Matt Carter,
Austin Stone Community Church

Dave and Jon Ferguson are the poster children for ministry reproduction. It's what they live and breathe. Their story of the lessons learned launching Community Christian Church and the NewThing Network will inspire and instruct anyone who longs for a genuinely reproducing ministry. But be forewarned, reading this book might do more. Who knows, it just might unleash the unique ministry dream God has birthed in your own heart as well.

—Larry Osborne,
pastor and author, North Coast Church

Jon and Dave Ferguson have been pictures to every young church-planter of the courage, faith, and sacrifice needed to start a missional reproducing movement in the church. They are passionate about helping people find their way back to God, and this book should be required reading for anyone who has ever wondered if they should start a church. If you are sitting with a dream, read this book at your own risk, but know that it will definitely push you to take the necessary step of faith which will unlock the greatest adventure of your life.

—Jeanne Stevens,
lead pastor, Soul City Church

Whether pastor, priest, or peasant, we all want to be a part of something bigger than ourselves. If you're tired of having God just for yourself, and desire to see your life and your church find their place in God's magnificent global renaissance, this book is for you.

—Hugh Halter,
author of *The Tangible Kingdom*, *AND*, and *TK Primer*

The church is a major part of God's heart for bringing his people back to his love. This book helps us to return to the reproducing-church movement, which is a fulfillment of his great commission. We need to see a greater movement toward reproducing churches around the world, and the only institution that can reproduce church is the local church.

—Marc Choi,
lead pastor, In2 Church

Exponential is filled with practical examples, compelling vision, and inspiring stories. It will provoke you to reproduce everything at a time when so many churches are not even adding. Jon and Dave are not just theorists. I've seen their ministry up close, and they deeply care that people find their way back to God.

—Ed Stetzer,
president, LifeWay Research

This book will be a great tool for young leaders and church-planters in Europe. It's simple, to the point, challenging, and encouraging. I love it.

—N.D. Strupler,
ICF Movement—Church Planting for Europe

Dave and Jon Ferguson are the real deal. I'm so grateful for their leadership and friendship. When our church made the move to multisite, they helped us navigate the new terrain. No matter where you are in your leadership journey, this book will stretch you and challenge you.

—Mark Batterson,
lead pastor, National Community Church

EXPONENTIAL

Other Books in the Exponential Series

≡XPONENTIAL
series

How You and Your Friends Can Start a
Missional Church Movement

EXPONENTIAL

DAVE FERGUSON & JON FERGUSON

ZONDERVAN®

ZONDERVAN.com/
AUTHOR**TRACKER**
follow your favorite authors

LEADERSHIP ✖ NETWORK®

ZONDERVAN

Exponential
Copyright © 2010 by Dave Ferguson and Jon Ferguson

This title is also available as a Zondervan ebook. Visit www.zondervan.com/ebooks.

This title is also available in a Zondervan audio edition. Visit www.zondervan.fm.

Requests for information should be addressed to:

Zondervan, *Grand Rapids, Michigan 49530*

Library of Congress Cataloging-in-Publication Data

Ferguson, Dave, 1962–
    Exponential : how you and your friends can start a missional church movement / Dave Ferguson and Jon Ferguson.
       p. cm.—(Exponential series)
       ISBN 978-0-310-32678-6 (softcovers)
       1. Church development, New. 2. Ferguson, Dave, 1962– I. Ferguson, Jon. II. Title.
    BV652.24.F47 2010
    254′.1—dc22
                                                      2010001882

Cover design: *Rob Monacelli*
Interior illustration: *Matthew Van Zomeren and Mark Sheeres*
Interior design: *Matthew Van Zomeren*

Printed in the United States of America

10 11 12 13 14 15 16 /DCI/ 24 23 22 21 20 19 18 17 16 15 14 13 12 11 10 9 8 7 6 5 4 3 2 1

To the two who believed in us
before we ever knew that God believed in us.
To the two who loved us unconditionally
before we ever understood the relentless grace of God.
To the two who were already giving their lives for the mission of Jesus
before we ever considered for what we would trade our lives.
Mom and Dad, thanks!

—Dave and Jon

CONTENTS

FOREWORD

If there was ever a word that captures a sense of the need for a change in the way we currently do church, it is the word *exponential*. The word itself expresses something of the heart, as well as the mathematics, of the missional paradigm. It conveys both a prophetic challenge to the prevailing ways of doing church in the Western world as well as an apostolic promise of real fruitfulness, should we take it seriously.

I have had the privilege of working with Dave and Jon and NewThing team for a while now, and what intrigues me about them is that they are not willing to settle with already great results; they desire to move to the next, and somewhat risky, edge. And this book, I believe, points us in the direction of where that edge is—toward exponential, transformative, missional Jesus movements.

Dave and Jon's story, and the story of NewThing, mirrors the story of the contemporary American church over the last decade or two. They are as many of us desire to be—successful leaders of a very large multisite church. The Ferguson brothers are at the forefront of what is happening in the American church and are informing opinion and action all over the world. But one doesn't get to this place simply by parroting the inherited wisdom. It demands that we further develop it without invalidating it. And because of this capacity to connect with current thinking as well as extend it, they embody the best of contemporary church thinking and practice, and yet they call us to go beyond current ways of thinking that limit our capacity to see the church as a missional movement.

Starting *missional* church movements is at the core of this new thinking. If the church-growth movement ushered in the era of the contemporary church, the megachurch, and the multisite phenomenon, then what the new missional paradigm will do is to stretch us by requiring that we take seriously again the sent-ness of all of God's people. The Ferguson brothers know that to do this, the church must move from addition to multiplication: it cannot *just* be about adding numbers to existing churches until they grow very large. It must *also* mean multiplying the actual number of churches, as well as empowering all of God's people in every sphere of life to be the church. This is going to take lots of new thinking and a whole lot of courageous action. And *Exponential* is a great example of that.

This is a thoroughly practical, genuinely innovative, and truly inspirational book, woven around a story of how a group of friends, captured by a grander view of God's kingdom, are on a journey to discovering what it means to be truly missional.

I am deeply honored even to be a small part of that journey.

—Alan Hirsch
author of *The Forgotten Ways* and
Untamed (with Debra Hirsch)
www.theforgottenways.org

INTRODUCTION

Reproduction: The Fibonacci Effect

The great mathematician Leonardo Fibonacci (c. 1170 – c. 1250) was asked to solve a math problem: if you put a pair of rabbits in a place surrounded by walls, how many pairs of rabbits can be produced from that pair in a year if every month each pair produces a new pair after it has been alive one month? Fibonacci began to crunch the numbers to solve the problem using the only tool he had — Roman numerals. Roman numerals were a clumsy tool at best, barely allowing him to add and subtract. Just to multiply or divide he had to use an abacus and then translate his results into Roman numerals. Frustrated, Fibonacci remembered the ten-digit Arabic numerals he was introduced to as a boy during his travels with his father and started using them to calculate:

The result of his calculations was an amazing sequence that became known as the Fibonacci Sequence:

Fibonacci calculated that after one year there would be 233 pairs of rabbits, or 466 rabbits, and that after two years of rabbit reproduction there would be more than 150,000 rabbits. After two and a half years there would be more than two and a half million rabbits! Not only did Fibonacci solve the problem of rabbit reproduction, he also, by introducing Arabic numerals to Europe, changed forever how we do math and how we count. No longer would we use Roman numerals; instead we use ten-digit notation, a much more efficient method for calculating exponential reproduction.

Jesus said, "You will receive power when the Holy Spirit comes upon you; and you will be my witnesses in Jerusalem, and in all Judea and Samaria, and to the ends of the earth" (Acts 1:8). Jesus has given his church the problem of rapid reproduction; how do we take his mission to the ends of the earth?

We are losing ground fast:

* Today, fewer than 20 percent of Americans attend church regularly, and only 22 percent have a positive view of church.
* Half of all churches in America did not add one person through conversion last year.
* Every week, forty-three thousand Americans are leaving the church for good.
* One hundred years ago, there were twenty-eight churches for every ten thousand Americans, and today there are only eleven churches per ten thousand.

If you do the math, we are not solving the mission problem given to us by Jesus.

What you are about to read is a way for us to go to the ends of the earth. If we rely on church growth at a single church with a single site, it is like Fibonacci using Roman numerals to solve the problem of rabbit reproduction. When it comes to rapid reproduction, old church-growth models are clumsy at best.

If we want to solve Jesus' mission problem of going to "Jerusalem ... Judea ... Samaria ... to the ends of the earth," we are going to have to find a new kind of math and a new way to count that results in rapid reproduction. That new math is exponential. The new way to count is by counting on you and your friends to start a missional church movement.

Let's get movin'!

PART ONE

MOVEMENTS START WITH 1

DO!

Every movement starts with one person. When you and your friends become apprentices of Jesus, you will follow in his footsteps and say to others, "Come follow me." The result can be the beginning of a missional church movement. For a Reproducing Leader Assessment, go to *www.reproducingleader.org.*

YOU

The Beginning of a Movement

BIG IDEA A missional movement can start with you.

- ✱ Our Dream on a Napkin
- ✱ The Story of Community Christian Church
- ✱ Five Reproducing Principles We've Learned

YOU

"You can do it." The moment I heard those simple words — "You can do it" — it was like someone had reached inside my soul and flipped on a switch. What had seemed impossible just moments before was now suddenly possible! Before you finish reading this chapter, I want you to have that same experience. I believe that sometime during the next several pages, God will reach inside *your* soul and convince you that what might seem impossible is *possible*, what you think is improbable can *happen*, and what you may have thought was just a pipe dream may very well be a *God thing*. But before we get to all that, let me back up a bit and tell you a bit of my story.*

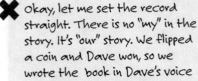

Okay, let me set the record straight. There is no "my" in the story. It's "our" story. We flipped a coin and Dave won, so we wrote the book in Dave's voice and added occasional color commentary.   —Jon

OUR DREAM ON A NAPKIN

As a college student, I had way too much time on my hands. Together with my friends, I would spend hours inventing games and pulling pranks on underclassmen, just to pass the time. "Lang Hall Fall Wall Ball" was a game we invented that combined handball and dodgeball and was played in the hallway of Lang

Hall. Though it does absolutely nothing for your GPA, a small rubber ball and a dormitory hallway can provide hours of entertainment and competition. When we weren't playing games in the hallway, we'd think of creative ways to fool unsuspecting freshmen. One of my favorite pranks in those years was sneaking into rooms and setting clocks five hours ahead, getting our helpless freshmen roommates to believe it was 6:00 a.m. when it was really 1:00 a.m. We'd laugh our heads off watching them shower, dress, and head out the door to the cafeteria, only to find it closed. But those years weren't just a time for playing games and wasting time. We also did our share of dreaming in college. Not just daydreaming through our classes but also really dreaming big about how God might want to use us.

A few years after graduating, I was sitting in Potter's Place, this little dive of a Mexican restaurant in downtown Naperville, thinking back on those college years. Together with my college roommate, Scott Alexander, my brother, Jon, and his friend, Darren Sloniger, we had just started Community Christian Church. The four of us had shared a common dream—reaching out to the Chicagoland area. We knew that it would take a very "complicated" strategy for us to actually reach all eight million people in the greater metro area of Chicago. So to get started, we had taken a map of Chicago and pinned it to a bulletin board on our dorm room wall. Then we divided Chicago among the four of us in the room and devised an innovative and "sophisticated" strategy for taking the entire city and the suburbs for Jesus. Each of us agreed to take a fourth of the metro area and accepted the mission of reaching a mere two million people. At the time, it was a grand idea and we were completely naive, but we actually believed it was *possible*.

As I sat in the Mexican restaurant that day remembering the God-sized dreams that had led us to plant our church, it got me dreaming again. So I pulled out a napkin and sketched out a completely new plan. I drew Lake Michigan, filled out the boundaries of the city of Chicago, and then began to draw circles, each representing different churches,—possible sites of Community that would be scattered all over the Chicago area. I was beginning to get a sense of a fresh vision, looking beyond my dream of four individuals dividing up a city to a dream of one church with many locations reaching various parts of the Chicagoland area. I thought about what I had drawn, then folded up the napkin and slipped it inside my journal.

That napkin stayed in my journal for the next four years. To be honest, I never showed the napkin to anyone and basically kept it to myself. Then one morning I was having breakfast with my friend Larry.* Larry was

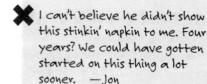
I can't believe he didn't show this stinkin' napkin to me. Four years? We could have gotten started on this thing a lot sooner. —Jon

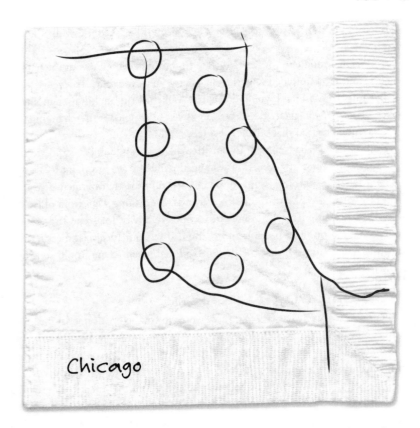

Chicago

a very successful entrepreneur. He drove a light blue Mercedes and was always dressed to the nines. In some ways, the trappings of wealth and the several businesses he had started impressed me. Larry was also finding his way back to God, and he had expressed some interest in how we did church. Even though he was still growing as a Christian, he was able to see some parallels between his entrepreneurial endeavors and how we had started our church from scratch. About halfway through my scrambled eggs and bacon, Larry asked me a very direct question. "So Dave, what is the dream?" He paused for a moment, and then he added a real zinger that I wasn't expecting. "If you could do anything, what would you do?"

There was silence on my end. I began thinking to myself, "Do I really tell him my dream? What if he thinks I'm crazy?" Even though it may seem innocent, a question about someone's life dream is really very personal. I knew that if I were to answer the question honestly and tell him the truth about my dream, it would be out there and I'd feel like I had to own it. I'd be forced to pursue it. So I didn't respond right away. I was afraid.

But Larry was persistent, and after a few seconds he asked me again, "Dave, what is the dream?"

And in that moment, for the first time in four years, I pulled out the napkin from my journal. I unfolded it on the table between us and said, "Larry, if I could do anything, this is what I would do." Larry looked at the napkin for a moment, looked up at me, and then said something that was simple yet life-changing.

"Dave, you can do that. Yeah, I can see you doing that."

Each of us has that moment in our life when we can look back and see that from that point forward, everything changed. And if I were to point to a single moment when everything changed for me, it would be that moment sitting at breakfast with Larry. With those simple words, everything went from off to on. What had just moments before seemed impossible was, for some strange and unexpected reason, now possible in my mind. I left our breakfast meeting that morning truly believing that the dream God had given to me would somehow come to life.

"YOU CAN DO IT"

I don't know if anyone has ever said those words to you before. If not, let me be the first: "You can do it." Yes, I'm talking to you. Yes, you—the one holding this book in your hands, the one reading the words on this page. I want you to hear this and believe that as sure as the day you were born, God has birthed within you a dream.

You may even have a hunch about that dream. Or maybe you are still searching and have yet to discover it. Perhaps, like me, you've tucked the dream away for the last several years and have not had the courage to say it out loud. You haven't talked about it with anyone. It might even seem a little foolish to you. Regardless of where you are at right now, I want you to hear those words again: "You *can* do it." If it were possible for me to sit across the table from you right now and speak to you face-to-face, I would love for you to hear those words personally spoken over your life.

Now, when I tell you, "You can do it," I don't want you to just take my word for it. I say these words to you because I want you to take Jesus at his word—to have faith in *his* word to you. Just before Jesus left this planet, he gave us, his followers, the mission of helping people find their way back to God. He promised us that we would have everything we would need to fulfill the mission he had for us: "You will receive power when the Holy Spirit comes on you; and you will be my witnesses in Jerusalem, and in all Judea and Samaria, and to the ends of the earth" (Acts 1:8). Notice again what Jesus says about this mission. Reread the verse for a moment.

* Who does Jesus say will receive power? *me*
* Who does Jesus say will be his witnesses? *me*
* Who does Jesus say will accomplish God's dream of world redemption?

me.

Jesus is quite clear as he speaks to his followers. He says "you." In other words, Jesus is saying to them and to us who follow him today, "You can do it." Sure, we have a million questions about how all of this will actually come true, but right now I want you to forget about the specifics and the details and just listen to what Jesus is saying to you. He is telling you that he wants *you* to do it. God is saying to you, to your friends, and to each of his followers, "*You* can do it." The movement that will eventually accomplish the mission of Jesus lives within you and me!

THE STORY OF COMMUNITY CHRISTIAN CHURCH

The naivete of our college-dorm dream to reach Chicago would somehow resurrect itself every time the four of us got together. Each of us was leading ministries at various places scattered throughout the Midwest. Our conversations were often spontaneous. They would happen on the phone or when we would hang out together on the weekends. Eventually

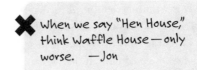

When we say "Hen House," think Waffle House—only worse. —Jon

this group of four friends started meeting together to seriously plan the launch of a new church. One of our meeting places was the exotic Hen House Restaurant in Dwight, Illinois.* It was there that we agreed on the specifics of a three-phased vision for Community.

OUR VISION

Phase 1: Impact Church

To be an impact church meant we would be a church that was relentless about impacting people who were living outside a relationship with Jesus. We were never interested in reaching people who were already attending church. Our intent was to reach people who were far from God. That is why our mission statement was "Helping people find their way back to God," and it has remained the same to this day.

Phase 2: Reproducing Church

Even in the beginning, we weren't content with simply growing one large church that would reach a lot of people. We thought we could reach more people by growing big *as well as* reproducing over and over again. At that time, the idea of a multisite church was virtually nonexistent, and so we assumed that we would accomplish all of this by planting lots of new churches.

Phase 3: Catalyst for a Movement of Reproducing Churches

Our vision was to have an impact far beyond the city of Chicago or even the United States. We hoped to one day see a movement of reproducing churches. Our team talked about this and committed it to prayer, but when we would share the vision with others, we would often only talk about the first two phases and leave this phase out. Why? I don't think we really believed that it was possible. But in our most courageous moments we would state this as part of our vision.

OUR MISSION

It took us only an afternoon to figure out a three-phase vision that we are still trying to accomplish, but it took us more than a year to settle on a phrase that best expresses our mission. It was about eighteen months into the life of Community that Jon and I heard Lyman Coleman retell the story of the prodigal son. With great conviction, he reminded us that we are all prodigals and that there are many prodigals in our communities who have yet to find their way back to the Father. Listening to Lyman share his passion for prodigals made our hearts beat fast, and we were convinced that we had just found our mission statement: "Helping people find their way back to God."

This mission statement resonates with the unchurched in their growing spiritual hunger. However, the churched will sometimes say, "Why do you say 'back' to God if we are trying to reach lost people?" The answer starts with the understanding that "in the beginning" God created a perfect world and had a perfect relationship with all of his creation, including man. This is evident by God's declaring that creation "is very good." But in the middle of this perfect community, man sinned and put relational distance between himself and God. Man went from intimacy with God to a state of lostness, and just like the father in the story of the prodigal son, our heavenly Father was grieved and desired for all of us to find our way back to him. Second Corinthians 5:18, 20 explains this: "It is all from God. He brought us back to himself through Christ's death on the cross. And he has given us the task of bringing others back to him through Christ.... So we are Christ's official messengers. It is as if God were making his appeal through us. Here is what Christ wants us to beg you to do. Come back to God!" (NIrV). God's love was so passionate that he came in the person of Jesus to provide the way back to that perfect relationship with the Father. As followers of Jesus, we are given the task of "helping people find their way back to God."

While the phrase "helping people find their way back to God" reflects the heartbeat of Community, two numbers remind us of whom we are working to reach: sixty-seven and twenty. If the world were a village of a hundred people, sixty-seven would be far from God, facing a Christless existence. And twenty of the one hundred would be living in extreme poverty. It is our mission to reach the sixty-seven and come alongside the twenty, helping all people find their way back to God.✱

 I know most of my comments are sarcastic, but this right here — "hpftwbtG" — that's a mission worth dying for. —Jon

GETTING STARTED

A few months after my wife, Sue, and I were married, we moved to the western suburbs of Chicago. At about that same time, my friend Scott invited a seminary buddy of his, Georgia Kurko, to join our team. With my wife and Georgia, our initial church-planting team had already increased by 50 percent! Darren and Scott shared an apartment, and my brother, Jon, moved in with me and my new bride. Georgia's apartment served as our multipurpose facility—all six hundred square feet of it. We used it for everything from children's ministry training to student ministry activities to equipment storage. Scott was the oldest person in our group at twenty-six, and Darren the youngest at twenty-one. We had no money to speak of, no people to help us, and, truthfully, no clue what we were doing! We were true entrepreneurs.

Every day for four months straight, we knocked on doors, getting to know the people in our new community. Marketing gurus now tell us that about 250 surveys provide you with a good random sampling. We knocked on more than 5,000 doors. We figured that if door-to-door surveys worked for Rick Warren and Bill Hybels when they started their churches, then we might as well try to do as many as we possibly could.

We asked people what they might look for in a new church. We asked them what they believed were the most significant needs in their community. We even asked them, "If you were to attend a church based only on the name, which church would you attend?" Then we showed them our short list of possible names to see which ones they liked best.

Every church planter thinks that it's the name of his church that will attract the crowds and change the world, and so they come up with all sorts of "cool-sounding" names. You'll even find some of those names among our NewThing churches, names like The Pursuit, Reunion, Restore, 242, Paseo, Crossing—all of them very cool-sounding. I'm not sure what they all mean, really, but I'm sure they are cool! Obviously, we also wanted a creative and hip name for our church. But my wife, Sue, kept insisting on Community Christian Church. "I like Community Christian Church," she'd say. "It's simple and makes sense … you should just call it Community Christian Church." I hated the name. It was boring, predictable, and lacked any sense of creativity. But she insisted and insisted. Finally, totally confident that unchurched people would support my view and prove her wrong, I added her suggested name to our survey along with my favorites. You can probably guess what happened. After surveying thousands of people in our community, we found that the name they liked best (by a ratio of ten to one) was Community Christian Church. And that's the name we've kept ever since.

FIVE REPRODUCING PRINCIPLES WE'VE LEARNED

Reproducing Small Groups

Long before we launched a celebration service, each one of us started a small group. We had only one problem. We had no people in our church. To solve this dilemma, we decided we'd each start a group and then show up at each other's group meetings so we could create a perception that there were at least a few people interested in this new church. We all discussed the same small group lesson and used the same icebreaker every night of the week. You can probably imagine how monotonous this was for us, hearing the same answers to the same questions from the same people night after night, and pretending like it was the first time we'd heard them. Looking back, it was a crazy way to start, but as a church planter, you just do whatever you have to do to get things going.

The key to reproducing each of those first small groups that we led was asking someone in our group to be our apprentice leader. An apprentice leader is someone who agrees to be developed and mentored as a leader and is eventually released to start a new small group. One of my first small group apprentices was a guy by the name of Jerry. Jerry was not even a believer, but he was actively searching for God, and that was good enough for me. Jerry eventually made a commitment to become a Christ follower, was baptized, and then immediately reproduced and started leading a new small group. Since that time, those small groups of eight to twelve people have reproduced countless times. Today we are a church with more than seven thousand attenders and a network of more than thirty thousand people celebrating every week with several thousand reproducing small groups.

Though we didn't fully realize it at the time, I cannot overstate the significance of insisting that every small group begin with a leader and an apprentice leader. Looking back, that one decision was foundational in establishing us as a reproducing church. Don't just skim over these words. I realize you may have heard this before. But take the time to highlight it if it will help you remember it. *As I look back, I am convinced that insisting every small group begin with a leader and an apprentice leader was one of the most important choices we ever made.* This is our first reproducing principle.

REPRODUCING PRINCIPLE 1

*Reproducing requires everyone
to have an apprentice.*

Reproducing Celebration Services

When we finally had our first public service, there were about forty people in small groups that made up our launch team (I'm not counting all the doubles, since our team was still attending every group!). We depended heavily on guerrilla marketing techniques like direct mail, newspaper advertising, billboards, and telemarketing. I'm serious; we actually did telemarketing for our church! I'm not proud of it. I don't recommend it. But we did it. Fifty-two thousand dial-ups! We somehow managed to get the word out about this new church, and a grand total of 465 people showed up for our very first service at Naperville Central High School. After all the energy we had invested to pull off that first service, I remember our tired team thinking, "We gotta do this every week now?!" And of course we did.

> **✖** It was July Fourth weekend. After that weekend, my wife, Lisa, and I started revising my resume.   —Jon

We began with a single celebration service at 10:00 a.m. on Sunday morning in the high school cafeteria. After our grand opening Sunday, we worked tirelessly to get as many people connected to our small groups as we possibly could. By the time summer rolled around, we had somehow managed to shrink that crowd of 465 down to a low of 130 adults and children.*

Even though we weren't seeing nearly as many people as we had hoped on weekends, that summer we made the decision to add a second service, just six months after we launched. I like to remind Jon that he didn't think we were ready to add another service. He likes to remind me that we had a grand total of about ninety adults sitting in a room that could easily hold five hundred. At the end of the debate, we decided to reproduce a celebration service and have one at 9:00 a.m. and another at 10:30 a.m. Why? Because we were convinced that an additional service would provide more space and another option that would help even more people find their way back to God.

About that same time, John and Cindy Arney, a couple in our church, had just given birth to twin boys. In preparation for the launch of our second service, I brought the twins onstage with me—one in each arm. I said to our young congregation, "This is what we are going to do in just a few months. We are going to reproduce. We will soon have two identical services, one at 9:00 a.m. and another at 10:30 a.m." This decision was based on another important reproducing principle.

REPRODUCING PRINCIPLE 2

Reproducing is proactive, not reactive.

The cafeteria at Naperville Central High School had room for more than four times the number of adults who were currently attending. With several hundred thousand square feet of space available, we had plenty of room for Kids' City, our children's ministry. We were using only a fraction of the parking available, so parking wasn't a challenge either. We weren't going to wait until the room was 80 percent full or we ran out of parking spaces before we reproduced.

 We reproduced another service because we believed that a new service would give more people more options. As long as we were prepared to care for these new people in our reproducing small groups, we believed God would send us people who needed to find their way back to him. This was the first time we actually put into practice the reproducing principle that we would be proactive and not reactive about our reproduction as a church. We intentionally decided that we would not simply wait for growth to happen to us—we would make room for people who weren't even there yet. We would make room for people while *anticipating* that growth would happen. And we've continued to reproduce celebration services ever since that day. We now have more than twenty-nine services every weekend, scattered across our various campuses in the Chicagoland area, and NewThing (our network of reproducing churches) has churches all over the world that are proactively reproducing celebration services on a regular basis.

Reproducing Campuses

Over the next several years, Community steadily grew to about seven hundred people by reproducing our small groups and our celebration services. This growth forced us to move from the cafeteria to a small theater at Naperville Central High School and eventually to a larger, seven-hundred-seat auditorium at Naperville North High School.

It was at that time that a real estate developer attending one of our small groups, who had recently become a Christ follower, asked me yet another life-changing question: "How can we get this experience of genuine community in the twenty-six properties we are developing across the Midwest?" We'll share more of the events that followed his question, but suffice it to say that the answer we came up with eventually led to a partnership and the building of a brand-new community center for the church. Our only challenge in building this new facility was that the center would be located two towns away from our current location, in a town called Romeoville. At the time, I just couldn't see how I could possibly ask seven hundred people to gather in a community where most of them didn't live. As we processed through this question, it raised a different question for us, one we had never considered before.

("What if we had one church that met in two different locations?")

I don't know which one of us first asked the question. My friend in real estate had one company with twenty-six locations, and I had my dream to reach Chicago on the back of a napkin in my journal. Regardless of which one of us first asked it, Community eventually decided to have two locations, and we became one of the first churches in the United States to be *one* church with *multiple* locations.

Of the seven hundred people who attended, only a few lived in Romeoville. So how could we start a new campus there? To start a new location, you need to have lots of people, right? Well, not quite. What you really need is not large *numbers* of people but the *right* person. Our venture into the world of multisite was forcing us to come to grips with yet another reproducing principle.

REPRODUCING PRINCIPLE 3

Reproducing is not about size;
it's about leader readiness.

If we could find the right leader, then the right people and the right number of people would follow. We found that Troy McMahon was the right leader for this new campus. He had proven his faithfulness as an apprentice leader, as a leader, as a coach, and as a director on our staff. Troy left his fast-track corporate climb in the business world to join our team and lead the charge in starting this new location. Along with Troy were 120 people who followed him to be a part of the launch team for our Romeoville campus.* Since the launch of that first campus, Community has launched ten other campuses and as of this writing has a total of eleven sites locally in the Chicago area. Along with our campuses, every one of the churches planted in our NewThing church-planting network is committed to reproducing sites and new churches.

 Troy was and is a great leader, but his fast-track corporate climb had him managing a plant where they made Hamburger Helper. —Jon

Reproducing Churches

As we continued to reproduce groups, celebration services, and campuses, God was clearly shaping us into something new—a reproducing church. A couple of years after our Romeoville launch, Dave Richa, our student community director, came to us and said he was interested in planting a new church in Denver, Colorado. Truthfully, I was a little put out that he didn't want to stay at Community. To be honest, it was kind of annoying that he had a vision for how to do church better than we were doing it. Dave took that vision to Denver, where he met with the pastors of several large churches, as well as a couple of church-planting organizations. They shared his vision and were enthusiastic about his coming to Denver to plant a new church. He returned to tell us that these leaders were not only excited about his vision; they were inspired enough to commit thousands of dollars to seeing it come to life. We couldn't deny that God was at work, and through these circumstances we learned another reproducing principle.

REPRODUCING PRINCIPLE 4

Reproducing isn't about our kingdom; it's about God's kingdom.

I remember standing in front of Community and telling our people, "If God is sending Dave Richa to start a new church in Denver, then God wants some of you to go with him." Over the next several weeks, people began to respond to God's prompting. It was amazing—thirty-five people sold their homes, got new jobs or transferred schools, and went with Dave to start this new church. The launch of this church became the first of what is now an international network of reproducing churches called NewThing.

Reproducing Networks

As we helped start even more reproducing churches and as existing churches began to align themselves with NewThing, we decided that we would host a semi-annual gathering of the lead pastors from these reproducing churches. There were only four of us at the first gathering, six at the second, and nine at the third. As we continued to reproduce, we began to believe that this little network of church leaders had the potential to become a *movement.* (The move from a network to a movement required us to recognize that what was happening was now much bigger than our church or even our church network.) Until that time, Community had been at the center of everything related to NewThing and was the driving force behind the reproduction of our new campuses and churches. To move to the next level, we would need to begin reproducing on the edges, having every NewThing church begin starting new campuses and churches. This realization opened our eyes to yet another reproducing principle.

REPRODUCING PRINCIPLE 5

Reproducing happens on the edge and at the center.

At that third NewThing gathering of nine leaders, we decided to expand from one network to three. I asked Dave Dummitt, lead pastor of 242 Community Church in Detroit, and Greg Lee, lead pastor at SunCrest Christian Church in northwest Indiana, to become network leaders and to find an apprentice network leader. A year later we reproduced three more networks led by Troy McMahon of Restore Community Church in Kansas City, Hank Wilson of Reunion Church in Boston, and Mark Nelson from Crossings in Knoxville. As we looked to the future and began formulating our vision to catalyze a movement of reproducing churches, we became convinced that a movement is created by the reproduction of networks. A movement is more than a single network of churches; it is what you have when those networks begin reproducing.

That brings us to where we are today. We are just starting to recognize where God has taken us and are starting to put each of these specific reproducing principles to work as we grow into a missional movement. Looking back, I'm amazed to see what God has done with a small group of friends from college who had a dream of helping people find their way back to him. And as I look ahead to the future, I see the outlines of a movement that has the unlimited potential of exponential reproduction.

Movements like this don't happen overnight. They are created through a process of reproduction, as people follow their God-given dreams, raise up apprentice leaders, start new sites and churches, and reproduce networks of churches. But it has to start with someone, and God is looking for someone. First Chronicles 16:9 says, "The eyes of the LORD search the whole earth in order to strengthen those whose hearts are fully committed to him" (NLT). Whatever your dream, wherever you are today, remember this: that someone can be you. Yes, a movement can start with you.

THE LEADERSHIP PATH

One Step at a Time

BIG IDEA The leadership path is a life-on-life process for developing leaders in a missional movement.

- ✱ Jesus and the Path of Leadership
- ✱ Troy McMahon's Story

When my brother, Jon, lived on the West Coast, he had the opportunity to participate in a three-hundred-mile bike ride down the coast of Southern California from San Luis Obispo to Orange County. Jon would be the first to tell you that at the time, he was at best a novice cyclist. To ride in the race, he had to borrow a beat-up old Schwinn ten-speed. But two things that he did worked to his advantage. First, he made the entire three-hundred-mile trek over the course of six days. He didn't try to go too far too fast or push too hard on any one day. And second, he didn't make this ride on his own. There were around thirty other cyclists, and they were all riding together. Even though Jon was a beginner, he's a pretty quick study, and it didn't take him long to figure out that if he positioned himself directly behind his buddy Amos, one of the more experienced and faster cyclists, he could maintain a decent speed. He didn't know it at the time, but cyclists even have a name for this approach; they call it "drafting." If you position yourself directly behind a faster cyclist, he will break the resistance of the wind for you, and as a result you will be able to maintain a higher speed with significantly less effort.

In the first chapter, I wanted to emphasize that the start of a new movement begins with you. And while I want to continue to encourage you with that truth, you also need to understand that it takes more than one person to make a movement a reality. You cannot do all of this on your own — you will need friends! In his book *An Unstoppable Force*, Erwin McManus gives one of the easiest-to-understand explanations of the church as a movement. Erwin reminds us of the scientific equation defining movement (momentum) as the mass of an object multiplied by its velocity.

$$\text{Movement} = \text{Mass} \times \text{Velocity}$$

Let's consider how this equation applies to our discussion, and why it suggests that successful movements require more than one person to really catch some speed. If one person is moving in the right direction by the leading of the Holy Spirit, I call that "spiritual velocity." Every one of us travels at a certain spiritual velocity, but to really gain momentum, you need to increase the mass. Movement is created when you influence other people to join you by inviting them to share life together and travel at a constant spiritual velocity. In other words, movement needs both speed *and* mass, and intentional leadership is required in order to influence the masses of people to live with any sort of spiritual velocity.

JESUS AND THE PATH OF LEADERSHIP

"So how can I expand my influence and grow my leadership around here?" That was the question Brad asked me as we sat down across from one another to talk about his leadership at Community. I realize that it's not every day that a potential leader tosses you a softball question like that one, so you just gotta love it when it happens. I particularly enjoy answering questions like that when they come from a guy like Brad, who has a huge leadership capacity. Without hesitating, I grabbed a crumpled-up napkin and started to answer his question by scribbling the illustration on the following page.

"Brad, the first step is for you to become an apprentice leader. And I'd like for you to be my apprentice in the small group that I lead on Wednesday nights." This meant that we would lead the small group together, and over the next six to eighteen months I would connect with him regularly until we both believed he was ready to lead a group on his own.

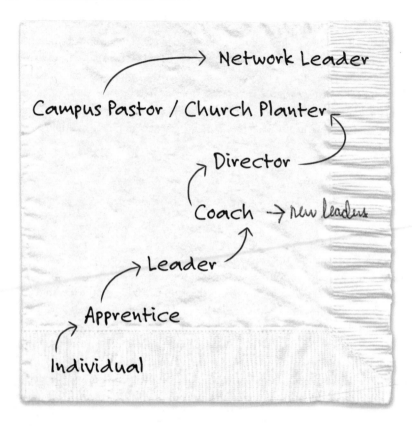

I went on to explain that eventually, when Brad began leading his own group, he would be responsible to raise up a new apprentice and reproduce new leaders. The goal of being an apprentice is that he would over time become a coach to others. (As a coach, Brad would then try to bring alongside himself the best leader he could find and train *him* to become a coach as well.) After successfully reproducing another coach, Brad could move into a director role or perhaps a staff position in our church, overseeing hundreds of people and working with his own coaches and leaders. I even told Brad that if he had the passion for it, I saw in him the gifting to be a campus pastor or a church planter with the potential to impact thousands and perhaps tens of thousands of people one day through a network of church plants.

The answer to Brad's question was not overly complicated. In fact, it was simple enough that I could scratch it out on a napkin and explain it to him over lunch. But it was challenging enough—and big enough—that Brad could give the rest of his life to pursuing that goal. Before we had even finished lunch, Brad said yes and agreed to become my apprentice, starting out on his own leadership path.

As you look at the scribbles on the back of my napkin, you might find yourself thinking, "Hold on! That looks like some kind of multilevel marketing scheme— a version of Amway for Jesus!" Nothing could be farther from the truth. This isn't a marketing ploy or a plan for building a bigger church; it's a life-on-life relational process for apprenticing leaders in the Jesus mission.✗ It's based on the same model that Jesus followed. Notice how Jesus began training his leaders by calling the twelve apostles: "Jesus went up on a mountainside and called to him those he wanted, and they came to him. He appointed twelve—designating them apostles—that they might be with him and that he might send them out to preach and to have authority to drive out demons" (Mark 3:13–15).

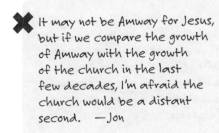

It may not be Amway for Jesus, but if we compare the growth of Amway with the growth of the church in the last few decades, I'm afraid the church would be a distant second. —Jon

- ✗ *Apprentice selection:* Jesus picked people "he wanted" (v. 13). Jesus' selection for apprenticeship was a relational process; he selected people he wanted around him.   ✗

- ✗ *Apprentice expectation:* Jesus "designat[ed] them apostles" (v. 14). *Apostle* means "sent one." Jesus was clear from the beginning that his expectation of an apprentice was that they would be sent out on mission.

- ✗ *Apprentice preparation:* Jesus' disciples were "with him" (v. 14). The primary means of training and developing these world changers was life-on-life relationships. Being with Jesus was their preparation.

- ✗ *Apprentice graduation:* Jesus concluded their apprenticeship by "send[ing] them out to preach and to have authority to drive out demons" (vv. 14–15). (The apprenticeship concluded when they could do what Jesus did.)   ✗

The change in the apostles wasn't just in what they could do; *it redefined who they were.* Their minds were transformed from being naive and ignorant about the real mission of Jesus to having a new understanding of the power of his gospel to change the past, present, and future. (Their hearts were reshaped; their self-centered love for "me and mine" was replaced with a love for those who were lost, lonely, and least likely to succeed.) They went from being a group of grind-it-out, one-day-at-a-time, working-class guys—sometimes timid and often afraid—to being a team of bold and courageous leaders who "turned the world upside down" (Acts 17:6 NKJV).

When I invited Brad into an apprenticeship with me, I followed the same process that Jesus followed: selection, expectation, preparation, and graduation. I was confident that by following this process, I would see the same changes in Brad that Jesus eventually witnessed in his apprentices, the apostles. I expected no more or less than what Jesus expected of his followers.*

 The conversation Dave had with Brad has been repeated thousands of times, and many of these conversations were with people who never once thought of themselves as leaders. —Jon

I wanted Brad to understand that this leadership path wasn't something new. It was a direction that many leaders before him had traveled, and if this was the path that God was calling him to walk, he could potentially impact thousands of people and catalyze a movement. Since Brad knew Troy McMahon, I took the time to share Troy's story with Brad to encourage him that he too could walk the leadership path that others before him had walked.

TROY MCMAHON'S STORY

As we mentioned in chapter 1, we like to say that when we discovered Troy McMahon, he was working the third shift, making Hamburger Helper. But the real truth is that he was working at General Mills, and they had him on the fast track to upper management. While Troy was successful in the marketplace, he also had a great passion for Jesus and shared our desire to help people find their way back to God. Over the course of twelve years, Troy started as a small group apprentice leader and moved through the leadership path, eventually leading a network of new churches. Today he is on his way to launching a new movement. He's a great example of what it looks like to follow the path of reproducible leadership. Let's retrace his steps on the path.

Troy and his family moved from Washington, D.C., to the Chicago area so that he could take a job with General Mills as an engineer in manufacturing management. Troy's good friend and the pastor of New Life Church, Brett Andrews, recommended that Troy check out a new church in Chicago—Community Christian Church. Several weeks after Troy and his family first showed up at Community, they attended one of our church picnics, where Troy and his wife, Janet, accepted an invitation to join a small group.*

Incidentally, while Troy was at New Life, he led Todd Wilson to Christ. Todd is now the executive director of the Exponential Network. —Jon

AN APPRENTICE LEADER

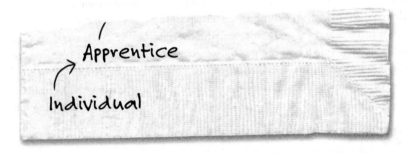

Troy loved what he was experiencing in his small group, and he expressed a desire to become an apprentice small group leader. Jon, who was directing Community's small group ministry at the time, connected Troy with a more experienced small group leader named Doug Blauser. After a couple of meetings together, Troy and Doug decided to launch a new group, of which Doug would be the leader and Troy his apprentice leader.

Troy quickly made his presence known at Community, and it was obvious that he was the kind of leader who could influence a lot of people. I asked Troy to join me for breakfast one morning to get to know him better, and it wasn't long before we were having breakfast every Wednesday at Bakers Square. It was during these breakfasts that Troy and I developed a strong friendship as we talked about life, leadership, and God's dream for Community.

A LEADER

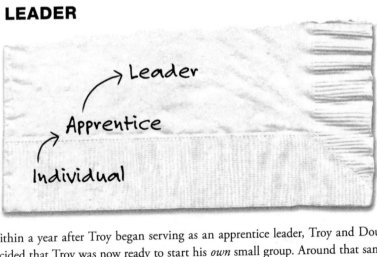

Within a year after Troy began serving as an apprentice leader, Troy and Doug decided that Troy was now ready to start his *own* small group. Around that same time, General Mills offered Troy a promotion that would require him to relocate to suburban Atlanta. Troy accepted the promotion, and later that spring Troy, Janet, and their baby boy moved to Cumming, Georgia. They quickly connected to a local church there and began leading a small group and serving in the student ministry.

When Jon and I were approached with the opportunity to partner with a real estate developer on a new campus in Romeoville (see chapter 1), we began to talk about someone who could lead that new site. I remember that we were in the lower level of the bank building where we rented office space, discussing this tremendous opportunity and thinking how good it would be if we could have Troy and Janet back at Community with us. The more we talked about it, the more we became convinced that Troy was exactly the kind of person we needed to lead this new site.

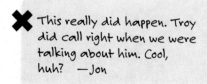

This really did happen. Troy did call right when we were talking about him. Cool, huh? —Jon

In fact, we decided that he *was* the person we wanted. Strangely enough, as we were having that very conversation, the phone suddenly rang. Do you want to guess who was calling us? It was Troy calling from Atlanta. We started laughing. We told Troy about the conversation we had just been having and how it seemed more than a coincidence that he had called. We believed that this was one of those God things and that the Spirit was leading us through these unusual circumstances.✶ Troy didn't give us an answer right then, but amazingly enough, a few weeks later Troy called us again to tell us that General Mills decided that they wanted him back in Chicago. God was putting the pieces in place for something new.

A COACH

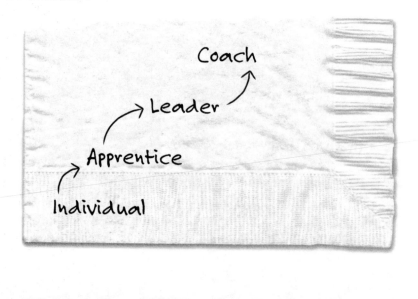

Within six months of our phone call, Troy and Janet (now with two sons) had returned to Community, they had joined my small group, and Troy had become my apprentice leader. Just like General Mills had Troy on the fast track to their upper management, we put Troy on a similar fast track at Community. I asked Troy to start over and become my apprentice so that we could

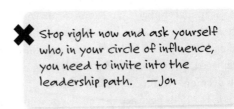

Stop right now and ask yourself who, in your circle of influence, you need to invite into the leadership path. —Jon

spend more time together focused on his leadership development process.✱ Troy agreed, and we began to meet regularly again, not just to guide our small group but also to dream about the future of Community as a church with multiple locations. Over the next several months, Troy moved quickly through the leadership path: he started leading his own small group, developed apprentices into leaders, and then began coaching those leaders. Within eighteen months of his move back to Chicago, I asked Troy if he would consider quitting his job at General Mills to come on staff at our church.

A DIRECTOR AND CAMPUS PASTOR

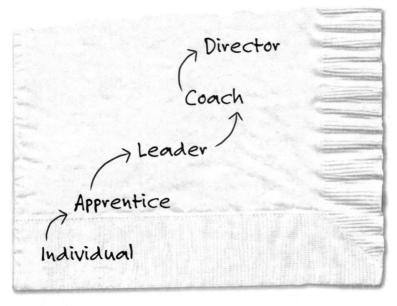

The next step for Troy on the leadership path was by far the most challenging for him. The step from being a coach to becoming a director is one that not only requires an expansion of leadership ability but also frequently requires an accompanying risk of vocational change. This is *not* a step that all people with high-capacity leadership gifts should take. Some of us will be called by God into vocational ministry, and some of us will be called into marketplace ministry. Both callings are a huge responsibility, and while Troy was leaving the marketplace to pursue full-time vocational ministry, we also had a guy (the man he replaced, Cliff Parrish) who was leaving our staff for marketplace ministry. Both decisions required significant faith on the part of these men.

For Troy, this next step meant that he would be leaving behind a high-paying and promising career in the corporate world for a new adventure with a new church that had God-sized dreams. I can make it sound good now, but for Troy and Janet, it felt like a big risk, and they wanted to know that God was in it. After much prayer, many conversations together, and some wise counsel from trusted friends, Troy came back to me and told me he was ready for the challenge.

 Dave's idea of helping Troy raise the funds was to give him a swift kick in the seat and say, "You can do it!"   —Jon

For Troy, the 50 percent pay cut wasn't the biggest hurdle; the biggest was that I was also asking him to raise half of his salary! (Of course, I told him about that after I found out that he was interested in the job.) After Troy got over his initial shock at the idea, we worked together to raise the needed funds for him to take that next step.✶

 Troy ended up stepping into the position that had been held by Cliff Parrish. Cliff had once worked for AT&T and had come to me with a dream for starting his own telecommunications company. Today Cliff runs a successful mission-minded business called RemoteLink (www.remotelink. com) that furthers the mission of Jesus through generosity, church planting, and economic development in third-world countries.   —Jon

Raising the money wasn't the only challenge for Troy. An even bigger challenge came when the launch of the second campus was delayed by several months. Managing a partnership between a church, a real estate developer, and a pension fund proved quite challenging. All of this meant that the opportunity we had signed Troy up for wasn't yet available, so in the transition period, Troy became our director of administration.✶

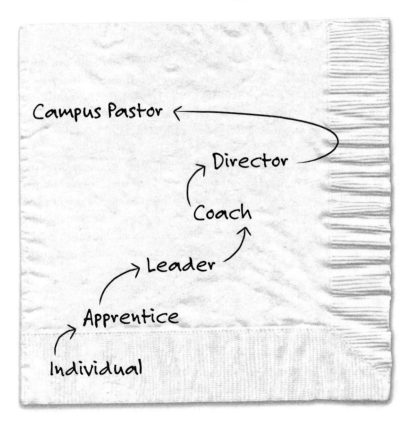

Campus Pastor

Director

Coach

Leader

Apprentice

Individual

After a few months, all of the pieces finally came together and we were able to launch our second site. We had talked, dreamed, and planned for such a long time about the launch of this new site in Romeoville, so we didn't surprise anyone when we named Troy to be the campus pastor. Troy called the first launch team meeting for the new site, and a whopping twelve people showed up. We had hoped for more. Fortunately, the launch team continued to grow over the next several months to well over one hundred people, and we were all just blown away when 552 people showed up at the first celebration service of our new Romeoville campus! I was excited for Community, and I was proud of Troy. In just five short years, Troy's influence had expanded significantly—from impacting ten people in a small group to impacting hundreds and thousands as our Romeoville campus pastor.

One of those people whom Troy impacted while serving as our campus pastor was Scott Knollenberg. Scott and his new bride, Michelle, had just moved into the HighPoint neighborhood where Troy had planted this new campus. Scott had recently finished his MBA, was being promoted at Caterpillar, and would be the first to admit that his life focus was entirely on advancing his career. Scott would also tell you that he was far from God at that point in his life.

One Saturday at the sand volleyball court at HighPoint, Scott met our new campus pastor, Troy McMahon, and they hit it off. At Troy's invitation, Scott came to one of our first celebration services and then joined Troy's small group. Within the next year, Scott made a commitment to be a Christ follower, was baptized, turned down a promotion and a transfer at work so he could stay in the community, and became Troy's apprentice leader in their small group.

Fast-forward nine years, and rather than moving through the ranks of corporate America, Scott expanded his influence, much like Troy. Though he was once far from God, Scott has walked the same leadership path that Troy walked, moving from an apprentice to a leader, from a leader to a coach, then on to a director on staff at our church. Today he is the campus pastor at our Romeoville campus. This campus has itself reproduced into two other campuses and a new church and now reaches out to more than a thousand people every weekend.

I want you to slow down for a moment and really think about what you have just read—really let it sink in. God took someone who was far from him, with *no experience* and *no seminary degree*, and now Scott is helping hundreds of people find their way back to God every week. My point is simple: if you doubt that this could happen to you—think again! If you are open to God's call on your life, God will use you and your friends to love the poor, feed the hungry, and bring Jesus to the people in your community who face a Christless eternity.

Starting the Romeoville campus was a kingdom-altering event. Not only did it give birth in our hearts and minds to the vision for two hundred locations in the greater Chicagoland area, it also sparked a multisite movement that would eventually impact thousands of churches around the world.

A CHURCH PLANTER

Over the next several years, Troy and I continued to meet weekly. We continued to grow in our friendship and also upgraded our meeting location from Bakers Square to Lou Malnati's, my favorite Chicago-style pizzeria. Troy would occasionally bring up the idea of starting a new church. Now, as much as I support the idea of starting new churches, I also hate it when my friends move away. Troy had become a close friend, so on many occasions I actually tried to discourage the conversation from heading in that direction. I still believe that I was right in discouraging Troy when he felt called to move his family from Naperville to Mexico and plant a new church south of the border. Troy was born in the Midwest, grew up near Kansas City, played football at Kansas State, and has lived his entire adult life in the suburbs. He didn't know Spanish from pig latin. While I believe that we need new churches all over the world (including

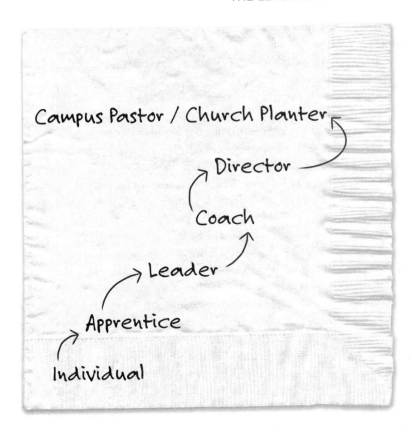

Campus Pastor / Church Planter

Director

Coach

Leader

Apprentice

Individual

Mexico), for Troy and his family Mexico made no sense, and I was glad to tell him so.

But I also remember that day at Lou Malnati's when Troy first talked about Kansas City as a potential location for a new church. This possibility was undeniably different. I had just been asked to be the vice president of the North American Christian Convention, which was being held in Kansas City, Troy's hometown. I had said yes to this role because the theme of the convention was church planting, and the leadership of the annual convention had decided that at this convention we would not just talk about church planting; we would actually launch a new church in Kansas City! I just knew that the time was right, and so I had to set aside my selfish reluctance and begin encouraging Troy to continue moving forward on his leadership path by planting this new church.

Troy will tell you that there were three experiences that confirmed to him that this was the right decision for him and his family. First, he received my blessing. I'm not really sure that this was necessary, but Troy insisted that he would not make a move forward unless I gave him my blessing. It was very honoring, and it forced me to move beyond my desire for close friends and look at the greater good of the kingdom. So I gave Troy my blessing.*

✖ "Blessing?" But the truth is, Dave finally said "Uncle." Troy is unstoppable. —Jon

Second, while he was attending the 2007 Exponential Conference in Orlando, there was an altar call and an anointing at the closing session led by Bill Hybels. I remember standing there watching Troy and Janet walk toward the stage and thinking to myself, "This is really going to happen." I knew that God was stirring things up, and they both sensed that the Holy Spirit was confirming this move back to their hometown to plant a new church.

Finally, as you may have guessed, I ended up inviting Troy to join me in Kansas City at the North American Christian Convention planning meeting. I told the planning team that I believed Troy was the person we wanted to lead the new church in Kansas City that would be launching through the convention that year. Within a few minutes more than three hundred thousand dollars had been committed by the leaders sitting around that table. Once again God had showed up in such a tangible way, and it was clear to us what he wanted to do.

That following spring, Restore Community Church was launched in Kansas City with 423 people and a vision to be a reproducing church. Troy was now well on his way to influencing hundreds if not thousands of people through Restore. But remember, this is not just about adding numbers. It's about exponential multiplication — leaders reproducing leaders. It's about reaching out to people like Scott Knollenberg, impacting people who in turn have the potential to impact thousands of others for Jesus.

A NETWORK LEADER

To ensure that Restore would be a reproducing church and would sustain a vision for reproduction, from the very beginning Troy brought on staff two apprentice campus pastors and an apprentice church planter. Within the first nine months of starting Restore, they had reproduced a new church in Haiti and had recruited a network of new church pastors in the States. Today, less than two years after its initial launch, (Restore is multisite: one church with two locations.) Troy is not only leading a reproducing church, but he is also one of NewThing's network leaders and leads four other church planters.

✗

✖ Finally, the end of our Troy McMahon tribute. Enough already.—Jon

That's Troy McMahon's story.* But I could have told

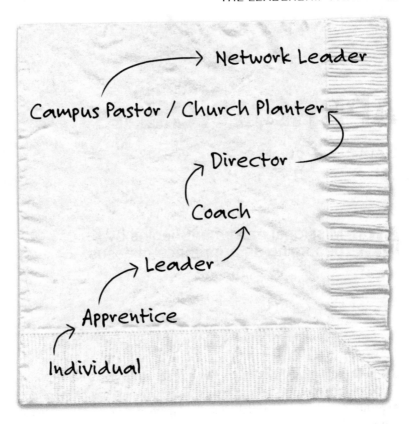

you Kirsten Strand's story. I could have told you Mark Nelson's story. I could have told you about John Ciesniewski, Brad Prunty, or Shawn Williams. You see, as remarkable as Troy's story sounds, it is not an exception — it's what we've come to expect from following the leadership path. There are now hundreds and thousands of people in reproducing churches all over the world who follow this path of leadership development in anticipation of God's calling them to one day lead a kingdom movement. Every one of them started at the same place Troy did — as an apprentice leader in a small group of Christ followers.

So where are you on this leadership path today?

And even more important, are you willing to take the next step on the path?

APPRENTICE

Come Follow Me

BIG IDEA Missional movement begins by becoming an apprentice of Jesus.

* Apprenticed to Jesus
* Dream Big
* Three Characteristics of a Jesus Apprentice

If a movement is to start with you and your friends, then it all begins with your becoming an apprentice. The core competency of any movement is *apprenticeship*. Apprenticeship is a fundamental principle of reproduction, yet it is so often overlooked. A gifted communicator can attract a huge crowd, a charismatic leader can create tremendous energy, and a talented writer can sell books by the millions. But if that teacher, leader, or writer wants to see their influence grow into a missional movement, they first must learn what it means to become an apprentice.

The very first action that Jesus took to start his movement was to recruit twelve apprentices. "Come, follow me," Jesus said, "and I will make you fishers of men" (Matt. 4:19). Jesus called twelve men into an apprenticeship and then taught them the basics of his message and his ministry so that they could do the same things he had done. Two thousand years later the Jesus movement has reached billions and billions of people, and it continues to impact new generations with an unchanging message. Through apprenticeships, people are empowered to reach their leadership capacity and influence as many others as possible to accomplish the mission.

APPRENTICED TO JESUS

You may have noticed that what I'm talking about sounds similar to what we often call "discipleship." I intentionally use the word *apprentice* as opposed to

44

disciple. While *disciple* is a brilliant word (and a word used by Jesus himself), it often does not mean to us what Jesus meant when he used it. I believe that *disciple* is a ruined word. When Jesus called people into discipleship, he was calling them for and preparing them to accomplish a *mission.*

> ✖ Don't shy away from the term apprentice. We've used it from day one and in a variety of ministries: students, kids, and adults. It does work. —Jon

When people use the world *disciple* today, though, it has almost nothing to do with our mission. Discipleship in the church today has more to do with consuming and absorbing cognitive content than it has anything to do with missional action. Being a disciple is more about an individual and his/her ability to get a passing grade on the subject matter, and less about being a follower of Jesus who lives in community with others for the sake of Christ's mission. I'm convinced that it will take at least another generation for us to recover the meaning of the word *disciple* so it is heard in the way Jesus meant for it to be heard.

The introduction of new language is a crucial step in reshaping paradigms and getting people to think differently about the movement of Jesus. Successful businesses are now seeing the importance of this principle. Ram Charan, in his book *Leaders at All Levels*, explains why the word *apprenticeship* has such power today: "Apprenticeship is at the heart of this new approach to leadership development. To understand why, you'll have to come to grips with a potentially controversial belief: leadership can only be developed through practice. Those who have talent for leadership must develop their abilities by practicing in the real world and converting that experience into improved skill and judgment. That conversion does not take place in a classroom."[1] In other words, you can choose to continue to use the word *disciple*, but that choice may prove counterproductive and result in producing the same kinds of static thinking you are trying to change. The word *apprentice* says that you not only are a learner but also are willing and ready to take action that will demand greater leadership responsibility in order to further the movement of Jesus. Apprentices don't just learn; they do what they have been taught and aspire to lead themselves.

Since the missional movement that we most want to advance is a movement originally started by Jesus, we must first and foremost become his apprentices. And just like his first followers, we must walk alongside Jesus and be guided and mentored by him. Now, you are probably thinking, "That sounds really nice and spiritual, Dave, but let's be honest—Jesus isn't here right now walking alongside me to give me the guidance and personal instruction that I need—so what should I do?" Believe it or not, Jesus anticipated your question. He even explains to us *how* he will apprentice us and bring his movement to life. In Acts 1:8, a passage we examined at the beginning of the book, Jesus shares his big dream with us and then gives us three characteristics that must be true of every one of his apprentices.

1. DREAM BIG

Jesus gave his apprentices a big dream when he told them, "You will receive power when the Holy Spirit comes on you; and you will be my witnesses in Jerusalem, and in all Judea and Samaria, and to the ends of the earth" (Acts 1:8). As big as it would have sounded to his followers, Jesus' dream was not just to reach Jerusalem, or even beyond that city to the area of Judea and Samaria. His dream was for his followers to be his witnesses and reach the very ends of the earth! He wanted them to venture beyond the safety of their hometowns and take this good news to new places. Now, that's a big dream! Being an apprentice of Jesus means learning to dream BIG.

I have found that when you dream big, it changes how you think, how you act, and it can even change those around you. Jesus understood the power of vision, and I've certainly learned a lot from his example. Another person who has pushed me to dream big is Lyle Schaller. He is one of the most prolific writers on church life, and he happens to live in the same town that I do. I love that old guy! Over and over again he will rib me by looking me in the eye and saying, "Dave, your biggest problem is that I have a bigger vision for your church than you do!" And strangely enough, every time he says that, my dream gets bigger!

Right now I'm thinking about what it will take for us at Community to be a church of two hundred sites in Chicago with one hundred thousand "3C" Christ followers.[2] And when Jon and I get together to talk about our vision to be a catalyst for a movement of reproducing churches, we try to dream big! We start these dreaming conversations strategizing about how to reach one billion people. Will we ever reach one billion people? Admittedly, the odds are against us.

But whether we ever see that dream fulfilled in our lifetime isn't really my point. The very act of dreaming big—allowing your heart and mind to pursue a vision that is bigger than you can handle—will change you in some very significant ways.

BIG DREAMS CHANGE YOUR QUESTIONS

I remember Carl George once telling me, "When you are really onto something, it will lead to more and more profound questions." I have found this to be true when it comes to the size of your dreams. The bigger your dream, the more you challenge and stretch your mind with tough questions. The size of your dream will often determine the types of questions you ask. Small dreams that are within your grasp and easily managed require one set of questions. Big dreams lead you to ask an entirely different set of questions, questions you would probably never ask otherwise.✴

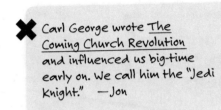

Carl George wrote <u>The Coming Church Revolution</u> and influenced us big-time early on. We call him the "Jedi Knight." —Jon

Over the last decade, our questions have changed and stretched with the size of our dreams:

- ✴ Ten years ago our dream was to have a church with two sites, so I had to ask, "How can I reproduce myself?" Now our dream is to have a church that has two hundred sites, and I ask, "How can I create a system for reproducing all of our leadership?"
- ✴ Five years ago our dream was to start a network of new churches, so I had to ask, "How can I attract, train, and deploy church planters?" Now our dream is to see a movement of reproducing churches, so I have to ask, "How can I create systems that reproduce networks and attract, train, and deploy apostolic leaders?"

The bigger the dream, the more profound the questions that you will ask. Some of the first questions I ask of a church leader who tells me that he wants to reproduce multiple sites are, "How many sites?" and "How big is your dream?" If they tell me that they want to reproduce two or three sites, the questions they need to ask are fairly simple. But if they say four or more, the questions become more challenging. At twelve sites, the rules change yet again, and the questions become even more complex. Enlarging our dreams forces us to ask the important and profound questions that will lead us to one day see the dream of Jesus—a church reaching the world—accomplished.

BIG DREAMS CHANGE YOUR PRAYERS

Big dreams also force you to ask questions to which you do not know the answer. When you have questions and you don't know how to answer them, who do you turn to? God! Big dreams force us to ask the types of questions that lead to greater dependence on God. If you were to read my journal, you would find it full of questions that I ask God:

"How are we ever going to find the leaders and artists for these new locations?"
"God, please <u>send us</u> apostolic leaders who have the passion and skill to not only plant a church but also start a church-planting network!"

I think God will do that — when we are faithful with what we already have.

If you don't have a dream that leads you to greater dependence on God, then you need to get a bigger dream!✶

BIG DREAMS CHANGE OTHERS

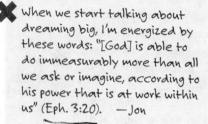

When we start talking about dreaming big, I'm energized by these words: "[God] is able to do immeasurably more than all we ask or imagine, according to his power that is at work within us" (Eph. 3:20). —Jon

Big dreams are also contagious. They are infectious. They not only change you, but they can also slowly begin to change your friends and those around you! Big dreams generate excitement, and they attract those who want to follow your example and step out in faith.

After my friend Larry heard my dream and said to me, "You can do it," we began to talk out loud about our dream of being a reproducing church with multiple locations all over Chicago. Within a couple of years we had a developer give us a $3.5 million community center to help start a new campus in Romeoville! The developer exercised bold generosity, responding to our God-sized dream.

A couple of years after that, an existing church gave us their building and property, worth over a million dollars, to use as a third site. This 163-year-old church hadn't seen more than fifty people in attendance in years, and when they reopened as a site of Community, we had over six hundred people show up for the first weekend! Our Montgomery campus has now reproduced and helped start three other campuses in the Chicago area *and* a church in Boston. This crazy big dream of a church with multiple locations all over Chicago invited a process of change and a step of faith for this tiny congregation. (Big dreams have the power to inspire faith, leading to change.)

While driving down Ogden Avenue with my teenage daughter Amy, I was reminded of this truth in a more personal way as well. Ogden is a main artery in the town of Naperville, with lots of big-box stores and strip malls. As we drove past a hardware store that had gone out of business, Amy looked at the empty building and said, "Hey, Dad, we should start a new location there!" Notice what she communicated to me in that little exchange. Because our church has always had a big dream of being a reproducing church, Amy has grown up seeing the whole world differently. Where most people would see nothing more than vacant buildings and urban blight, she has been raised and taught to see potential sites for reproducing churches. As an apprentice of Jesus, when you start to dream big, it will begin to change others: from the high-capacity donor to the risk-taking leader—it will even affect your teenage daughter!

BIG DREAMS CHANGE YOU

Other than my conversion as a Christ follower, I can honestly say that the biggest change agent in my life has been this dream of two hundred locations in Chicagoland and becoming a catalyst for a movement of reproducing churches. Because I have embraced this dream, I now have different questions that drive me. I discover I am constantly drawn back to ✖ develop greater dependence on God. And I find myself surrounded by people, leaders, and high-capacity influencers who are also passionate about being a part of this big dream. The dream now defines my identity, my relationship with God, and my closest relationships in ministry.✗

> ✖ This dreaming stuff does come more naturally to us than to some people. But even if you don't consider yourself much of a dreamer, take a few minutes to reflect on this question: "What is your God-sized dream?" —Jon

Before we move on, let me say something that I hope you will take ever so seriously. Are you ready?

I find that most of us have a dream buried somewhere inside us. The problem is not that we lack the ability to dream; it's that our dreams are often far too small. As apprentices of Jesus, we need to dream dreams that match the heart of our leader and teacher. As our dreams get bigger, our doubts will inevitably grow. But remember what we talked about earlier: you can do it! Jesus has said that with God alive and working in you, you really can do what he asks you to do. You just need to find the courage to believe what God has said to you and ✗ speak out loud the dream that God has given to you—share it with someone and make it real.

START SMALL

I've just told you that every apprentice needs to dream big, but ironically, you chase your biggest dreams by starting small—with yourself! The starting point for every apprentice who wants to pursue a big dream is the recognition that the goal is not just to reproduce your role or function but also to reproduce *who you are*. To accomplish a big dream, you'll need to realize that everything about you will be reproduced over and over and over again. What you say will be repro- ✗ duced. What you do will be reproduced. What you don't do will be reproduced. All of it—good and bad, strengths and weaknesses—will show up in the lives of the people who follow your leadership.

When we started Community, the one hill we were ready to die on was our mission of helping people find their way back to God. I can remember nights when I would literally dream about people coming to know God through Jesus. It was our obsession, and we lived it out passionately. I remember when my friend Ed Stetzer joined me for lunch on a Sunday after a celebration service at Community. "Thirteen times," he said. "Thirteen times what?" I asked Ed. "Thirteen times—from the moment I walked in the doors to the moment I walked out—I heard it. From the stage, in the hospitality area, even mingling with people, over and over again I heard, 'Helping people find their way back to God.'" Ed added, "People know the mission."✻ What started as a burning passion that God put into our hearts is something I now regularly hear in the prayers of the people of Community: "Lord, use me to help more and more people find their way back to you." And God is answering those prayers! At the time of this writing, Community is seeing an average of more than a person per day choosing to follow Christ and getting baptized.

> ✖ I was at lunch with Stetzer too. I even paid for it. But do I get a mention in this paragraph? Nope! —Jon

So how do you actually become an apprentice? How does the dream become a reality? That's a great question! Right before Jesus left this planet, he was standing before his apprentices and said to them, "Friends, you can do it! We can take this movement to the edges of the world. I'm not going to abandon you. I will continue to apprentice you and all those who will receive me. Here is how you and all those who come after you will get it done." Then he explained, "You will receive power when the Holy Spirit comes on you; and you will be my witnesses in Jerusalem, and in all Judea and Samaria, and to the ends of the earth" (Acts 1:8). These words show us the three primary characteristics of a Jesus apprentice: Spirit led, missional, and reproducing. We use the following symbols to help us remember these characteristics:

THREE CHARACTERISTICS OF A JESUS APPRENTICE

When Jesus gave his followers the "to the ends of the earth" dream, he also promised them that he would give them someone who would be essential to accomplishing that dream—the Holy Spirit. Followers of Jesus must be Spirit led if they want to be involved in fulfilling his dream of reaching the world.

1. Spirit-Led Apprentice

"You will receive power when the Holy Spirit comes on you ..."

Being Spirit led is the most critical quality in the life of an apprentice of Jesus. So what does it mean? Being Spirit led is simply *hearing from God and obeying what he says.* Sounds simple, right? It is, but it's also incredibly challenging. I continually tell our people at Community that if I were granted one wish for them, I would wish that every one of them would hear God speak to them each day. I was recently talking with another pastor, Perry Noble, the lead pastor at NewSpring Church. Perry has a way of making something profound very simple and easy to understand. He said to me, "Leadership is as easy as listening to God." And he is right about that! Listening to God (and leadership) is often surprisingly simple and yet very difficult at times. There is not a doubt in my mind that the big dream of Jesus could be accomplished if each and every one of us would simply stop and listen to God each day.

When my daughter Amy was a preschooler, there was a particular week when it seemed as if she were constantly disobeying us, over and over again. We would tell her to turn off the television, and she would just sit there, ignoring the fact that we had spoken. At other times we would tell her to go wash her hands and come to the dinner table, and she would just ignore us and keep playing, refusing to come to the table. There were other times when we would tell her to quiet down a bit and not talk so loudly, because her little brother was napping, and she'd go ahead and wake him up, talking louder than ever. Sue and I grew increasingly frustrated and kept wondering why there was such willful disobedience. "Why doesn't she obey us anymore? Why isn't she listening to us?" As first-time parents, this was a tough season for us.

I decided to have a heart-to-heart talk with our three-year-old Amy. In the Ferguson household, the phrase "Obey the first time" had been repeated over and over, so I thought I would begin there. I got down on one knee with Amy and started talking calmly about how she needed to obey the first time. As I was speaking to her, this strained look came over her face and she leaned in toward me. "Dad, talk so I can hear you," she said. Then she repeated herself: "Dad, talk so I can hear you." It suddenly hit me. What if my little girl couldn't hear me? What if she *wasn't* being willfully disobedient? What if I was misreading the situation?

We took Amy to her doctor to have her hearing checked. Dr. Nelson did a tympanograph to measure the vibrations within the ear cavity, and the tympanograph showed us a flat line—there were no vibrations in Amy's ear. In other words, she was hearing only about 5 to 10 percent of everything that was being said to her. A flat line meant that the ear wasn't receiving sound vibrations. Fortunately, we found out that this wasn't a permanent condition, that her ear was actually full of fluid and that it could be remedied with medication.

This set of circumstances got me to think about the act of spiritual listening and what it really means to be a Spirit-led follower of Jesus. Thinking about my experience with Amy at the doctor's office, I asked the question, what if a tympanograph of my spiritual listening came back from heaven as a flat line? What if we discovered that we are really living our lives hearing only 5 to 10 percent of what the Father is saying to us? What a tragedy it would be if we were to get to heaven and hear God say to us, "I was speaking, but you weren't listening to me!"

1. God Speaks When You Least Expect It

I've discovered that often God will speak when you least expect it. When Troy McMahon called our office at the exact same time that Jon and I were saying, "I wish Troy were still here; he would make a great campus pastor," it was clear to us that God was speaking. After the grand opening of Community, we realized that we couldn't keep transporting all our equipment in our cars, and our team prayed and asked God for a van. The very next day, we got a call from someone who didn't even go to our church, asking us if we knew anyone who could use a free cargo van! Again it was clear to us that God was speaking.

More recently, at an all-staff meeting following a day of prayer and fasting, we heard God speak quite clearly to our leaders. We had just gone through one of the toughest financial seasons ever in the life of Community, so I asked our staff to pray and fast together about some hard decisions we would have to make. When our team reconvened, I asked, "Did anyone feel like they got any direction from God?" Everyone hesitated, and then Steve raised his hand and said, "In these tough financial times, I think God is saying, 'Don't shrink the vision; increase the vision!'" This sounded counterintuitive, but it was confirmed by several other people. Once again it was clear to us that God was speaking, as we expanded

As a result of that day of prayer and fasting, in spite of being way behind financially, we decided to give away one weekend's offerings to four key missional causes outside of Community. That weekend we gave away more than two hundred and fifty thousand dollars. We did this again the following year and gave away over four hundred thousand dollars. —Jon our vision to include reaching new people and places we never had before. Soon afterward we began seeing record giving and unprecedented generosity.*

God Speaks through Spiritual Disciplines

2.

God also speaks through the everyday spiritual disciplines that draw us close to him. The place where I am most likely to hear from God is in my journaling. It is my goal each day to open up the Bible and read a chapter with an ear for the voice of God speaking specifically to me. As I read, I underline any verses that seem to resonate in my heart or bring conviction. Next I write out those verses with some observations, thinking through how they apply to me and my life. Then I write out my prayers to God. Last, I just sit quietly and see if God brings to mind thoughts that I need to take action on. If I sense that God has brought something to mind, I write it down in my journal to remind me to take action.*

> ✖ Several years back I went to New Hope in Honolulu and spent some time with Wayne Cordeiro at a pastors practicum. The single most important takeaway? How he had his people journaling every day. We stole the idea and made our own 3C journals. —Jon

?

This simple discipline of reading the Bible, journaling my thoughts, praying, and listening for God to speak has been the primary way that I hear from God. If you opened the pages of my journal, you would see how over the years God has brought people to mind with whom I should partner, shown me how I should organize initiatives, and given guidance as to whether I should say yes or no to opportunities. There is a direct correlation between my journaling, the Spirit's leading me, and the missional movement that God has given me to lead.

God Speaks from Moment to Moment

3.

Finally, there is also a moment-to-moment rhythm to being Spirit led. First God speaks, and then we step. God will often speak to us throughout our day, and when we hear his voice, we must take the next step by simply following what he says. Jesus explains this rhythm to his followers in John 10:27 when he compares us to sheep and identifies himself as our Shepherd: "My sheep listen to my voice; I know them, and they follow me." Jesus is teaching us that we should make listening to his voice a priority; for us to truly know him, it is essential that we listen. The apostle Paul writes in Galatians 5:25, "Since we live by the Spirit, let us keep in step with the Spirit." After we have heard from God, we must take steps to follow. The rhythm of being Spirit led is quite simple: every moment of every day is composed of God's speaking and our stepping. When God speaks, we step. This moment-to-moment rhythm is a key characteristic of an apprentice of Jesus.

Being Spirit led is a way of saying that we are constantly listening for God with a posture of willing obedience. The word _obey_ in the original language of the Bible comes from the same Greek root word which means "to listen under" or "to hear." When parents have kids who don't obey, often they will complain and say, "They just don't listen to me." But what they really mean is, they don't _obey_. I believe that the reverse is also true. Often when we don't _obey_ God, it is because we just aren't _listening_.

2. Missional Apprentice

" ... and you will be my witnesses ..."

Jesus goes on to describe his apprentices by saying that they will be his witnesses. The word _witness_, in the original language of the New Testament, is _marturious_. If you say it slowly, you can almost hear the word _martyr_, can't you? The two words are closely related. When Jesus tells his followers that they will be his witnesses, he is not saying that they will simply talk about him in the presence of others. No, it goes much deeper than that. Witnesses were frequently tortured and killed as a means of forcing them to disclose the truth. In other words, Jesus is saying that you and I must be prepared to die for his mission. He is saying that we must be ready to trade our lives, whether one day at a time or in one final act of surrender, to see the mission he has given to us fulfilled. Jesus was being very candid and reminding his apprentices that following him would be risky!

But then again, isn't life full of risks? Risks are something we take every day. And many times, we do it without even realizing it! Are you planning on driving sometime in the near future? Let me warn you—driving can be very risky! One out of seventy-five people who drive will be injured in an automobile accident. Do you plan on using the bathroom in the next twenty-four hours? Risky! Every year, 270,000 injuries happen in bathrooms. (And there are other risks if you avoid using the bathroom.) On the other hand, some things that we think are risky aren't risky at all. For example, if you are a single woman and you are thinking that it is far too risky to ask out a single guy, you should know that 71 percent of guys will say yes if you ask them. That's not risky at all! Guys are easy! (But beware; 78 percent of all stats are actually made up on the spot.)

When it comes to taking risks, the important question you need to ask is, when was the last time you took a risk and trusted God? When was the last time you courageously followed Jesus and did something that was clearly beyond your own abilities? When was the last time you followed Jesus so closely that it was uncomfortable, maybe even a bit scary?

If you saw Sher, a twentysomething suburban girl, sitting in a dark Chicago alley near Union Station with four people who live on the streets, you might think, "That seems kind of risky; what is she doing there?" The answer is simple. Sher is an apprentice of Jesus. God spoke to her, and she stepped out to take a risk to serve the mission of Jesus.

A couple of years ago, as Sher's birthday was coming up, she decided that she didn't want to have a party for herself. And God gave her an idea. She talked it over with Tyrone, a homeless friend of hers, and he confirmed that it was indeed a good idea. So Sher began to enroll her small group of young adult friends in the plan. They decided that they would throw a birthday party for the people who lived on the streets of Chicago near Union Station. There would be cake, treats, and gift bags with gloves, socks, knit caps, fruit, and prepackaged snacks.

On Sher's twenty-sixth birthday, she headed down to Union Station with thirty of her friends from the suburbs and joined up with fifty of her friends living on the streets of Chicago for the most unlikely birthday party ever. Together they ate birthday cake, opened gifts, shared laughs, and partied. Not everything went smoothly. When Shaun, who lived on the streets, pulled out a box cutter and threatened to cut someone if he didn't get the gift he wanted, it could have brought an abrupt end to a festive event. But Sher calmly asked Shaun to give her the box cutter, and much to her surprise Shaun handed it over. The party continued and became the first of many "risks" that Sher and her friends would take to further the mission of Jesus.

Over the last several years, their mission to the streets has witnessed incredible highs and lows. They've seen some of their friends die, shared a Chicago-style pizza together on Thanksgiving, been verbally attacked, and even been treated to lunch by some of the very people they came to serve. If you were to ask Sher, "What are you trying to do?" she would tell you, "We aren't there to really 'do' anything; we're just trying to continually offer ourselves to others relationally. And doing that requires taking constant risks." *

I did a consultation a couple of years ago with one of the largest churches in the United States. They had reached a plateau in their growth and were considering going to multiple sites. Their leaders were all very excited. Their enthusiastic talk had me convinced that they were ready to take the risk. But as the meeting closed, the youngest leader, a friend of mine, pulled me aside and said, "Dave, we are a long way from doing this."

> ✖ Sher is now launching a second missional community among the homeless in the UpTown neighborhood of Chicago. She is reproducing leaders and continuing to take significant risks. Gotta love that!. —Jon

I was confused by his comment and asked, "Why?" He admitted, "At this point we are afraid of failing; we are afraid of the risk."

I find that there are two common fears that keep us and our churches from taking risks for the sake of mission. The first is our fear of failure. We say to ourselves, "I'm afraid it just won't work ... and I can't accept the possibility of failure." The second fear that keeps us from taking risks is closely related—it's the fear of loss. We work for years to build a large church or successful career, and our "success" can become the very thing that gets in the way of our taking more significant risks. We tell ourselves, "I've accomplished too much to lose it all." If it is a fear of failure or loss that is holding you back, let me remind you of the grace of God. Walking faithfully in obedience to God is what matters, not your success or failure in the eyes of the world.

And if you are struggling with the fear of loss, let me remind you that we aren't here to build a kingdom in the here and now; we're to think of our mission in light of eternity. Is your fear of losing what you have right now keeping you from God's bigger dream for your life? Remember the master's words to the servant with one thousand dollars who buried the money out of fear? The master said, "That's a terrible way to live! It's criminal to live cautiously like that!... Take the thousand and give it to the one who risked the most. And get rid of this 'play-it-safe' who won't go out on a limb" (Matt. 25:26–30 MSG). Faith is risky business; it's a refusal to play it safe!

3. Reproducing Apprentice

"... in Jerusalem, and in all Judea and Samaria, and to the ends of the earth."

"Come, follow me,... and I will make you fishers of men" (Matt. 4:19) was a calling to follow Jesus, but at the same time it was an invitation to be trained and prepared for a greater responsibility, to be a part of the Jesus mission. When Jesus later told his followers, "Go and make disciples" (Matt. 28:19), he was giving them a command to reproduce others like he had done with them. From the earliest days of their apprenticeship with Jesus, his followers were sent out and involved in his mission. Jesus would send them out with another friend, with the intention that each of the twelve would also begin exercising his authority and expanding the mission by training others: "Calling the Twelve to him, he sent them out two by two and gave them authority" (Mark 6:7). Jesus did the same thing with the seventy-two: "After this the Lord appointed seventy-two others and sent them two by two ahead of him to every town" (Luke 10:1). And Jesus is still sending people out—including you! He sends each of us out with "authority," an authority that puts us in a position of influence and leadership.

Yes, that's right. I said *leadership*. Don't let that intimidate you. I'm not talking about an office or a title. When I use the word *leadership*, I'm referring to the influence that God has given you with others. That authority or influence, even if it's with just one other person, puts you in a place of leadership.

Who are the people that God has placed in your sphere of influence? Is it a friend? A neighbor? Someone in your church? Somebody in your neighborhood or a person at work? When we started Community, God brought my brother Jon alongside me, together with three friends from college and my wife, Sue. We were just a handful of friends.* Not only were we apprentices of Jesus ourselves, but each of us also went out in response to his mission and found an apprentice to influence. That's the heart of ✖ our story at Community. We were just a handful of friends who came together with a willingness to risk anything and everything as the Spirit led, and we did that by influencing one person at a time.)

> "My brother Jon alongside me"? What am I, a lapdog? I'm all about this apprentice thing, but that sounds a little condescending, don't you think? —Jon

As you have seen in this section, we began quite simply: reproducing small groups. Today there are hundreds of small groups that make up Community, and thousands more that make up the NewThing network of churches. Again, we also committed ourselves to reproducing our celebration services. We reproduced our first service within six months of our launch, and we now have more than thirty services. As the Spirit has led us, we have started new campuses and churches and continue to reproduce at a pace that allows us to double the number of new churches in our network every year and reach tens of thousands of people around the world.)

Jesus wants you and your friends to be a part of his movement. And that happens when you, as an apprentice of Jesus, commit to reproducing your life at every level of influence that God gives to you. You may be influencing leaders, artists, small groups, teams, venues, campuses, churches, or even networks. But the basic principles are the same at every level: listen to God's Spirit, take risks ✗ for the sake of mission, and commit to apprenticing others.)

CHAPTER

4

REPRODUCING LEADERS

The 2-2-2 Principle

BIG IDEA **A leader must develop four key relationships to start a missional movement.**

- Everything Rises and Falls on Leadership
- Four Relationships Every Leader Needs
- Tammy Melchien's Story

You and I are leaders. People will follow us. And yet if we're really honest, there are times when we do anything *but* lead. We resist the calling. We sidestep responsibility. We look for a way out. And sometimes we miss great opportunities. At other times we simply delay the inevitable and put off leading, but that lost time can prove incredibly costly. I believe that the first step toward getting back on the leadership track is identifying the actions we take and the attitudes we express that indicate a clear lack of leadership.

EVERYTHING RISES AND FALLS ON LEADERSHIP

There are twelve indicators that leadership is lacking. Leadership is lacking when:

1. I wait for someone to tell me what to do rather than taking the initiative myself.
2. I spend too much time talking about how things should be different.
3. I blame the context, surroundings, or other people for my current situation.
4. I am more concerned about being cool or accepted than doing the right thing.

5. I seek consensus rather than casting vision for a preferable future.
6. I am not taking any significant risks.
7. I accept the status quo as the way it's always been and always will be.
8. I start protecting my reputation instead of opening myself up to opposition.
9. I procrastinate to avoid making a tough call.
10. I talk to others about the problem rather than taking it to the person responsible.
11. I don't feel like my butt is on the line for anything significant.
12. I ask for way too many opinions before taking action.

I hope you will take the preceding list to heart,* because I believe that everything you do will rise and fall on the quality of your leadership. Just a few months ago I was glued to my Twitter account, looking at the first

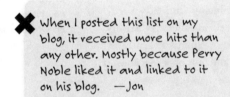

When I posted this list on my blog, it received more hits than any other. Mostly because Perry Noble liked it and linked to it on his blog. —Jon

pictures of a plane safely resting in the waters of the Hudson River. As the full story unfolded, credit for miraculously landing the plane in the Hudson River was given to the strong leadership displayed by pilot Chesley "Sully" Sullenberger. After landing, Sully guided his crew and passengers safely onto the wings, and there were zero casualties. His ability to effectively lead was literally a matter of life and death for the 155 people on US Airways Flight 1549.

The decisions, the actions, and the ideas of leaders make the headlines every day. But there are many acts of leadership that don't make the news. Consider how a manager responds to a disgruntled customer at Starbucks or how a first-grade teacher tries to motivate her class to read more books. Even if we aren't reading about these stories or seeing them in the headlines, it's still all about leadership.

When Community opened our second campus, in Romeoville, we identified and developed a whole new cadre of leaders to come alongside our new campus pastor. We not only asked them to go to this new campus; we also asked them to backfill the places they were leaving, so we wouldn't have a leadership void left behind. We sent out some of our best leaders: Tom and Sue Natiello, Doug and Marilyn Blauser—people who were leading small groups and coaching small group leaders at our current location. Four years later we launched our Carillon campus, targeting seniors in an active adult community just north of our Romeoville campus, and again it required reproducing leaders.

Two years ago we launched our Plainfield campus. We identified a campus pastor, selected a target date, found a location, developed a marketing strategy, and chose service times. But after all the planning was complete, there was still the hard work of identifying and developing leaders who would carry out the vision for this campus. Even up to the last few days prior to the launch of that campus, our focus was on being sure we had leaders in place to launch successfully.

Every time we launch a campus, a celebration service, or a church, it's all about *helping people find their way back to God*—that is our mission. But we know that the only way we can accomplish that mission is by having our leaders catch the vision for investing themselves in someone else who can also lead. At every turn in Community's development as a reproducing church, we recognized another key reproducing axiom: Everything rises and falls on leadership.*

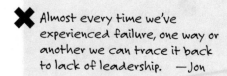

Almost every time we've experienced failure, one way or another we can trace it back to lack of leadership. —Jon

REPRODUCING PRINCIPLE 6
Everything rises and falls on leadership.

Here is why this reproducing axiom is so important: There are thousands of churches in the United States that are multisite and thousands of others that have planted churches, nationally and internationally. That said, there is a significant difference between launching a new campus—or even a new church, for that matter—and becoming a *reproducing* church. Occasionally you will find a church that is able to launch new locations because of its size or because of significant financial resources. This is not a reproducing church. A reproducing church is a church that is *repeatedly* launching new small groups, teams, services, campuses, churches, and even networks. And there are really no shortcuts to doing this. More than anything else, it demands the intentional and systematic reproduction of leaders.

FOUR RELATIONSHIPS EVERY LEADER NEEDS

We've discovered that as a leader, you will need four key relationships in order to successfully reproduce again and again.

1. A Reproducing Leader Needs Followers

The idea that a leader needs followers may seem obvious, but we find that it is often overlooked. I can't tell you how many times I've thought, "This person looks like a leader, walks like a leader, and talks like a leader," and then we've placed him in a leadership position before we've seen if he can actually attract a following and learn to be an apprentice himself. How I regret doing that now.

Several years ago a talented young man started attending our church. One of our campus pastors immediately identified him as someone with tremendous leadership potential. He had strong people skills, and he could cast vision and strategize with tremendous insight. When we would sit down and talk about ministry strategy and direction, he could quickly articulate for me the next steps we needed to take. And nine times out of ten, he was spot-on. Not only that, he was a great communicator—a truly gifted teacher.

So what did we do? What any pastor in his right mind would do—we offered him a position on our staff. And he accepted. We soon found out that while he did some things very well, his real gift was "talking church" with the best of them. Yes, he could cast a compelling vision. And because of that he was great at attracting a crowd. But the sad truth we discovered was that he was unable to develop a following. His ability to truly lead was seriously crippled.*

> ✘ Unfortunately, this wasn't the only time Dave hired somebody before we put them to the test of developing a following. And guess who had to let them go? —Jon

There is a difference between *attracting a crowd* and *developing a following.* Crowds are temporary. They come and go. They're fickle *especially singles* ✗ and unpredictable. But followers are in it for the long haul. When Jesus enlisted his disciples, he drew them out of the crowd and challenged them to follow him and do life with him (Matt. 4:19). While having a following is not the only test of leadership, you can be sure that if there are no followers, there is a lack of leadership.

Crowds are	Followers are
temporary	lasting
fickle	loyal
unpredictable	committed
transitory	consistent
fleeting	faithful

We have found small groups to be the best place to put this principle to the test, because only a person who is capable of developing followers will be successful at leading a small group. And if a person has proven capable of developing a following in a small group, one of those followers in the group can be a future apprentice leader.

2. A Reproducing Leader Needs Apprentices

We challenge every leader to have at least one apprentice—someone he or she is working with and developing to become a leader as well. There is a simple apprentice-developing process that applies to any leadership role. It's based on a principle found in 2 Timothy 2:2, where the apostle Paul writes to his apprentice Timothy, "The things you have heard me say in the presence of many witnesses entrust to reliable men who will also be qualified to teach others."

In his book *Organic Leadership*, Neil Cole describes Timothy's apprenticeship with Paul as he comments on this passage: "Paul passed on to Timothy truths that were so profound that he would not forget them. They gripped his life and never left him. At the same time, however, the things Paul passed on were simple enough that Timothy could in turn pass them on to others who could then pass them on to others."[3]

This process of developing apprentices is based on what we call the "2-2-2 Principle." In this passage from his letter to Timothy, Paul speaks of reproducing leaders into the fourth generation:

First generation	Paul
Second generation	instructs Timothy
Third generation	to invest in "reliable men"
Fourth generation	"who will also be qualified to teach others"

Pause for a moment and let the significance of this principle sink in. Apprenticeship is not about finding people who can help us do tasks more effectively. We're *not* talking about preparing people to simply replace us so we can move on to something else. At the heart of biblical apprenticeship is a mindset of reproduction: reproducing our leadership so the mission will be carried on to future generations.

We love using the word *apprentice*, because it conveys the idea that the person in that role is aspiring to something more. They are in a temporary role, being trained for something else. An apprentice is not a coleader or an assistant leader; an apprentice is someone who is being equipped and trained to become a leader, who will then be responsible for leading others.

Ram Charan, in his book *Leaders at All Levels*, writes, "Apprentices are people who learn from doing ... practice, feedback, corrections, and more practice. [The apprentice model] is designed to give each promising leader the opportunities that are right for him or her at the fastest pace of growth he or she can handle, defining the learning needed in each new job and making sure the learning in fact took place before helping the leader take the next step or leap forward. With this approach, leaders develop increasingly sophisticated and nuanced versions of their core capabilities in an astonishingly short time."[4]

> ✗ Just so you know, this is not just theory that we're writing about here. Right now I have two apprentices that I meet with weekly, and he has one. —Jon

In Acts, Luke makes an easily overlooked point about Paul's interaction with his apprentice Timothy. He writes that "Paul wanted to take him along on the journey" (Acts 16:3). What do you think it would have looked like for Paul to take Timothy with him? While there are many ways in which an apprentice needs to be developed and equipped, we have found a simple process that has proven successful time and time again in a variety of leadership roles or functions—five basic steps that you can follow to take someone "along on the journey" and equip them for leadership. Your ability to utilize these five steps will largely determine the impact of your leadership.*

So let's make this practical. Take a moment to think of someone in your sphere of influence whom you are currently developing, or someone you would like to develop as a leader. What would it look like to walk that person through the following five steps? *everyone have a timothy + a Paul*

1. I do. You watch. We talk.

2. I do. You help. We talk.

3. You do. I help. We talk.

4. You do. I watch. We talk.

5. You do. Someone else watches.

The Five Steps of Leadership Development

1. *I do. You watch. We talk.* As an experienced leader leads a team, an apprentice takes time to observe him or her. Within a few days the two should meet to discuss what the apprentice has observed. This debriefing time should include three simple questions: (1) "What worked?" (2) "What didn't work?" and (3) "How can we improve?" This time of debriefing needs to continue throughout the process.

2. *I do. You help. We talk.* In this phase of development, the leader gives the apprentice an opportunity to help lead in a particular area. For example, if someone is being developed to lead a student ministry small group, the leader might ask that person to lead the prayer time while the experienced leader leads the remainder of the time together. Again, this experience should be followed up with a one-on-one to talk.

3. *You do. I help. We talk.* Now the apprentice transitions from supporting or helping the leader to taking on most of the leadership responsibilities of the team or group. If a person is being apprenticed to lead a team of sound technicians, he or she will operate the sound system and provide leadership for the other sound technicians. The more experienced leader now begins releasing responsibilities to the new, developing leader. As in the previous steps, the leader and apprentice leader should meet regularly to debrief the ministry experience.

4. *You do. I watch. We talk.* The apprentice process is almost complete as the new leader grows increasingly more confident in his or her role. Consider how this step might look in a children's ministry. A children's group leader, at this point, would give his or her apprentice the opportunity to fulfill all the functions of leadership, with the more experienced leader now looking on and watching the new leader in action.

5. *You do. Someone else watches.* This is where the process of reproducing comes full circle. The former apprentice is now leading and begins developing a new apprentice. Ideally, the leader who has developed and released several apprentices will continue to work with those leaders in a coaching capacity.

If there is one section of this book that I want you to photocopy and send to somebody else, it is this section on the five steps. If you memorize anything from this book, memorize these five steps. If you're tempted to steal anything from this book and claim it as your own, claim these five steps. I admit that I did. Honestly, I have no idea where they came from, but I am pretty certain that I didn't make them up myself. These five steps are the key to developing and reproducing leaders, and they have the power to help you and your friends start and spread a movement!*

Every leader will have a relationship with an apprentice, but in addition to this relationship, every reproducing leader also needs the input and accountability of *peers*.

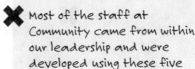

Most of the staff at Community came from within our leadership and were developed using these five steps. —Jon

3. A Reproducing Leader Needs Peers

In his book *The Five Dysfunctions of a Team*, Patrick Lencioni says the best form of accountability is what he calls "Peer-to-Peer Accountability." He says the healthy competition that is experienced among peers, combined with the natural desire to not let them down, makes the peer relationship an ideal environment for leadership development.

At our church, reproducing leaders find peer-to-peer accountability in something we call "leadership huddles." Huddles are monthly gatherings of leaders in small groups that include four basic activities: (1) praying for each other, (2) sharing wins, (3) disclosing challenges, and (4) exchanging best practices. These huddles are led by a coach, a leader of leaders.) very important

Even before we launched our first public celebration service at Community, we held a monthly gathering for leaders called Leadership Community. We got this idea from Carl George's book *Prepare Your Church for the Future*. In the book, he describes a monthly gathering of leaders that includes three key elements: vision, huddle, and skill.

- **×** *Vision.* This is a large gathering of all of your leaders to celebrate where God is at work, to honor new leaders, and to look ahead to where God is asking you to go next. This is usually led by the lead pastor.
- **×** *Huddle.* This is a small group of leaders (four to five) who come together for the purpose of encouragement and accountability. This is led by a coach.
- **×** *Skill.* This is a midsize gathering of leaders for the purpose of ongoing training, equipping, and development. This is often led by ministry directors or leaders and coaches who are skilled trainers.

We consider these three elements to be like vitamins or supplements that every leader needs on a regular basis. While we have found a monthly gathering to be the best way to provide them, the format may vary. But in any case, leaders' experiencing these three aspects of development must remain a high priority in a reproducing church.*

 Dave thinks people come for his vision. They really come for Eric Bramlett's new leader song. For an example of his antics go to YouTube and search on "bramlett chan." If you're ever in Chicago on the first Saturday of the month, you need to check out this big party. —Jon

Initially, our Leadership Community was a small group of ten to twelve leaders, but as we've grown and added more campuses, our Leadership Community has also grown. Now when all of our campus leaders come together for Leadership Community, we can expect up to five hundred leaders and apprentice leaders. As this gathering of leaders has grown, the planning and programming demands of the Vision and Skill times have changed as well. When there were just a handful of us, we would sit around a table or in just a few rows, and it had a very casual, conversational feel. As we've grown, the Vision time has become much more of a production, with a cue sheet and detailed planning. The Huddle time remains roughly the same as it was and will likely stay this way as long as our ratio of leaders to coaches remains low.

What is the value of these times? Our Leadership Community gatherings provide an opportunity for our leaders to be together, sharing experiences, struggles, challenges, and joys. Good leaders quickly learn that they need wise counsel from other leaders. Have you ever noticed that Solomon, the wisest man who ever lived, wrote more about the importance of wise counsel than all the other biblical writers combined? Have you ever wondered why? I think the answer is simple: Solomon was the wisest man in the world, and true wisdom recognizes that it doesn't know everything—it seeks counsel from others (see Prov. 1:5; 12:15; 15:22; 19:20). Reproducing leaders will need to seek wise counsel from their peers. This is the third key relationship that every leader needs.

4. A Reproducing Leader Needs a Coach

When you finally become a reproducing leader, you will inevitably develop a following and begin to surround yourself with a group of peers for support and accountability, as we just discussed. But in addition to seeking counsel from your peers, you will also need to seek out a coach who can provide a different perspective, challenging you in ways that will further your development as a leader.

Several years ago Glen Wagner joined our staff. He was a gifted communicator and strategist. He had already planted three churches and was sought out by executives and companies for coaching and strategic planning. Early in the tenure of any new staff person, we look for an opportunity to sit down with them and get their initial impressions and observations about our church. We've found that an "outsider's" perspective can be invaluable. I sat down with Glen to talk over some of this with him, and I remember there was one particular thing about our church that impressed Glen the most. (He told me he was amazed at how much we valued one-on-one development of our staff.) At first I didn't understand what he meant, so I asked him to elaborate. Glen explained that he'd never been in an organization or church that placed such a high priority on connecting with one another in one-on-one meetings for ongoing coaching and accountability.

I was surprised by Glen's observation. I didn't realize that what we were doing was all that unusual. I assumed that this was how most churches and organizations developed their people. After all, what was the alternative? Was there another way to do it? What Glen helped me to see was that this practice of one-on-one coaching had indeed become deeply ingrained in our culture.

I believe that the prominence of this one-on-one development is really just an outgrowth of our emphasis on apprentice development at all levels. We equip and develop our staff the same way we equip and develop all of our leaders, through one-on-one coaching.

Every leader needs a coach. Whether you're a small group leader, a missional team leader, or a leader of a group of students, you need someone who will provide ongoing care and trusted counsel. A good coach can often oversee the development of a small group of leaders, but usually no more than five at a time. The coach connects with each of his or her leaders regularly for one-on-one meetings, as well as meeting with them in a group that we call a leadership huddle. The huddle combines an opportunity for peer-to-peer accountability with the beneficial insight and wisdom of a more experienced leader, the coach. In chapter 8, we'll discuss this coaching role in greater detail.

Developing a leadership layer of nonpaid coaches (leaders of leaders) has long been a priority for us. The temptation we often face is to try to solve the challenge of caring for our leaders by hiring more paid staff. Eventually, though, we came to the realization that in order for us to continue to grow, reproduce, and care for the number of people God continues to send us, we just couldn't afford to hire and pay enough staff to carry out the task. That's why we now emphasize that every leader in our church needs to have a coaching relationship.

Tammy Melchien, who has been on our staff for several years at Community and is now preparing to lead the launch of a new campus, has been on an amazing journey as a developing, reproducing leader. She has benefited from each of the four key relationships. Here is her story in her own words:

TAMMY MELCHIEN'S STORY

I started my leadership journey as a campus minister at Eastern Illinois University, where I served for six years. We had over three hundred students involved, but I knew that my primary responsibility wasn't the students; it was pouring my life into seven female leaders who would in turn invest in the lives of their peers. Joy, Jo, Danah, Stephanie, Leah, Stacia, Shawanda—each was a life I knew I was called to help develop.

I would meet with each girl individually and with all of them as a group on a weekly basis to talk about life, study the Bible together, and develop our vision and strategy for reaching the campus. Nothing gave me more joy than to see them grow in their faith and ministry skills. When they graduated, I knew we were releasing well-equipped leaders into the world.

I relied heavily on my own mentors and peers for wisdom, encouragement, and accountability. Even though these people were scattered at various colleges and universities all over the country, we would still try to meet several times a year and were in regular contact through email and phone calls. Every month, I drove six hours (round trip) just to have lunch with one of my key coaches, Monica, who served at a campus in a neighboring state.

When I began to sense that God was leading me to take a next step in my ministry, I turned to Monica for guidance. She spoke words into my life that released me from my current position and began to give me a new vision for how God could use me in a different arena. Any concerns that I had about leaving the students and a ministry I loved were dispelled when the decision was made to hire one of the girls I had developed to replace me. Danah had been one of my first student leaders, and I had the privilege of apprenticing her for three years. When she stepped in to replace me, I knew that the ministry was being left in good hands. I am thrilled to say that seven years later she is still there, pouring herself into the lives of young women.

So where did I end up? Well, at Community, serving in a multisite children's ministry. Let's just say that children's ministry is probably the last thing I ever imagined myself doing! I knew absolutely nothing about leading a children's ministry (or a multisite church, for that matter). The campus pastor I reported to during my first year at Community played a huge role in my development. We would spend an hour every Sunday sitting on the couch outside the worship center during the second service at our campus. I gleaned so much during those informal chats, learning about the DNA and vision of our church. Glen Wagner, the lead children's ministry director at the time, also coached me. He helped me to see how my leadership gifts could translate into the children's ministry environment. He helped me to discover that even though I was now serving children and not college students, my role was still the same—leading followers and developing apprentices.

When Glen decided to move on, I stepped into his role as the lead children's ministry director. And as I stepped up to replace Glen, those following behind me stepped up as well. I turned over the children's ministry leadership at the two campuses I was overseeing to two of my apprentices, Scott and Mary. In my new role, I focused on developing the children's ministry directors at each of our campuses. But I also felt that a huge part of my role was to create a team atmosphere where each of these directors felt connected to the others, so that peer development, collaboration, and support would be maximized.

One of my greatest joys in leading this ministry has been experiencing the tight-knit camaraderie we share on our children's team. It truly is a team where peers have each other's backs and where our leaders partner together in life and ministry. Not only do I believe this peer support has made our weekly ministry to over twelve hundred kids more effective; it has greatly reduced the rate of staff turnover in our children's ministry.

Now, after seven years at Community, I am standing at yet another crossroads. I am sensing God leading me to take a new step on this leadership path. Once again I turned to my mentors, and with their guidance and after much prayer I am preparing to lead the launch of a new Community campus. Recently I became an apprentice to the campus pastor at one of our locations. As I prepare for this new role, I am also developing several people to replace me in my roles in our children's ministry.

Coaches, peers, apprentices, and followers. A leader's story of development is summed up in these four key relationships. And as

I move on to the next new thing that God calls me to do, I know that though the faces will change, the roles will remain the same. And I will continue to trust that God will use me and the people he has surrounded me with to advance his movement.*

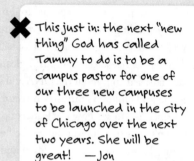

This just in: the next "new thing" God has called Tammy to do is to be a campus pastor for one of our three new campuses to be launched in the city of Chicago over the next two years. She will be great! —Jon

REPRODUCING ARTISTS

The Crucial Creative Class

BIG IDEA Attracting and reproducing artists is essential to starting a missional movement.

* Artists Catalyze New Communities
* Artists Help Sustain New Communities
* Attracting and Reproducing Artists
* Creating a Culture That Attracts Artists
* Creating a Culture That Develops Artists
* Five Factors for Reproducing Artists

If you asked me to give you the absolute essentials for spreading a missional movement of reproducing churches, I would narrow it down to two things:

1. Reproduce more and better _leaders_.
2. Reproduce more and better _artists_.

Obviously, we need leaders who grow people up in Christ, mobilize them for the mission of Jesus, and apprentice the next generation. But we also need artists who can lead and facilitate the large group gatherings of worship and the celebration of our God. Yes, I know this is a gross oversimplification. Still, simplifying it in this way gives us an important focus. I am convinced that if we can get these two essentials right, everything else will fall into place.

ARTISTS CATALYZE NEW COMMUNITIES

Richard Florida, author of *The Rise of the Creative Class*, presents his groundbreaking research to city planners and real estate developers, explaining that if they want to revitalize a region, they must begin by attracting the creative class. He writes, "The creative centers tend to be the economic winners of our age ... in the form of innovations and high-tech industry growth. The [creative centers] also show strong signs of overall regional vitality, such as increases in regional employment and population."[5] Florida goes on to demonstrate that throughout North America there is a direct correlation between the size and concentration of the creative class and the vitality of the community.✱

✖ The only reason we know about Richard Florida's book is because we have breakfast with our friends Nick Ryan, a real estate developer, and Perry Bigelow, a home builder, every Wednesday. —Jon

There is a lesson here for the church: if we want to see vitality in our churches, we need to attract artists and others in the creative class. So how do we do that? Florida gives a key suggestion that is equally applicable to our church context: "Creative people are not moving to these places for traditional reasons: sports stadiums, freeways, urban malls and tourism.... What they are looking for above all else is the opportunity to validate their identities as creative people."[6] In other words, we must become churches that make room for creative people to be creative!

Artists and creatives are often the ones leading the way forward, catalyzing the creation of new faith communities. In 2 Chronicles 20, we have this amazing picture of the Israelite army being led into a victorious battle over three heathen nations—by a choir! Or consider the story of Jericho, where God commanded the musicians to blow trumpets and march around Jericho for seven days until the wall came crashing down. Creatives and artists will often be the ones leading the way forward, taking new territory for the mission of Jesus.

If you are still skeptical about what I'm saying, think about launching a new site or a new church without musicians, vocalists, or technical artists of any kind. It would be quite a challenge. Then consider what it would be like trying to start a new incarnational church *without* the help of missional imagination. I'll be blunt: it's not going to happen!

ARTISTS HELP SUSTAIN NEW COMMUNITIES

The same artists who help to catalyze these new communities of faith will also be the ones who sustain new reproducing churches. Currently, Community has eleven sites and twenty-nine adult celebration services each week. In addition, we have seven Student Community and twenty-one Kids' City large group gatherings each week. We utilize the gifts of more than four hundred amazing artists every week so that people can join together and celebrate what God is doing in their lives.

As I look a few years ahead to the future, I anticipate that we will be adding at least two new campuses per year and four new celebration services each year. This means that there is an ongoing need for somewhere between seventy-five and one hundred new artists each year, just to sustain this level of growth. If I look beyond our church to the NewThing Network, we'll need a whole army of creatives to march ahead of us. Having artists and creatives on our teams will help to sustain these new communities.

If hundreds of creatives are needed for a reproducing church, and thousands more for a reproducing network (and even more than that for a movement), then what is the key to attracting and reproducing enough artists to keep up with the demand? As Richard Florida has suggested, you'll need to be a place that validates artists' identities as creative people. We have found that the creative class will often gravitate to communities where art and the artist are valued and appreciated. And wherever the creative class gravitates, there will be the creating of culture. These will be the physical and philosophical places where new communities of faith emerge.

ATTRACTING AND REPRODUCING ARTISTS

You might be thinking, "Attracting and reproducing is great, and I want to do all that, but what about *excellence*?" To some it might feel as if the idea of reproducing artists is too forced, lacking creativity, and that it will stifle artistic excellence. It's sort of like the two ends of a tug-of-war.

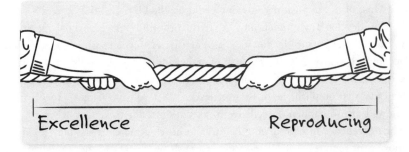

Some view the process as a win-lose situation, like this tug-of-war. When you pull hard on the reproduction side of the rope, you get lots of new artists, but in the process you lose your artistic excellence. Conversely, when you pull hard on the excellence side, you will only be able to trust a few talented artists to do the work, and you will be unable to reproduce quickly. Those who adopt this paradigm will always end up sacrificing one value for the sake of the other.

I think there is a better model for attracting and reproducing artists. Think of the process like riding a bicycle. A bicycle has two pedals, and in order to create forward motion, you need to push both of the pedals, but you do it one pedal at a time.

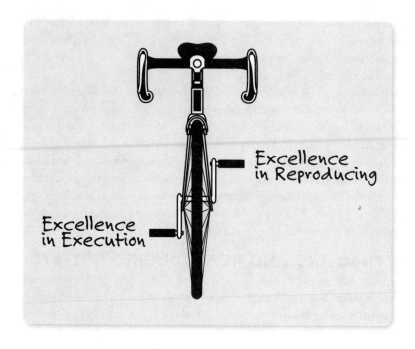

Most of us are pushing only one pedal on the bike, and that makes it very hard to develop any momentum. We frequently find ourselves choosing either to limit the opportunities for stage and artistic expression to just a handful of accomplished artists or, in the spirit of artistic development, to let anyone have a chance to "give it a try." I would suggest that neither option will effectively lead us to accomplish the mission of Jesus. We need to develop a process that allows both to happen. Excellence in execution tends to attract other artists, while excellence in reproducing helps us to develop more artists. Developing a movement requires that we learn how to push the pedal of artistic quality *and* the pedal of artistic development in tandem. As we gain speed, we will learn to alternate the pedals so quickly that it seems as though we are pushing both pedals at once.

Sounds great, doesn't it? But how do we do this practically, while keeping our balance as we pedal? I have two key suggestions for you, relating to *seasons* and *standards*.

1. *Seasons.* In every church, there are peak seasons when you have an influx of newcomers. Typically, these seasons are around "back to school," Christmas, and Easter. During these seasons, you want nothing to get in the way of people finding their way back to God, so you intentionally focus your time and energy on excellence in execution. During other seasons of the year, you are free to focus more on the reproduction of artists.

2. *Standards.* It's a good idea to create a standard of excellence that you will never compromise. This standard is in place to make sure that poor execution doesn't distract people from the voice of God when celebrating. You should continue to hold up this standard while you are reproducing.

Now that we have a better grasp of the fundamental relationship between attracting and reproducing artists in our communities, let's take a look at how to go about creating a culture that is attractive to artists and conducive to reproducing.

CREATING A CULTURE THAT ATTRACTS ARTISTS

There are five keys to developing a church culture that attracts creatives.

Cultural Key 1: Take Risks

The greatest gift we can give to any artist is a culture that is willing to take risks. My friend Eric Bramlett, who coauthored our book *The Big Idea*, taught me ✗ everything I know about the importance of letting artists take risks. I can still remember a Starbucks conversation in which he explained it to me this way: "Art by its very nature requires risk, the risk of expressing your most intimate creative thoughts and ideas on a canvas or dance floor or through music in front of large crowds. The crowds show up to watch the artist and can either cheer with raucous applause or boo and heckle with catcalls. Art is a risk!" ✳

As I listened to Eric that day, I began to see why most churches tend to repel artists. Many churches are not known as great-risk-taking organizations. Some churches even pride them-

 One time we had a service where we took a creative risk using fire. The fire was so out of control, we had to evacuate the room. —Jon

selves on wearing the label "conservative." Churches would rather be right than risk failing. Churches like this will not attract artists.

We are now at a place in our church where we routinely take artistic risks. We have done musical theater, hip-hop, a full orchestra, and even a kazoo band. We have done services where we tattoo everybody—and services where we anoint everyone. Many of these risks have worked marvelously—and some have been huge failures.

Our Yorkville campus recently took a risk when they put together the now infamous Bass Extravaganza. What is a "Bass Extravaganza," you may ask? Well, imagine every person on the stage playing a bass guitar, and you've got the picture. That's right, all bass guitars. (And a drum kit, but we'll let it slide. After all, it has a bass drum, right?) A whole lot of practice and careful arrangement of the songs were required to make this happen. The benefit of that extra time invested was that we not only had a rockin' Sunday morning but also saw a strengthening of relationships within the band. Prior to this weekend, one band member was on the fence in terms of his time commitment. After being part of something this fun and crazy, he saw the value of his contribution and has been a key artist ever since. Artists love it when we take risks, and our people love it when we create interesting experiences for them to invite their friends and neighbors to.

Cultural Key 2: Develop Relationships

All of us are created by God with a strong desire to live and thrive in our relationships with other people. But I've noticed that artists' need for connection is often greater than that of the average person. Their need for relationship is not just a basic desire to connect with others; it is often necessary for the development of their art, since much of creating art is a collaborative process. Theater, for example, is a collaborative form of art that requires not only other actors but also artists who design the stage and set. Music often requires collaboration between musicians playing different instruments. If you want to create a place for artists, it's important that you develop a means of bringing them into relationship with other artists.

A great way we've found to do this is to hold an open mic night. Choose a bar or cafe where you and your team of artists can hang out with other artists. Not only will your relationships with your artists improve, but your artists will begin developing relationships with others, independent of you and your ministry. This is huge. Plus, the community you create in that place may even begin to attract other artists.

Cultural Key 3: Give Them a Role

On more than one occasion, I have shown up to speak at one of our locations and noticed a band member who looked new. I'll say, "Thanks for playing with the band," and then ask, "What's your name, and how long have you been playing?" What happens next is amusing to me. First they tell me their name, and then they say, "This is my third week here. Last week I auditioned, and this week I'm playing." Then they look at me and say, "And who are you?" And I just say, "Dave," and leave it at that. We give artists a role on one of our teams as soon as possible. Artists contribute by creating art, so allow them to begin doing so as soon as possible.★

"I just say, 'Dave,' and leave it at that." Those words are begging to be mocked. Please email me your best dig at Dave for saying that. Type "Dig" in the subject line and send to jonferguson@ communitychristian.org. —Jon

Cultural Key 4: Plan to Reproduce

There is an old saying you've probably heard many times: "Birds of a feather flock together." I've found that this is probably more true of artists than of any other affinity group. Musicians want to be with other musicians. Dancers want to be with other dancers. Techies want to be by themselves. Oops, that is another story! To ensure that you are attracting artists, make sure that you create within your culture an expectation that every artist reproduces another artist. You may call it shadowing, understudy, second chair, or apprenticeship, but it is an understanding that we not only do art; we also bring other artists alongside us and help them develop their gifts. (Develop an *expectation* of reproduction that will build on the natural inclination artists have to be together and gives them a missional direction and focus.)

Cultural Key 5: Rock It Out!

Don't miss this last one. If you want to attract artists, you have to rock! Don't turn the volume down, rewrite the lyrics, and play it safe. Rock! Be good at what you do. Own what you do. Be passionate about what you do. Go all out with what you do! I'm not talking about a style of music here; (I'm talking about giving your artists freedom to express themselves with passion. Go all out! Get excited about what they do. Cheerlead in the moment. Let them rock! Artists respect that,) want that, and need that! If they have the opportunity to be in a place where they can really do what they love, you won't be able to keep them away. When you think about your artists, remember the immortal words of Dewey Finn (played by Jack Black in the movie *School of Rock*): "Dude, I service society by rocking, okay? I'm out there on the front lines liberating people with my music."★

Risks, Relationships, Roles, Reproduce, and Rock—five Rs. Rick Warren will be proud. —Jon

CREATING A CULTURE THAT DEVELOPS ARTISTS

It's all well and good to read that you should expect your artists to reproduce other artists. You've probably come to expect that from this book by now. But deep in your heart you're wondering, "How do you develop a strategy for helping artists reproduce and develop *that actually works?*" Well, let me tell you that you are in for a surprise! What you are about to read are three time-tested strategies that we have been using for several years in the development of hundreds and hundreds (if not thousands) of artists. In other words, this stuff works.

Strategy 1: Artist Leadership Path

The first strategy is a clear leadership development path for artists. You may be thinking, "Hold it, you just used the terms *artist*, *strategy*, and *leadership* all in the same sentence. Whatever it is you are talking about—it won't work." Yes, I realize that artists are different, but they're not *that* different. The same leadership path that we use for developing our leaders can also be used for developing our artists.

> Apprentice → Artist → Apprentice Leader → Leader → Coach → Director

A great example of this is Tony Germann. It had been a very long time since Tony had been in church when he showed up at our Romeoville location. Tony had played in lots of bands and is a terrific musician, and he was really surprised to find a church that played "real" music, the kind of stuff he loved to play. I met Tony on his first visit to the church, and his wife "outed" him by saying, "Tony is an awesome guitar player." Bill Carroll, who was our arts champion at the time, got his contact info and had him auditioning for our band within a month. Tony moved right past the apprentice stage and was regularly scheduled as an artist. Tony not only was a very gifted musician, but he also showed some great leadership gifts, so over the next four years he advanced further along the artist leadership path. He started leading one of our bands, began coaching our band leaders, and is now the arts director at our Romeoville campus.

Developing and hiring artists from within the church has real benefits over hiring from outside. First of all, most of the congregation have already seen these people grow, have watched them move through the development path, and have been cheering them on. Second, you know these artists' strengths and weaknesses, you're prepared to help them grow, and you are excited to make them part of the team.

While Tony's story is amazing, it's not unique. I could tell you a similar story about Chris, BT, Jeff, Charissa, and many, many others. Use the leadership path to cast a vision for your artists and show them how an artist can not only continue doing their art but also begin leading other artists and reproducing.

Strategy 2: Apprenticeship

It is essential that you are apprenticing new artists. We try to bring every new artist into our ministry through an apprenticeship. The apprenticeship works with our artists in the same way that it works with our leaders.

Step 1: I do. You watch. We talk.

Step 2: I do. You help. We talk.

Step 3: You do. I help. We talk.

Step 4: You do. I watch. We talk.

Step 5: You do. Someone else watches.

If you came to our church this weekend, it would not be unusual for you to see the apprenticeship process played out live on our stage. You might hear Bill, who is leading worship, say, "I want to introduce you to my apprentice worship leader. Instead of playing backup, he is going to be leading this next song and I will be backing him up. So let's all join in as Chris leads this next song." Then you would see Bill step to the back and Chris come forward, and in front of several hundred people Chris would lead a song for the very first time.

An interesting dynamic occurs when you apprentice a new worship leader like Chris. First, it reinforces that we value and believe in artist development and reproduction. Second, we find that people are rooting for Chris to do well his first time onstage. He gets support and encouragement from the congregation. Finally, Chris gets the opportunity to lead worship in front of several hundred people, and that experience helps him to feel comfortable in front of the congregation.

In the case of Bill and Chris, we saw Chris go from being a gifted artist working as a bartender to being a regular on the band schedule, leading band rehearsals, and then overseeing other band leaders. Chris is now the arts director at our Plainfield campus. I just love it. And check this out — the last time I was at our Plainfield campus, Chris was onstage introducing Seth, an apprentice worship leader who would lead worship for the very first time himself.

Apprenticing like this can happen with musicians, vocalists, actors — even techies. Once the value of reproducing artists is in place and a clear path for development is explained to them, the reproduction of artists begins happening through apprenticeships.

Strategy 3: School for the Arts

It was one of those aha moments when I knew that what I had seen could help further the mission of Jesus. I had just come from Naperville Music, where they were offering a "Rock School" (this was before the movie *School of Rock*, but if you have seen the movie, you'll know where I'm heading with this). The Rock School was a semester program for adults and students who had some musical experience and had always wanted to be in a rock band. For example, if you used to play the drums in high school or if you used to sing in the school chorus, you could sign up and they would place you with other musicians and vocalists and make up a band. Over the next several months, one of the teachers from the school would work with your band on a weekly basis to help you and your bandmates perform a set of two to three songs.

Instead of a recital at the end of the semester, though, they would rent a local theater, deck it out with the best AV equipment, and add a few fog machines. There were about a half dozen bands each semester, with six to seven people in every band, so once everybody invited a few friends and family members to the final show, they would have a crowd of around two hundred to three hundred people. Then they would ask the local cable provider to put the show on cable TV. Add it all up, and what do you get? You get the chance to be in a rock band with lights and fog, performing before a big crowd, broadcast on TV—you can be a rock star for a night!

After seeing this, I kept thinking, "Wow, we *have* to do this!" I knew that if we could provide something similar to the Rock School, when it was all over, we would be able to offer people additional opportunities to keep playing through our Kids' City, Student Community, and adult ministries. This had huge potential to help us develop and reproduce our artists.✱

My junior high son, Graham, just participated in our "rock school" last week, and he loved it. The concert was held at an outdoor amphitheater. —Jon

So I shared this idea with one of our artists, Rachel Carroll, and she started our School for the Arts. We initially began with nine private music teachers in piano, voice, percussion, and guitar, as well as some group classes in painting, acting, and music theory. That first semester, we launched with about 90 students at our Naperville campus. The school has now grown to 30 teachers and 410 students at four of our campuses. Additionally, the teachers are paid by the income from the school, which makes the School for the Arts self-funded.

Use any one of these strategies—or all three—and begin creating a culture that will reproduce the artists you need to launch a missional movement.

FIVE FACTORS FOR REPRODUCING ARTISTS

The following five factors can change the way you think about reproducing artists. A few of these insights come from Bill Carroll, who was one of our arts directors and is now in Paris, France, preparing to plant a NewThing church. Are you ready? Here are five factors that will help you reproduce your artists and creatives.*

✖ Even as we speak, Bill is probably strolling the streets of Paris, looking for a place to relax over coffee and a pastry. Church planting is so hard. —Jon

Factor 1: Think 30 Percent

I want you to remember the number thirty. That's the percentage of people in your church who *could be* engaged in the arts. Three out of every ten people who show up every weekend could be playing, performing, or supporting the arts in your community. Does that percentage seem high to you?

Over the last few decades, the conversation about the arts and the expectation of artistic excellence in the church have dramatically increased. Correspondingly, the level of creativity and excellence has also increased. While this is a good shift overall, what is not so good is that many church leaders have bought into a false standard of excellence. They tend to think that there are relatively few artists who can meet the acceptable standard for good quality. But it's just not true.

Think about all the people in your church who once played an instrument in high school or college. How many people were in dance troupes or theatrical groups or took painting lessons? Think about all the people who used to play in a garage band or "back in the day" played in a local bar band. The best estimate is that about 30 percent of your people have some background in the arts, and they have the potential to be engaged, using those gifts and skills in ministry.

Factor 2: Say, "We Need Artists"

I can't tell you how many times I've heard from new artists, "I didn't audition because the artists were really good and I didn't think you *needed* anyone else." Keep in mind that while you want to have a high standard of excellence in the arts, artists need to be told that they are needed! Find different ways to say that you need them. Say it from the stage, in your weekly program, on your website, and even in casual conversation. However you choose to communicate with people (both inside and outside of your church), make sure you are letting them know: "We need artists."

Factor 3: Insist That Your Artists Recruit Other Artists

We recently met with the lead team of a very large church that was struggling with artist development and recruitment. The number of new artists was greatly lagging behind the growth of the church. Their arts team admitted, "We barely have any new artists." We asked their arts director, "What are you doing to recruit new artists?" She said, "I put a monthly ad in the church program." Then, after a long silence, we said, "And …?"

Saying in the church program once a month that you need new artists will not get the job done. Such ads often get a response from a very small number of people, and they will typically be one of two types of artists: either those who think they are good and are not, or those who have performed with other churches. The former are no help to you, and the latter make up a small fraction of the artistic talent in your community. Remember, your focus is on recruiting that 30 percent who played in high school or college a few years back or those who played in the bar band before they got married and started having kids. We've found that the best way to get to *those* artists is through other artists.

Every one of our band leaders knows that as soon as a service ends, they need to scan the front of the stage for people standing around checking out the band's equipment and studying guitar effects pedals. Those are your musicians. If you are trying to do all your recruiting through one person, you will never get the job done. Every member of the team needs to be out there recruiting and needs to understand that the development of new artists is a top priority.

Our artists know that they are responsible to keep their ears open for potential artists at all times. Often new artists are recruited when they say something like, "I used to play in this band …" or, "I loved dancing …" Many times it's the spouse that will "out" them and talk about how good they once were. As soon as our artists hear something like that, they know they have found someone who needs to get more involved in the artistic community.

Factor 4: Follow Up Fast

Once an artist expresses an interest, you need to follow up fast. The only thing worse than not developing and reproducing artists is ignoring a gifted artist who expresses an interest in serving. I encourage every person in the arts to follow up no later than *the day after* a new artist expresses interest. Send them an email, give them a quick phone call, or drop a note in the mail telling them what the next step is to getting involved.

Every day that you don't respond to an artist after he or she expresses interest increases your odds of not having that person involved by about 15 percent. So if you talk to a potential new artist on Sunday and wait until that Thursday to follow up with them, the chances that they will get involved have decreased by almost half. Recruiting may be the most important thing you have to do that week.

Factor 5: Let Pagans Play

Many of our artists play in local bands and perform in theater companies. Since we encourage people at all stages of spiritual growth to use their art for God, we have lots of artists who are recruited by other artists and begin doing their art at our church before they become Christ followers. We're not only okay with that; we encourage it. Our Romeoville campus has been very successful in encouraging people playing in outside

 One of my favorite worship leaders at the Yellow Box (one of our Naperville campuses) is a guy who started playing in our band long before he was a Christ follower. If he keeps tracking, he'll be an arts director someday soon. —Jon

bands to come to church to play in the worship bands. They have recruited two entire bands that way. Not only that, but as a result of the relationships that have been formed in these bands, a number of people in them have actually come to follow Jesus!✱

The next time you're in a public place, take a look around. If you are in a public place right now, go ahead and take a look at the people around you. Think to yourself, "Thirty percent of the people I see have significant artistic gifts." That's three out of ten. And sadly enough, most of them don't think they have a place in the church. Yet these are the very people that you need, along with your friends, to catalyze and sustain a missional movement. So go over and ask one of them to join you!

Now.

Seriously.

PART TWO

REPRODUCING TRIBES OF 10–100

A missional church movement spreads by reproducing tribes of ten to one hundred people. These tribes we call groups and teams are ever-including and ever-expanding. It is tribal leaders who sustain the movement by leading and coaching these groups and teams.

REPRODUCING GROUPS

The Eternal Community

> **BIG IDEA** Reproducing small groups connect the unconnected and spread a missional movement.
>
> * Connecting the Unconnected
> * Developing 3C Christ Followers
> * Reproducing Groups and Leaders
> * Why Small Groups Are the Best Place to Reproduce Leaders
> * Myths about Reproducing Small Groups

It was a typical Tuesday afternoon. Jon had left the Yellow Box for home a little earlier than usual. It was about four in the afternoon, and he was driving south on Massachusetts Avenue about a block from the opening of the cul-de-sac where he lives. What first caught his eye were the police cars. Then he saw the yellow tape.

The story unfolded quickly. John and Sheri Scherer had lived in their home on Massachusetts for several years. Sadly, this was a family who kept to themselves. Hardly anyone knew them. But as the events of that day unfolded, we learned a lot more about John and Sheri.

Their ten-year marriage ended in divorce, and John's world spiraled downward quickly. His drinking resulted in a DUI, the loss of his job, and eviction from his nearby apartment. No one realized just how desperate he was until his sister-in-law arrived at the house that day, where Sheri and their six-year-old daughter, Rachel, lived. She went there after Sheri failed to show up for work. What she found was everyone's worst nightmare.

She discovered Sheri's lifeless body in an upstairs bedroom. Rachel was nowhere to be found. The next day, John's SUV was in a head-on collision with a semi on Interstate 80 in rural Iowa, killing John and his daughter, Rachel. The truck driver said that during a driving rain, the SUV unexpectedly crossed the median and gave him no time to react.✶

 It was surreal to see this unfold right outside my house in my neighborhood. It seemed more like something I'd watch on the ten o'clock news. —Jon

My brother Jon says, "This tragedy left many of us in my neighborhood asking, 'What could we have done to keep this from happening? How could we not have seen this coming? Why didn't they reach out for help?'"

The truth is that people just like the Scherers live around us every day—people who look just like you and me, people who are doing life *all by themselves*. And more than anything in the world, they need to experience life-giving community.

THE POWER OF COMMUNITY

Some of my favorite research on the power of community is the Alameda County Study.[7] A group of researchers tracked the lives of seven thousand people in Alameda County, California, over a nine-year period. What they found is pretty interesting.

- ✶ People with *weak* relational connections were *three times* more likely to die than those with *strong* relational connections.
- ✶ People who had bad health habits, like smoking and eating the wrong kinds of food, but had strong relational ties lived significantly longer than people who had great health habits but lived more *isolated* lives.

In other words, the study confirms the wisdom of John Ortberg when he says, "It's far better to eat Twinkies with good friends than to eat broccoli all alone!"

In another study, from the *Journal of the American Medical Association*, 276 people volunteered to be exposed to the common cold virus. (I can't help but wonder who would say, "I want a cold; pick me!") In this study, researchers discovered that

- ✶ people who had strong relational connections were four times better at fighting off illness than those who didn't;
- ✶ people with strong relational connections were significantly less susceptible to catching cold, had fewer viruses in their system, and produced less mucous.

It might sound a bit gross, but we now have the research to finally prove that unfriendly people really are snottier than friendly people!

Loneliness and desperation are not God's dream for us. God never intended that we would try to do life by ourselves, on our own, without help from others. At Community, our answer to the problems of loneliness and social isolation is for every person to be connected to a life-changing community of people, a group that can get you through any challenge or situation that comes your way. These communities are far from perfect—they're composed of messed-up, broken people just like you and me. But they work because the people in these groups intentionally encourage one another to grow in their relationships with God, each other, and the world around them. Our small group strategy has been built around three core values: connecting the unconnected, developing 3C Christ followers, and reproducing groups and leaders.✶

 Much of the content in this theology of community came from a great series we did called The Story of Everything. Tim Sutherland, our lead teaching guru, is brilliant on this topic. —Jon

VALUE 1: CONNECTING THE UNCONNECTED

The Garden

From the very beginning, God's dream was to satisfy our relational, emotional, and spiritual needs through *community*—a relational oneness that we experience vertically with God and horizontally with other human beings. That's what Adam and Eve experienced—complete relational connectedness with God and with each other. But look at what happened: "They hid from the LORD God among the trees of the garden" (Gen. 3:8). When Adam and Eve sinned, their oneness with God and with each other was lost, and our experience of healthy community came to a screeching halt. Since that time, God has been relentlessly pursuing his people, giving us opportunities to return to him and experience that same community that Adam and Eve enjoyed in the garden. Dallas Willard writes, "God's aim in human history is the creation of an inclusive community of loving persons, with Himself included as its primary sustainer and most glorious inhabitant."[8]

God designed us to feel like something is missing when we're *not* connected with him and with others. Throughout the Scriptures, we see that God utilizes small group structures to provide care for his people and to help people learn what it means to experience true community with one another and with him.

Old Testament

In the Old Testament, we find that God's people, the nation of Israel, were organized around large and small groups. Israel was divided into tribes, and the tribes were broken down into families or clans, and the families or clans were subdivided into single family units.

When Moses, the leader of the Israelites, found himself running out of steam, on the verge of burnout, and unable to meet the needs of the people he was commissioned to lead, his father-in-law, Jethro, suggested he try a small group system to better meet the needs of his people: "Select capable men from all the people — men who fear God, trustworthy men who hate dishonest gain — and appoint them as officials over thousands, hundreds, fifties and tens. Have them serve as judges for the people at all times, but have them bring every difficult case to you; the simple cases they can decide themselves. That will make your load lighter, because they will share it with you. If you do this and God so commands, you will be able to stand the strain, and all these people will go home satisfied" (Ex. 18:21–23).

Notice what Jethro was promising to Moses. Not only would Moses save himself from a nervous breakdown, but the people he was leading would actually be more *satisfied*. A small group structure could meet the people's need for increased care.✴

Ever wonder why it was Moses' father-in-law who suggested this plan? It makes me wonder if he was tired of getting an earful from his daughter, Moses' wife. —Jon

Jesus

In the New Testament, Jesus spent the majority of his time with his small group of followers. The primary focus of Jesus' ministry was investing in his small group, his missional team of disciples. When asked what the greatest commandment was, Jesus boiled it down to two things: love God, and love others (Matt. 22:37–39). It's in the context of a small group that we are best able to fulfill this two-part command, the summary of all of God's teachings.

The diagram on the following page highlights our tendency to drift toward a pseudo-spirituality or pseudo-community, when God's desire is for us to experience genuine community with him and with others.

The Early Church

Finally, when we look at the early church in Acts 2, we read that they gathered in two places: "Every day they continued to meet together in *the temple courts*. They broke bread in *their homes* and ate together with glad and sincere hearts" (v. 46,

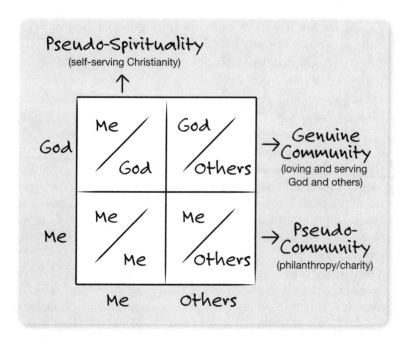

emphasis mine). The temple court was a public place where large groups of people gathered. But the early church also met in homes, where people gathered in small groups to enjoy a meal together and share the Lord's Supper.

If you take a careful look at what are often called the "one another" passages in the New Testament—the commands and encouragement from Paul and the other apostles that specifically address relationships in the church—you'll find a clear reminder of the importance and necessity of small groups. It is only through small groups that we are able to facilitate the kind of community that God wants you, your friends, and your church to experience.

A Vision for Connecting the Unconnected
God's people have been charged with the mission of connecting the unconnected ever since his dream of perfect community fell apart in the Garden of Eden. Let's pause for a moment to think about this mission of connecting the unconnected. I'll begin with what is likely an easy question to answer: do you plan to be alive in five years?

I'm guessing your answer is yes. Now I want to ask you a few questions to which you may *not* have answers:[9]

✻ In the next five years, would you like to influence the people around you in a life-changing way?

* Can you think of anything more life-changing than for someone to choose to follow Christ?
* So if you'd like to influence people in that way over the next five years, what is your plan?

Maybe you already have a plan, or maybe—like many people—you're sitting there thinking to yourself, "What plan? I never really thought about making a plan." If this describes you, and you don't already have a plan to influence others to follow Jesus, let me give you one to consider.

 If you were to start a small group today, and within a year start another group, and each new group you started would start a new group of its own every year, at the end of five years, how many people do you think would be directly or indirectly impacted in a life-changing way by your actions? At the end of five years, you would have thirty-two groups impacting somewhere around 320 people. Now, <u>that's a plan!</u>)

This is what is staggering to me: currently at our church we have about three hundred adult small groups. If each of these small groups lived out this plan, we'd see more than 96,000 people involved in life-changing communities in just five short years. Now, I know that all of this seems like a lot of talk about numbers, and maybe you're not into numbers. If that's the case, try to remember that the 96,000 figure represents *individual* people as well. The individuals who make up this group of 96,000 may be your neighbors, friends, or coworkers—people who right now are facing a Christless eternity!

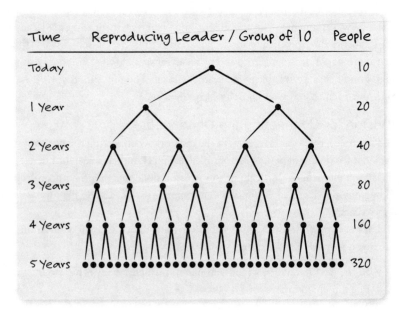

Imagine what could happen in your church and in your community in five short years if you and your friends caught a vision for connecting the unconnected through small groups!*

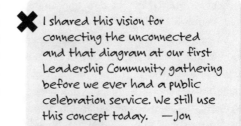 I shared this vision for connecting the unconnected and that diagram at our first Leadership Community gathering before we ever had a public celebration service. We still use this concept today. —Jon

VALUE 2:
DEVELOPING 3C CHRIST FOLLOWERS

While there are many experiences that contribute to biblical community, three emerge from the description found in Acts 2:42–47 and provide the basis for the second value that guides our small groups at Community: developing 3C Christ followers. We expect anyone who wants to deepen their relationship with Christ to continually grow in these three C experiences:

* Celebrate
* Connect
* Contribute

Each of these experiences has a corresponding focus on a particular relationship, and they all serve to deepen our walk with Christ. These three Cs are embedded into the activities and the culture of our small groups.

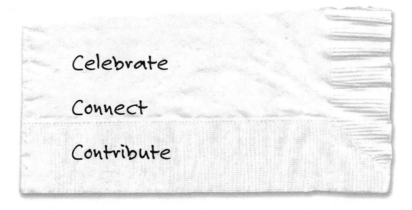

Celebrate

Connect

Contribute

Experience: Celebrate (God-Us)

The group that formed the very first community of Christ followers was a celebrating community. Acts 2:46–47 (NLT) says, "They worshiped together ... each day," and then goes on to describe how they chose to worship and celebrate: "[They] shared their meals with great joy and generosity—all the while praising God."

Did you catch that? "All the while praising God." Celebration wasn't just a weekly event; it was a *lifestyle* and an integral part of community life together. The first Christ-following community celebrated the great things God was doing in their midst.

Small groups need to be centers of celebration. We can celebrate the simplest of blessings, like a job promotion or a birthday. We can also celebrate the more significant "wins" in life, like a renewal of wedding vows or the adoption of a child.

Experience: Connect (Church-Us)

Another popular word that characterizes the kind of community people long for is *connect*. The first church community was unequivocally and tightly connected to one another and to God. They were so connected that the Bible says they were together daily: "Every day they continued to meet together" (Acts 2:46).

In our fast-paced, fragmented lifestyles, the very thought of connecting daily seems absurd. Most people in our communities and churches would think, "You've got to be nuts! A celebration service once a week and a small group gathering once a week or every other week is already a stretch. You want us to connect *every day*? Not a chance." But this kind of regular, daily interaction was one of the dominant characteristics of this attractive community.*

In *Organic Community*, Joseph Myers describes four patterns of belonging based on a theory developed by Edward Hall: public, social, personal, and intimate. Myers concludes that healthy community occurs when our connections, or "belongings," are greatest in the public realm and decrease in each succeeding realm as we discern those with whom we can experience a significant level of intimacy relationally. Myers suggests that connections in all four of these spaces contribute to our health and connectedness. I would agree with him and add that an increase in the frequency of time spent with the same people in these spaces will result in the greatest depth of community.[10]

Experience: Contribute (World-Us)

The third word that characterizes a healthy community of small groups is *contribute*. Acts 2:44 says that the members of the first church community "shared everything they had" (NLT). Verse 45 says, "They sold their possessions and shared the proceeds" (NLT). This was a group of people who could stand up and say, "If you've got a genuine need, we will help you." And the early church took this call seriously! Consider the contrast between the example of Barnabas, who sold a piece of property and gave the proceeds to the church to help the poor (Acts 4:32–37), and the story of Ananias and Sapphira, who misrepresented their gift and ended up dead (Acts 5:1–10).

Within the context of a small group, contributing most often occurs when the group members serve one another. Contributing is also something that occurs outside the group as the group serves the local community by meeting particular needs. For example, a small group may choose to serve in a homeless shelter or in a school, mentoring children who are struggling academically. (We find 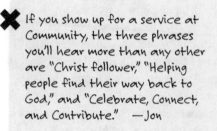 that groups who come together *without* an external "contribute" component or missional focus often fail to experience the same depth of community as do the groups who seek out opportunities to contribute to a particular cause and work together.*)

> If you show up for a service at Community, the three phrases you'll hear more than any other are "Christ follower," "Helping people find their way back to God," and "Celebrate, Connect, and Contribute." —Jon

Michael Stewart at Austin Stone Community Church conveys the importance of pursuing mission within the context of community: "This wonderful, beautiful community we find in Acts 2 was a direct result of pursuing Jesus and his mission. At Austin Stone we have realized that when you aim for Acts 2 community, you will get neither community nor mission. But if you aim to pursue Jesus and His mission, you'll get both mission and community."

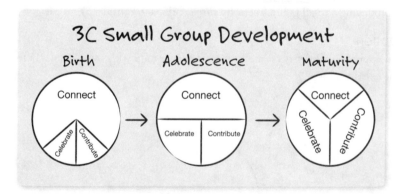

Both small groups and missional communities (see chapters 6 and 7) are places where people experience the three Cs of celebrate, connect, and contribute. The amount of emphasis that is given to these three experiences will vary depending on the type of group and the season of that group's life or development.

For example, a small group of young married couples will initially place a heavier emphasis on connecting as they get to know each other. However, as the group continues to meet, the emphasis on connecting will be more natural and less necessary, and the focus on contributing to those within the group or to a cause outside of the group will grow. What is important is that every group is intentionally growing in all three of these experiences.

VALUE 3: REPRODUCING GROUPS AND LEADERS

When living organisms are healthy, they naturally reproduce. God's intention for his church is that it would be a healthy, living organism that not only grows but also continually reproduces. In Mark 4, Jesus tells a story about four types of soil and a farmer who scattered seed. Have you ever noticed that the seed that fell on good soil didn't simply produce a plant—it produced a crop and multiplied "thirty, sixty, or even a hundred times" (Mark 4:8)? In the animal kingdom, species become endangered and can even go extinct when they die at a faster rate than they reproduce. Sadly, this will be the fate of the church as well if we fail to reproduce. Just as healthy organisms will reproduce—one cell at a time—healthy churches can reproduce one small group at a time.

 While all of this sounds good, just how do small groups actually become reproducing communities where leaders are developed and released? We've already covered the importance of apprentice development (a key piece of this model), and I want to emphasize again that small group reproduction is really all about _leader_ development. That said, when it comes to the basic "how to" for reproducing a small group, there are three options to consider.

Option 1

An apprentice leader is released to start a new group with some members from the existing group.

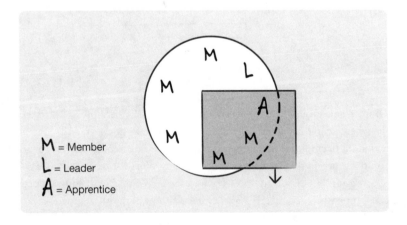

M = Member
L = Leader
A = Apprentice

Option 2

An existing leader is released to start a new group with some members from the existing group.

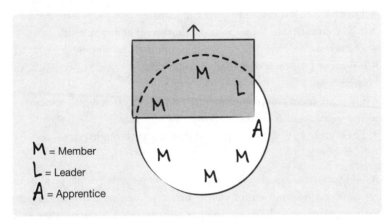

M = Member
L = Leader
A = Apprentice

Option 3

A "turbo group" is started in which all members are apprentices, and they all are released to start new small groups.

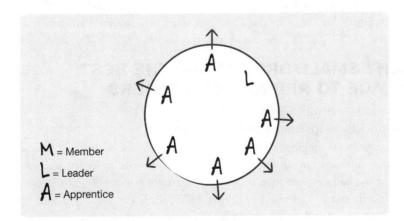

M = Member
L = Leader
A = Apprentice

Reproducing with Term Groups

In addition to the three options for reproducing an existing small group, we have begun to experience the benefits term groups bring to reproducing groups and leaders. Our term groups typically operate on a seasonal basis for a specific period of time. We usually have three to four terms every year when new groups are launched from scratch to welcome newcomers. Nelson Searcy, a church planter in New York City and the author of *Activate*, calls these groups "time-bound" groups. He gives seven advantages to starting these types of small groups:[11]

* They have a clear beginning and end date.
* It is often easier for people to make short-term commitments.
* The schedule allows time for group promotion and sign-ups.
* It is easier for people to get into a group when everyone is starting at the same time.
* There are more group options—new topics are offered each semester.
* The schedule matches the academic calendar year.
* These groups allow for the growth that comes through a stress-and-release cycle.

As long as there are always groups available for new people to join, term groups can be a great option for your church. As the end of an existing group draws near, plans must be made to start new groups for the next term. The date for the beginning of the new group provides a great goal for small group reproduction—and it begins a helpful discussion about the need for new leaders. One of the greatest advantages of term groups is that they force the reproducing conversation between the leader and apprentice leader.

In addition to being the primary place where people learn to fulfill Jesus' great commandment to love God and each other, small groups have proven to be the best place for us to grow and develop our leaders.

WHY SMALL GROUPS ARE THE BEST PLACE TO REPRODUCE LEADERS

Reason 1: Small Groups Are a Great Place to Take Leadership Risks

There was a young guy here at Community who was one of the most successful small group leaders in our church when it came to reproducing leaders and groups. But if you had a conversation with Rick, you would probably say that he doesn't necessarily talk like a leader and doesn't walk like a leader, and if you knew him as a high school student, you might say he was even a little annoying at times. But this young guy loved people and he loved Jesus, and he invested over and over again in apprentice leaders who were then released to start new small groups. In just four years he reproduced fourteen groups, and we loved him for it.✻

Now, that's a success story, but it doesn't always work that way. Sometimes people we think are a four, five, or six on a leadership scale become a three, two, or one when we place them into a leadership role, even after they've been

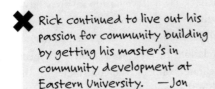

Rick continued to live out his passion for community building by getting his master's in community development at Eastern University. —Jon

apprenticed. However, one of the great advantages of developing and releasing leaders in small groups is that small groups lessen the leadership risk because the impact of a poor leadership decision is confined to a smaller number of people. Even if a leader fails miserably (which I have seen only a handful of times), it will have a negative impact on only a small number of people. Small groups are a great place to take leadership risks.

Reason 2: Small Groups Are a Great Place to Receive Honest Feedback

Receiving the kind of honest feedback a developing leader needs can be extremely difficult. And this is increasingly true as your influence grows. When you are responsible for larger numbers of people and are perceived to have more authority, you are less likely to receive constructive criticism. This is one reason why so many leaders in positions of great influence fail. Few people have the courage to speak the truth to them.

A small group provides a great environment for leaders at all levels, especially new developing leaders, to receive honest feedback. In a small group are people you trust, people you've grown to care for deeply, and conversely, people who care for you. Even so, the leader must take the initiative and create an environment where it is safe to communicate the truth. I encourage leaders to ask their group members to complete this sentence on a regular basis: "If I were the leader of this group, I would ..."

Reason 3: Small Groups Are a Great Place to "Get Church"

Inexperienced spiritual leaders often don't "get" church—or rather I should say that they don't "get" *healthy* church. They often have a difficult time understanding biblical principles like servant leadership. If most of their experience in leading others has been in the marketplace, they may be used to motivating people through compensation or inappropriately leveraging their authority. Small groups help even the most experienced marketplace leaders understand that leadership is really about influence and serving, not their position or title.

I had a conversation with a small group leader a while back who was complaining that her small group was not committed. She said they weren't participating consistently, they weren't doing their "homework," and they didn't seem to want to grow. She was complaining about her followers as if she had nothing to do with their lack of response to her leadership. It was making me crazy. She clearly wasn't getting two key leadership principles: (1) real leadership involves serving others, and (2) real leaders take responsibility for the actions of their followers.

Small groups are a microcosm of the church. As we mentioned earlier, anyone who wants to grow in his or her relationship with Jesus Christ is expected to grow in the three experiences of celebrate, connect, and contribute. All three of these experiences need to occur within the context of a small group. A leader will "get" church when he or she learns to effectively lead a small group in each of these experiences.

Reason 4: Small Groups Are a Great Model for Reproducing Campuses

I would guess that you've been a part of a small group that reproduced at some point. Think back on your experience. If you were to make a list of what is needed to reproduce a small group, what would you include? Here is my quick list:

* ✱ leader
* ✱ host
* ✱ site
* ✱ vision
* ✱ strategy
* ✱ prayer

Now let me ask you—how did it feel when you launched that new group? How did it feel to be a part of the new group that was started? How did it feel to be a part of a group that released others to start a new group? Typically, there is a mix of emotions: sadness over having to leave a healthy group, but also excitement about the opportunities to help new people experience a life-changing community.✱

Reproducing small groups is very much like reproducing campuses and churches. It requires leadership, vision, strategy, a host site, and a number of other factors. Small groups provide a great model for leaders who wish to understand, in practical ways, what it means to reproduce campuses and churches. When we made plans to launch our first campus, we referred to the expe-

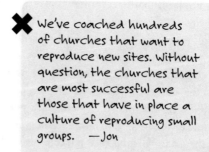

We've coached hundreds of churches that want to reproduce new sites. Without question, the churches that are most successful are those that have in place a culture of reproducing small groups. —Jon

riences people had in reproducing their small groups, to help them understand what they were going to experience when reproducing a new campus.

MYTHS ABOUT REPRODUCING SMALL GROUPS

Joel Comiskey is one of the leading authorities on small groups in the church today. In his book *Home Cell Group Explosion*, he researched the fastest-growing small-group-based churches in the world. More than seven hundred small group leaders completed his twenty-nine-question survey, designed to determine why some small group leaders succeed and others do not when it comes to connecting the unconnected and reproducing their small group.

Factors That Do Not Affect Small Group Reproduction

He first discovered some factors that do not appear to have any effect on reproduction.

1. The leader's gender, social class, age, marital status, and education were not factors in his or her ability to reproduce a small group.
2. The leader's personality type was not a factor in his or her ability to reproduce a small group.
3. The leader's spiritual gifting was not a factor in his or her ability to reproduce a small group.

So what factors, according to Comiskey's research, actually affect group reproduction?

Factors That Do Affect Small Group Reproduction

1. *The leader's prayer life.* The one factor in the survey that seemed to have the greatest effect on whether a group reproduces is how much time the leader spends praying for group members. The leader's devotional life consistently appears among the three most important variables in the study.
2. *The leader's setting goals to multiply.* The seven hundred leaders surveyed were asked, "Do you know when your group is going to reproduce?" Possible answers were "yes," "no," or "not sure." Leaders who know their goal and know when their groups are planning to reproduce consistently reproduce their groups more often than leaders who do not know their goal.
3. *The leader's receiving effective training.* Comiskey's research also found that small group leaders who felt that they had been trained to reproduce their small groups did so more rapidly. However, training was not as important as the quality of the leader's prayer life.
4. *The group's evangelistic efforts.* Comiskey found that there is a direct correlation between the number of visitors in a group and the number of times a leader reproduces the group. In other words, if you have lots of newcomers, you're more likely to reproduce your group.

5. *The group's "outside" meetings.* I call this the fun factor. The research found that groups that met more frequently *outside* of the regular small group gathering—just for fun—were more likely to reproduce than those that didn't.[12]

Let me ask you a question right now: do you believe this research? Do you believe that a person's education, personality, or spiritual gifts may have nothing to do with his or her ability to lead a small group to thrive and reproduce? Do you believe that if you were consistently praying for the members of your group, it would result in greater life-change and increase your likelihood of reproducing leaders and groups? If you do, what steps are you ready to take today to align your daily activities with your deeply held convictions?

God's dream is for everyone to experience life-giving biblical community, and he has left it up to his followers, people like me and you, to connect the unconnected, bringing that life-changing community to those who need it most.

A few years ago there was a small group at Community made up of couples in their early thirties, with the exception of one older couple in their sixties. At the end of their gatherings, the group would break into two smaller groups for prayer—men in one group and women in another. One evening, the husband from this older couple told the men he really wanted to buy a Christmas present for his daughter whom he'd become estranged from, but his life insurance premium was due, and he couldn't afford to cover both expenses. He asked the guys to pray for him about this difficult choice he had to make. He was in a quandary because he wanted to reconcile with his daughter and was seriously considering sacrificing his life insurance to do it.

After group that night, the younger guys got together and decided to pitch in to cover the cost of his life insurance premium. It wasn't a lot of money for them, but to the older man it was a significant part of his income. The following week the younger men gave him enough money so he wouldn't have to sacrifice his life insurance. When they handed him the cash, he looked at the ground, began to shake a little, and started to cry. He said he'd never received anything like this before and felt so blessed that a bunch of guys half his age cared about him in such a profound way.

Two months later, while he was working, he died of a massive heart attack. The man's wife asked the group to plan and lead her husband's memorial service.

 Small groups are the epicenter of community life in a church. For a long time we at Community have believed that God will send us only the number of people for whom we can adequately offer care. There may be other ways to care for and develop people in their relationship with Christ, but we continue to find that reproducing small groups are the best context in which to nurture and grow followers of Christ.

REPRODUCING MISSIONAL TEAMS

Communities with a Cause

"COULD WE START SOMETHING FOR PEOPLE WHO WON'T COME TO CHURCH?"

"I'm not sure I can get them to come to church with me." I was surprised to hear Kathy say this, because every week she brings people who are far from God to our church services. Often I will look out into the crowd at a weekend service and see an entire row of people sitting next to her, and I know these are people who are still getting started on their spiritual search for God. Kathy is as passionate about helping people find their way back to God as I am. So when Kathy described these teenage girls in an eating disorder group she was leading and said, "I'm not sure I can get them to come to church with me," I had to listen. She went on to tell me that the girls were overwhelmed and terrified to come into a room with several hundred people. She said that some of the girls would get into the building but would stay out in the lobby the whole time. Then Kathy asked me, "Could we start something for people who won't come to church?"

Kathy's question took me back several years to the time when our church first became a multisite church. Our motivation at the time wasn't to be innovative but to be a church that would "go into the world." We were passionate about the mission of Jesus, and if that required us to start a new site in a nearby neighborhood, we were going to do it. But Kathy's question that day in our café challenged me in a new way. As I considered it, I just knew that the answer *had* to be, "Yes!" *

Over the last *twenty* years we have learned from churches like Willow Creek, Southeast Christian, and Saddleback how to grow a megachurch. And today

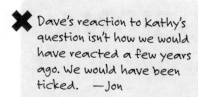

Dave's reaction to Kathy's question isn't how we would have reacted a few years ago. We would have been ticked. —Jon

there are more megachurches in the United States than ever before. Over the last *ten* years we have learned from churches like LifeChurch.tv and Seacoast how to have one church in multiple locations. And today we are seeing more and more churches growing through multiple sites (don't worry—we'll explore the emerging multisite movement at length in chapters 9 and 10).

Now, what is happening through multisite churches is very good news. But it's not *enough* good news. And here is why: my best estimates tell me that at least one-third to one-half of the American population will *never* come to churches like the ones you and I attend. Up to 50 percent of the population will *not* come to a church-owned facility no matter how cool or engaging it looks and feels. Even multiple sites won't completely solve this problem. So what's the solution? I believe that in the next decade we will need something more than megachurches and multisite churches—we'll need *reproducing* churches filled with missional teams that go to the people and don't just expect people to come to them. These volunteer-led teams will be a part of every church that wants to reach an increasingly diverse world. We can no longer be content asking people to come to us. We need to go to them!

"I THINK I ACCIDENTALLY PLANTED A CHURCH"

Shawn is one of the most thoroughly churched guys around. He can't remember a time in his life when he was not involved in a church. Shawn liked church but, somewhat similar to Kathy, had a growing frustration that many of his closest friends had no interest in church activities and would not come with him to a service. If he asked them to go water-skiing with him, they would always say yes. His friends would even rearrange their schedules and do whatever it took to be out there on the water. But if Shawn asked them to go to church with him, the answer was always no.

This got Shawn thinking a bit—and gave him an idea. With the blessing of his church, he changed his Sunday routine from going to church to going water-skiing. He invited a couple of his best buds along—and of course they said yes.

That first Sunday as he played hooky from church, he went skiing with two of his non-Christian buddies. He was about to get in the water when he got an attack of the "guilties." So he said to them, "Guys, you know I'm Baptist, and I'm feeling kind of guilty for not being in church today. Do you mind if I read a bit of Scripture first?" His friends seemed a little uncomfortable, so he read the shortest psalm he could find. Then Shawn said, "We Baptists pray for needs, so does anybody have any prayer requests?" One guy said he was unemployed, and the other guy said his grandma was in ICU. So Shawn prayed for the guy's job and the other guy's grandmother and then asked God to bless the day and the boat. Then they went skiing.

The next Sunday, at Shawn's encouragement, his two friends brought a bunch of buddies. Again he read a little Scripture and got ready to pray. But this time he said, "We Baptists like to see if there are any answered prayers." The one friend said, "You know, I did get a job this week. Thanks!" And the other friend jumped in, saying, "My grandma was released from the hospital this week." Then Shawn asked if there were any other prayer requests. After the guys heard those kinds of results, a bunch of hands went up. Shawn prayed for each person and asked God to bless the day, and then they went skiing.

Shawn and his friends now do this weekly with more than sixty people. They gather near the dock, have breakfast, read a bit of Scripture, pray for each other, take up an offering to give to the poor, and then go water-skiing. Recently they started bringing spare boat parts so if they come across someone whose boat has broken down, they can help out.

Shawn looks back on this and says, "I think I accidentally planted a church."

GOD IS ALWAYS GOING AND SENDING

Whenever someone is lost or alone, God's reaction is always to "go" and to "send." When the Gentiles were without knowledge of the one true God, God sent Abram, telling him to go to a foreign land: "Leave your country, your people and your father's household and go to the land I will show you. I will make you into a great nation and I will bless you" (Gen. 12:1–2).

When God saw that we were far from him, the Bible tells us, "God didn't go to all the trouble of sending his Son merely to point an accusing finger, telling the world how bad it was. He came to help, to put the world right again" (John 3:17 MSG). And what instructions did Jesus give to those he apprenticed? Scripture says, "The Lord appointed seventy-two others and sent them two by two ahead of him to every town and place where he was about to go. He told them, 'The harvest is plentiful, but the workers are few. Ask the Lord of the harvest, therefore, to send out workers into his harvest field. Go! I am sending you'" (Luke 10:1–3).

Over and over again we see that our God's reaction to the lost, lonely, and "least of these" is to go and to send. So when Jesus told his followers, "Go and make disciples of all nations" (Matt. 28:19), he was not saying anything radically new. He was simply reminding them, once again, that the mission of a Christ follower is to go.

Be honest. Isn't there something inside of you that knows you are supposed to be out there beyond the walls of the church facility? Isn't it a bit unrealistic to insist that the world should come to us and fit inside our church buildings? If you believe that Jesus told you and me to go because he really meant for us to go—and not just invite people to church—why don't you and your friends start a 3C community and begin reproducing missional teams? Well, why not?

MISSIONAL TEAMS: 3C COMMUNITIES

In the same way that Shawn's church gave him permission to focus on his unreached friends, we need to give the people we lead permission to start a missional team. These missional teams can practice the simple three Cs (celebrate, connect, and contribute) where they work, in their neighborhoods, at cafés, at local hangouts, where they work out, and where they play in a sports league. At Community, we often refer to our missional teams as 3C communities.*

When I talk about missional teams or 3C communities, inevitably someone will ask, "I do setup and teardown; is that missional?" Someone else will say, "I'm on a team that provides care for our toddlers every weekend during the celebration services; is that missional?" What people are wanting to know is whether the teams that serve within the four walls of the church are missional. Absolutely. If your team contributes to the mission of helping people find their way back to God, then it is missional. We certainly need to get outside the walls of the church, but we also need to make sure that those

 In raising the value of missional teams serving outside the church walls, don't minimize the ministry of someone like Mary Stuart. She has been on a team holding babies during the celebration services at Community since the beginning. And she knows she is contributing to the mission. —Jon

things that happen within the walls of a facility owned or rented by a church are missional. If you and your team are contributing to the mission, then you are missional; if you are not contributing to the mission, then you need to start!

What makes a missional team distinct is that it has a *cause-related* focus. In the previous chapter, I gave you a small group model that includes the three Cs but has a greater initial emphasis on *connecting* than on celebrating or contributing. By contrast, a missional team will be comprised of the three Cs but will ultimately have a greater emphasis on *contributing*.

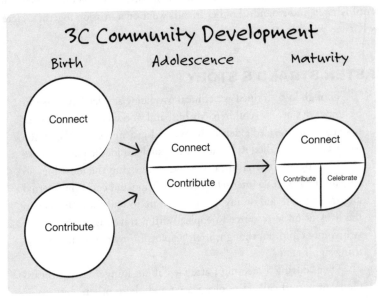

3C communities are the kinds of gatherings that focus on serving people and are able to reach people who would never walk through the doors of our churches. The following model shows the development of a 3C community:

1. *Birth.* The missional team will experience all three Cs but will be birthed in one of two ways: (1) through an affinity or connection with a particular group of people (for example, Shawn birthed a 3C community to reach his skiing friends); (2) through a cause to which you and your friends want to contribute your time, talent, and resources (for example, Kathy started a 3C community for teenage girls with eating disorders).

2. *Adolescence.* Regardless of whether your 3C community is birthed with a focus on connecting or contributing, the next phase is to encourage people who are connecting to contribute, and to encourage those who are contributing to connect.

3. *Maturity.* As a 3C community matures, it will continue to focus its efforts on connecting and on contributing to the cause. However, there will also be an increased emphasis on celebrating, as some begin to find their way back to God and as others grow in their relationship with Christ.

Kirsten was living the American dream: a six-figure salary, happily married with two great kids, and living in Naperville—a city that repeatedly receives awards as one of the best places in the country to raise a family. Surrounded by the blessings of success, she still was feeling depressed, lost, and unfulfilled. That is, until Kirsten and a handful of her friends went on a mission together. Here is how Kirsten tells her story:

KIRSTEN STRAND'S STORY

Though I was trained as a clinical psychologist, I left my career to be home with my two children. My husband worked as a regional sales manager and traveled extensively. We had just moved to Naperville —or Oz, as we called it, because it was such an idyllic place to raise children. By all external measures, we were living the ideal life. So why did I struggle so intensely with depression and constant internal angst? God had laid on my heart the desire to make a difference in the lives of underresourced people. With a traveling husband and two young children, though, I felt helpless in my ability to do anything significant.

Then, during a meeting I attended about hunger relief, I heard God's profound call. His voice wasn't audible to others, but it was to me. God asked me to start a movement of Christ followers who would live out Matthew 25 and be Jesus to the poor. I remember praying, "God, why me? Why not someone in a position of leadership who could really do something?"

After this epiphany, my husband and I spent many months praying. During that time, we became convicted that God was indeed calling our family to a different lifestyle. It was time for a seismic life change. Scott left his company and went back to school to get a degree to teach in low-income schools. I worked part-time jobs to pay the bills and served relentlessly as a volunteer leader at Community. I enjoyed working as a volunteer but faced many challenges and frustrations. There were the obvious financial challenges; we went from making a six-figure income to our kids qualifying for free and reduced lunch. Tears streamed and arguments with God raged. How could I ever grow this ministry into the impact-making ministry for which he had given me a vision?

I spent three years talking to anyone who would listen to me and learning about community development and the needs in our area. I began to surround myself with a team of friends and key people who were also passionate about the mission of bringing restoration to neighboring East Aurora. I had a core volunteer team of about twenty friends who were as committed to this work as I was. After I spent three years volunteering and leading, Community hired me to give birth to Community 4:12 (Eccl. 4:12), a ministry with the mission of "uniting people to restore communities." We all fell in love with East Aurora, an underresourced and primarily Hispanic community just miles away from our largest campus in affluent Naperville.

We planned a <u>Christmas Gift Mart</u> for our first event. We wanted to provide the dignity of not just receiving a "handout," so we collected new donated toys and set up a mart where parents could shop for toys for pennies on the dollar. Then all the money we raised was donated to the school. For that first event, we had 120 volunteers and raised eight hundred dollars for the school.*

 This Gift Mart is one of the coolest things ever. Last year fifteen hundred volunteers provided fourteen thousand toys for more than thirty-five hundred people in East Aurora and East Joliet through this event. If you'd like to get the scoop on how to make an event like this happen, contact Kirsten at kirstenstrand@ communitychristian.org.
—Jon

We continued organizing community events and began after-school clubs to build relationships in the neighborhood. I attended any community meeting I could find and began building partnerships with other churches, schools, and nonprofits. I spoke at small gatherings to fuel a passion for serving the underresourced. The ministry grew, but God wasn't finished challenging me yet.

Through this informal training, I learned that one of the key principles of Christian community development is "relocation." If you are going to serve in a community, you really need to live there and be a part of it. I kept arguing with God: "That principle couldn't apply to me—I have two young kids." Surely God didn't want them moving into a community known for violence, poverty, and low-functioning schools.

But that is exactly what God wanted.

Once my husband finished school, he was hired as a third-grade teacher in East Aurora. While he got to know the community through teaching, we continued to grapple with the idea of moving our family. After a year of anguished prayers, we decided to make what we perceived at the time to be a significant sacrifice. We moved to East Aurora. Little did we know that moving would be the greatest blessing we'd ever experienced.

We have now lived in East Aurora almost three years. In that time, the work of Community 4:12 has grown exponentially. Our credibility and acceptance in the neighborhood grew immediately when our elementary-aged children became a part of the school system we were fighting to change. We were no longer working for "them." We were working for "us." Our credibility at Community also grew as people realized this was not just some feel-good ministry we were doing—we were out to truly restore a community.

The heart for compassion and justice has begun to explode at Community. Five years ago we had about one hundred volunteers and a budget of five thousand dollars. Today we have more than two thousand volunteers and an annual budget of more than two hundred and fifty thousand dollars. Community 4:12 has expanded to partner with six elementary schools, a middle school, and a high school. We run after-school programs, tutoring programs, a parent-training program, community events, and a bimonthly coffeehouse, and we facilitate an advisory board whose purpose is to unite churches, organizations, and businesses around a common vision. We have acquired permanent 24/7 ministry space in East Aurora and just launched a campus of Community that is bilingual. We have recently reproduced the ministry in another underresourced community on the east side of Joliet, Illinois.

Today my soul is at peace. While it is a constant challenge to balance ministry, motherhood, and leading a growing ministry, I am doing what I know God designed me to do. When I look back over the journey and try to look ahead to the future, I am humbled, because there is no way to explain what has happened, except to say that God is using me and a few of my friends to spread a missional movement.

HOW TO REPRODUCE 3C COMMUNITIES

Beyond the four walls of our churches, in the neighborhoods and workplaces where the least, lonely, and lost live, are the places God is sending us to. Jesus didn't say to his followers, "Bring the world to us." He said, "*Go into* all the world." I believe one of the best ways that we can go into the world is by reproducing 3C communities, and there are some practical steps we need to take to begin the process.

1. Believe That Acts 1:8 Was Meant to Be Accomplished

Read those last words of Jesus in Acts 1:8 once again: "You will receive power when the Holy Spirit comes on you; and you will be my witnesses in Jerusalem, and in all Judea and Samaria, and to the ends of the earth." As we've already discussed, Jesus said this because it's his mission for the church—and he meant for it to be accomplished! I will say it one more time, but make sure this sinks in: we need to believe that Jesus' mission was meant to be and can be accomplished!*

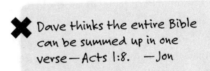

Dave thinks the entire Bible can be summed up in one verse—Acts 1:8. —Jon

Amen

Once we believe this, it changes how we think about the strategies and tactics of our local church ministry. It forces us to come to grips with the simple fact that we cannot build facilities big enough or fast enough to keep up with what God wants to do. We need every follower of Christ engaged and mobilized in the movement.

2. Ordain Every Christ Follower to Start a Church

A while back, I stood in front of hundreds of leaders at Community and told them the story of Shawn, the guy who accidentally planted a church. I told them

Kathy's story and her powerful question, "Could we start something for people who won't come to church?" And I told them I wanted Community to start lots of 3C communities to reach all kinds of people that we were not reaching. Then I said to our people, "As your pastor, I give you my permission to go and plant churches." At that moment, I felt an overwhelming sense of God's approval.*

> Every year we have an anointing service where we commission new leaders. It really is a marker event in the lives of those new leaders. —Jon

Set aside a time for you and your friends to take a second look at the mission of Jesus, given to us in Acts 1:8. Ask them if they really believe it was meant to be accomplished. Tell them that this mission will require more than simply inviting your friends to join you; it will require that you go to the world. Then ordain them. Bless them. Give them permission to do what Jesus has asked them to do.

3. Teach People to "Go" and Not Just "Bring"

Some people find joy in the quiet sounds of nature, but Donna Sauer tells me that the roar of motorcycles ignites her engine and brings her happiness. Donna loves bikes (more specifically, she loves Harleys!) and she loves bikers. Bikers are her crowd, and that is where she feels most at home. Now, her biker friends are a distinctly spiritual group, and they look out for each other, but Donna says, "What they really want in life is found in Jesus, and most of them are so far away." A couple of years ago we gave Donna permission (she didn't really need it, of course) to skip church on Sundays and to start something to reach her biker friends. And she did.

Donna began her own weekly rides where she invites anyone who likes motorcycles to meet her for breakfast and a ride. The group meets every Sunday morning at a local restaurant called Elmer's Doghouse. Over the last year more than two hundred different riders started their engines and hit the road with Donna. Her simple goal is to love them, help them love each other, and look for opportunities to pray for her friends.

Along the way, she organized this group of bikers into a difference-making community. *Her* biker friends invited *their* biker friends, and more than 225 bikers came together to lead a ride that raised twenty-seven thousand dollars to fight ovarian cancer. At the beginning of biking season this year, more than forty of her biker friends joined her at Community's Montgomery campus for the first annual Bike Blessing. Campus pastor Carter Moss gave a talk geared just for Donna and her friends and then was given the privilege of praying with each biker. After the blessing, the riders took off on scenic country roads to a lunchtime destination.

Donna shared with us, "The blessing ride was a fantastic way to kick off the new riding season. I am going to continue to lead the Sunday rides and hope that the group continues to grow and find their way back to God."

If we are going to reproduce 3C communities, we must be willing to give people like Donna permission to skip our worship services to create their own alternatives that will help people find their way back to God.

4. Plant the Gospel before Planting a Church or Starting a Group

Missional teams will think gospel planting before church planting or even starting a group. Missional teams will go and live among the people with a readiness to serve them. From that context, they will ask two important questions (in this order):

1. What is good news (gospel) for these people?
2. What is church for this people group?

A missional team does not presume to know the answers to these questions before they live as Christ among them. My friend Alan Hirsch says that most churches mistakenly operate in this order:

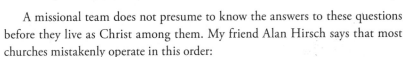

Ecclesiology → Missiology → Christology

Instead, we should be operating like this:

Christology → Missiology → Ecclesiology

Too often we go into a situation or a community and presume to know the form that is most needed to release the functional power of the gospel. We first must plant the gospel in the hearts and lives of people and then see what form of ecclesia emerges from the transformed community. If we begin with the premise that we are starting a "church," it will often come loaded with intuitional and cultural assumptions. (Churches should grow out of the mission, not the other way around.)

5. Recognize That Missional Teams Must Be Both Incarnational and Apostolic

To this day, Kirsten Strand is passionate about the East Aurora neighborhood. She was so passionate about the mission of restoring the community that her family relocated there, and others have followed. That is what it means to be incarnational, to move into the neighborhood like Jesus describes in John 1:14: "The Word became flesh and blood, and moved into the neighborhood" (MSG).

If a missional team is apostolic, then it will recognize the "going" and "sending" of leaders as a priority. Every missional team needs to be thinking about their current context *as well as* the next place God wants to work. That, in a nutshell, is what it means to be apostolic.

Like small groups, missional teams also have at least three ways of reproducing (see models for reproducing groups on pages 96–97):

1. The *apprentice leader*, when ready, will go and start a new team.
2. The *existing leader* can be sent out to start a new team, and the apprentice leader becomes the new leader for the existing team.
3. A *team of apprentice leaders* is formed for a short amount of time with the understanding that they will all go out and start new works to further the mission.*

One of Kirsten's apprentice leaders is Bob Lowe, a passionate community advocate who spent much of his career working for the YMCA. Over time it became obvious that God was at work not only in East Aurora but also in the east side of Joliet. Since Kirsten and her team were both incarnational and apostolic, it was also obvious that Bob was the guy to lead this new expression of Community 4:12 in this new community.

 Last month, Eric Metcalf started a missional community turbo group with twenty-five future 3C community leaders. Among the communities to be served are a homeless community, a golfers' community, a community of business executives, and a tennis players' community. —Jon

If missional teams do not think in terms of apprenticeships and reproducing leaders, their work will always be limited to one place for one period of time. However, if a missional team will think apostolically and emphasize reproduction, their impact will grow exponentially. All successful movements are both incarnational and apostolic.

6. Provide Missional Teams with Coaching and Training

Our first attempt at mobilizing people for missional teams was a false start. We did a good job of inspiring a few people. We told some stories to help people get it. We asked one of our campus pastors to oversee these teams, and we even put a few dollars toward it. Our intentions were good, but the biggest mistake we made was not providing the necessary infrastructure to support missional teams. Missional teams, like every other kind of group or team, need two types of support: coaching and training. In chapter 8 you will learn all about coaching and why that is necessary to spread a missional movement.

The kind of training missional teams need before they start is primarily in developing a missional *imagination*—helping people see the possibilities that God has already put before them. A great example of this type of training is found in the work of Forge, founded by Alan Hirsch (see *http://forgeamerica.com*). Alan and his team are experts in helping leaders develop a missional imagination and see possibilities in their current context. In addition, Hugh Halter and Matt Smay have developed some outstanding adult-learning modules that can be accessed via the Web and used to train leaders while they are engaged in mission (see *www.mcap.info/*).

7. Get Comfortable with Chaos and Failure

Here are the brutal facts: if we give our leaders permission to go out and start missional communities and churches that will reach people for Jesus, it will not be perfectly organized and it will certainly not be one hundred percent successful. During a recent retreat with our campus pastors and strategic team, I asked everybody to wrestle with this question: "How would Community be different in two years if everyone literally obeyed Jesus' command to go into all the world?" The two most common responses: "It will be really messy" and "We will have a lot more failure."

Several years ago we launched a campus in a new neighborhood between our Yellow Box Campus and our Montgomery Campus. There were many things about this launch that were similar to other launches. We believed this was a God thing because we were invited into this community by the developer himself. One of Community's most respected staff persons was identified as the campus pastor for this new launch. For several months preceding the launch we worked to develop a strong relationship with the local elementary school. In spite of what we believed were our best efforts, eight months after the launch, this new campus was closed.

As we've gone over and over what led to this failure, we now recognize several strategic mistakes we made in launching this campus. Our launch team was too small, we did not have enough small groups in place before we launched, and we failed to recognize the cultural differences in this community. The people who lived in the neighborhood were primarily Anglo, but the school where we launched had a majority of Spanish speakers. While our outreach efforts targeted this Spanish-speaking community, our weekend celebration services did not. We will launch in this community again. And when we do, we will take a different approach with a new metric for success that is appropriate for reaching this unique community.

As hard as this decision was for me personally I know it was much more painful for our campus pastor and launch team, who gave every last ounce of energy and prayer they could to make it work. When we announced the closing of this campus, I was so proud of our leadership community. We brought the campus pastor and launch team on stage, acknowledged them for their commitment and hard work, and then prayed for them. I took the opportunity to let everyone know that if we're going to be on mission with Jesus, it will demand that we try new things. Sometimes those new things will fail. And that is okay as long as we're faithful. After that, every one of the three hundred leaders gave them a long and tear-filled standing ovation.

A genuine missional movement will demand that we create a metric that goes beyond counting nickels and noses to discover new ways of tracking community development and personal transformation. This will mean having to reorganize some of our existing structures. It will also involve taking more risks and involving leaders who are different from the kinds we've worked with in the past. And when someone goes out and fails, we will learn to bring them home and celebrate the faith that it took to take that risk. If the call of Jesus is to go, then we need to be faithful and go. Our churches will need to become more comfortable with chaos and failure — if they want to be faithful to God.

I sometimes imagine a conversation with Jesus that goes like this:

Jesus: "Dave, welcome to heaven."

Dave: "Wow, this is awesome!"

Jesus: "Yeah, I told you it would be. How many people did you bring with you?"

Dave: "Well, there are all those people who came to Community."

Jesus: "Great. But what about the people who never came to Community?"

Dave: "I invited them, but they just wouldn't come to church with me."

Jesus: "I invited you to join me in heaven …"

Dave: (silence)

Jesus: "… but for that to happen, I had to go to you."

Dave: (more silence)

REPRODUCING COACHES

Leading Life-Changing Conversations

BIG IDEA The coach-leader relationship is crucial to sustaining a missional movement.

- ✗ A New Coaching Model
- ✗ Checking a Leader's RPM'S
- ✗ Three Primary Coaching Tasks
- ✗ Coaching Conversations
- ✗ Six Coaching Questions
- ✗ John Ciesniewski's Story

COACH K.

It's one of the most memorable shots in the history of college basketball. Duke University is playing the University of Kentucky in the East Regional finals of the 1992 NCAA tournament. It's a matchup between two perennial powerhouse basketball programs. There are 2.1 seconds on the clock. Kentucky leads 103–102. The referee hands the ball to Grant Hill. Christian Laettner fronts his defender just above the key at the other end of the court. He then leaps to grab the length-of-the-court pass from Hill, dribbles once, turns around to his right, and sinks the game-winning shot as the buzzer goes off. Duke wins 104–103. I have seen that shot countless times. And I never get tired of watching that play.*

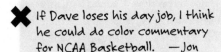 If Dave loses his day job, I think he could do color commentary for NCAA Basketball. —Jon

That's what we often remember—the play on the court: Laettner catching the pass, taking two dribbles, turning around, and sinking the shot. What we don't often think about is what *preceded* the shot: the crucial seconds before Laettner took his position on the court. What we so easily forget is that just moments before that play ensued, the Blue Devils huddled around Coach Mike Krzyzewski, mapping out what each player needed to do in order for that play to be successful.

Here's what Krzyzewski said about that huddle: "I instinctively realized that I had to get them to snap out of the daze they were in and I had to make them believe, positively, that they could win this game. Then I had to get them all singing out of the same hymnal. And it all had to be done in less than two minutes."[13]

Mike Krzyzewski is one of the greatest coaches in the history of college basketball. His Duke Blue Devils are consistently among the top teams in the country. Year after year the team changes, assistant coaches take over other programs, players come and go, and many graduate to the NBA after playing only a couple of years—yet Coach K. remains. He is the constant factor that makes the Blue Devil program one of the most successful in college basketball. Solid, dependable coaching is the consistent factor in dynasties.

Let me draw a parallel here. We were in a season at our church that felt like a championship run. Our Naperville campus had just moved into a new building (affectionately known as the Yellow Box) and was seeing record-breaking attendance, and we were beginning to launch additional campuses. Amid those victories and celebrations, we were also feeling the growing demand of caring for the large number of people that God was sending. And we were increasingly aware of our need to develop a growing number of leaders who would be able to care for these people.

We felt tremendous temptation at that time to throw money at hiring additional staff, but we were wary of that quick fix to handle this challenge. Still, we knew that if we weren't going to have additional staff, it would require us to begin putting a focused effort into developing an unpaid layer of leaders. We call them coaches. Developing coaches (leaders of leaders) may be the single most overlooked yet vital task in spreading a missional movement.

A NEW COACHING MODEL

A coach is a leader of leaders whose intentional investment in the lives of other leaders encourages those leaders, challenges them, and holds them accountable to grow in their skills as leaders and in their journeys as Christ followers. We have seen God use the relationship of coach and leader to disciple and grow people far beyond their (and our) expectations. When the relationship is good, both the leader and the coach benefit and become more effective in fulfilling their God-given leadership responsibilities.

(Because the *relational investment* of a coach is of greatest importance, it is ✗ crucial that the leader-to-coach ratio is low enough that the coach is able to effectively invest in the life of each leader.) We have found that even the most effective coaches are only able to invest in a maximum of five leaders, and many of our coaches work with as few as two or three leaders. Naturally, if a coach is leading a group or team in addition to his or her coaching responsibilities, that will also limit the number of people he or she can effectively coach. In other words, keep your leader-to-coach ratio *low*.

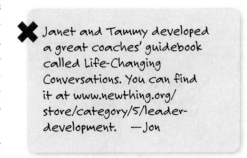

Janet and Tammy developed a great coaches' guidebook called Life-Changing Conversations. You can find it at www.newthing.org/ store/category/5/leader-development. —Jon

Our staff, led by Tammy Melchien and Janet McMahon, created a simple, effective model that helps us train and develop the coaches at Community.*****

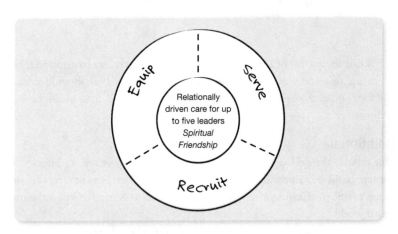

Equip

Serve

Recruit

Relationally driven care for up to five leaders
Spiritual Friendship

At the heart of the model is a focus on "relationally driven care." The one constant in a healthy coaching relationship is a growing friendship between the coach and the leader. Notice in this model that relationally driven care is surrounded by a solid line representing the constancy of that relationship. The three tasks that flow out of the relationship are separated by dotted lines to indicate that the emphasis placed on these tasks will vary depending on the needs of an individual leader and their group or team.

CHECKING A LEADER'S RPM'S

One way our coaches develop and maintain a strong relationship with their leaders is by focusing on what we call the RPM'S. This is an acronym based on Luke 2:52, where we read, "Jesus grew in wisdom and stature, and in favor with God and men." RPM'S help our coaches remember the four key areas where they need to be providing relational accountability and encouragement in the lives of their leaders.

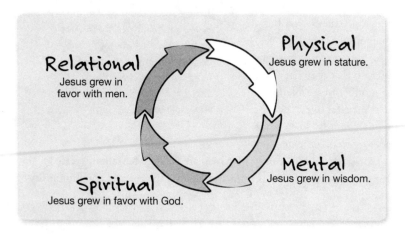

While these areas of a person's life are interdependent, we have found it helpful to use this acronym as a reminder to the leader that they should intentionally focus on each one of them at times to be sure that all areas of life are being addressed.

Relational

Our relational world typically includes the people with whom we interact on a regular basis: our immediate family, friends, neighbors, coworkers, and small group members. (Getting to know your leaders means getting to know their relational world.)

Here are some questions a coach can ask to find out how a leader is developing relationally:

* ✻ How are your relationships at home?
* ✻ What about your marriage, dating, or family life is going well? What's not going so well? What would you like to change?
* ✻ Who do you consider your closest friend? How is God using that relationship to grow you?
* ✻ What are your relationships at work like?

✷ Which of your relationships give you energy and life? Which are the most challenging or draining?

Physical

The leader's physical well-being is often the most overlooked aspect of his or her life. Yet diet, exercise, sleep, and rest are all vital to our ability to lead effectively. If we are serious about developing the whole person, we have to help our leaders see that their physical well-being can affect their ability to lead with passion and energy for the long haul.

Here are some questions a coach can ask to learn more about a leader's physical health:

✷ What does a good night's rest look like for you?
✷ On a scale of 1 to 10, how would you rate your current energy level?
✷ What are you doing to maintain good health when it comes to exercise and eating habits?
✷ Is there anything about your physical health that you'd like to change?

Mental

Another often-overlooked aspect of coaching is the development of our leaders' minds. In order for our leaders to continue to stay sharp and be lifelong learners, they need to be challenged. A good coach will ask them how they are growing and stretching their minds, while keeping them accountable and finding out how they are guarding themselves against things that can be dangerous to their minds and potentially lead to temptation and sin.

Here are some questions a coach can ask to learn how a leader is developing mentally:

✷ What have you been learning lately?
✷ How are you applying what you are learning from the weekend celebration services? Your small group? Leadership Community?
✷ What magazines, books, or websites do you read or access? How are they helping you grow your mind?
✷ What thoughts have been dominating your mind? Are they drawing you closer to God? Are they pulling you away from him?

Spiritual

In chapter 6, we referenced Joel Comiskey's research, in which he discovered that the most significant factor in a leader's ability to grow and reproduce his group is his devotional life. It is imperative that a coach help her leaders discover and act on whatever it is that helps them grow deeper in their relationship with Christ.

Here are some questions a coach can ask a leader to learn how they are developing spiritually:

- ✱ How would you describe your relationship with Christ right now?
- ✱ What does it look like when you are feeling closely connected to God?
- ✱ Which spiritual disciplines seem to help you draw closer to Jesus? Prayer? Journaling? Worship? Solitude?
- ✱ How could I hold you accountable to practicing those disciplines?
- ✱ What has God been saying to you lately through his Word? The Holy Spirit? Other Christ followers? Prayer?

THREE PRIMARY COACHING TASKS

There is no substitute for the time and work it takes to develop a strong relationship between a coach and a leader. That must be the primary focus of coaching. Out of that core relationship flow the three primary coaching tasks of equipping, recruiting, and serving (see figure on p. 119).

Equipping

It is the coach's responsibility to ensure that the leader is given the necessary tools and resources to be effective. These may come in a variety of forms, including books, blogs, websites, podcasts, and training opportunities. The coach may not be the primary provider of equipping for the leader. However, she will need to be in tune with the particular needs of an individual leader and help the leader find the resources necessary for her to be equipped to lead successfully.✱

 Okay, so clearly we are trying to be gender sensitive in this section. Which is good. It's important to be sensitive to the weaker sex ... I'm joking! Just for the record, we are cool with women coaching and leading at all levels. —Jon

Recruiting

Two of the most important and challenging tasks a leader must carry out are recruiting people to be part of his group or team as well as identifying and recruiting apprentice leaders so the group will reproduce. These tasks can also be overlooked or neglected as a leader gets focused on leading his group and/or carrying out the functions of that team. A coach will provide the much-needed guidance and focus to help the leader remember to identify and recruit apprentices as well as additional team or group members.

Serving

The greatest gift a coach can bring to a leader is to be available when needed. On occasion a coach will need to come alongside a leader, and they will serve together. This may happen during a crisis or when a leader is experiencing personal challenges and is uncertain of his ability to lead in a particular situation. (Leaders need to know that their coach cares for them enough to sacrifice his time ✗ and resources in order to help them be successful.)

COACHING CONVERSATIONS

More than anything else, successful coaching demands meaningful conversations between the leader and the coach. These conversations will provide additional vision, encouragement, and ongoing development for the leader.

Envisioning Conversations

These are four of the most important letters in the leadership alphabet: I-C-N-U.

Slowly say those letters to yourself. Now say them quickly. Have you ever had someone say, "I see in you the characteristics, qualities, and strengths of someone who could do something great for God's kingdom?" Has anyone ever looked you in the eye and simply said, "I-C-N-U!" Those four letters represent four of the most powerful words one person can say to another.

Jesus knew these letters. To one of his apprentices he said, "And I tell you that you are Peter, and on this rock I will build my church, and the gates of Hades will not overcome it" (Matt. 16:18).

When he said, "You're Peter," it was a play on words, because *Peter* literally means "rock." Jesus was essentially saying, "I-C-N-U someone strong and solid and reliable, like a rock." And that was a huge thing for Peter, because he tended to be anything *but* reliable.

But Jesus was saying even more than that. He was saying, "Not only do I-C-N-U a rock; I'm going to build on you something more radically influential than you could ever dream of. Even death won't be strong enough to stop what I'm going to do through you." Jesus said all of this to someone whose past was checkered with impulsiveness and flaking out. When the pressure was on, Peter tended to fold like a card table. But Jesus cast a vision for his life. He called out something new in Peter when he said, "I-C-N-U strength, reliability, and dependability." And over time, that's exactly the kind of person that Peter became as he led the early church—strong, reliable, and dependable.

Developing leaders need to be on the receiving end of envisioning conversations. They need someone to come alongside them, look them in the eye, and with all the confidence in the world say, "I see in you ..." They need to know that you believe God has a dream for using their time and talents to spread a missional movement.

This is what Larry did for me as he sat across the table from me at Potter's Place. He looked me in the eye and said, "Dave, you can do it." That's what our leaders need, and that's one of the most important conversations a coach can have with a leader.

Empowering Conversations

Coaches also need to have empowering conversations with their leaders. These are conversations where a coach is asking a leader to take the next step in his leadership journey. We refer to these conversations as "making the ask." An "ask" is that pivotal conversation when you sit across from someone and ask him to step up and lead, often for the first time or in a more significant and influential way. Over the past several years there have been a lot of conversations at our church about making the ask. The focus of these conversations has been about the difference between making a "big ask" versus a "mini-ask." ✱

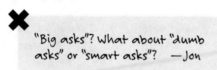

"Big asks"? What about "dumb asks" or "smart asks"?   —Jon

What is the difference between a big ask and a mini-ask, you might ask? Jesus made big asks. He asked his disciples to go into hostile communities, cast out demons, call for repentance, and heal the sick, all while taking nothing with them—no bags, no money, not even an extra jacket. This was not a mini-ask. When it comes to the asks we make of potential leaders, we tend to minimize them—asking for the bare minimum rather challenging leaders to a significant opportunity.

What happens when we make mini-asks?

When we fail to make the big ask and settle for a lower level of commitment, we place the development of that leader in jeopardy in a number of ways.

* *We minimize that person's potential.* When we dumb down a leadership ask, people go into whatever was asked of them with low expectations. We think we're doing this person and the church a favor by getting the person to say yes to the ask, so we make it seem manageable or more doable. We figure getting them in is the desired outcome, rather than fulfilling God's dream for them to reach their greatest potential.

* *We minimize the vision.* When we lower the bar on leadership asks, we make the mission of helping people find their way back to God seem insignificant, hardly worthwhile. Consequently, we are less likely to attract high-capacity leaders. Jesus' challenge was to "follow me." He told us up front that we might need to leave behind houses, family, and friends to do it. What if, instead of challenging his followers to a high

level of commitment, Jesus had said, "What I'm asking you to consider is not that big of a deal, really. It will only take a few hours out of your week to follow me." When we ask someone to step up to leadership or ask them to take another step forward in their leadership path, we are asking them to join a missional force that is called to change the world. That is a huge vision, and it demands a big ask.

✶ *We minimize God.* When we make mini-asks of developing leaders, we are putting tight parameters on what God can accomplish through someone. Who says God can't change the world through you? If we ask people to step up to a task that is small and manageable, we should expect only small, manageable results.

Here is a good equation to remember when you need to have an empowering leadership conversation:

Need + Vision = Inspiration

Need - Vision = Desperation

How many times have you heard or maybe even delivered a desperate call for more people to work in the toddler room? It usually sounds something like this: "We have a huge need for more workers in the toddler room during our 8:00 a.m. celebration service. It only requires one hour a week and little or no preparation. Just show up and keep them from hurting themselves."

Be honest. Are you inspired by that opportunity? It sounds pretty desperate, doesn't it? Now ask yourself, "How often do I present a need without a missional vision?" That same need could be communicated with a little bit of vision, and it would sound completely different: "We have a great opportunity for you to serve the families of our toddlers during our 8:00 a.m. service." We know that the safety and security of a child is important, especially to newcomers who may be taking their first steps on their way back to God. Not only that, you have no idea who you may be holding in your arms in the toddler room — future leaders, difference makers, men and women who will go on to make a huge impact for God's kingdom."

To which *ask* would you be most likely to respond?

Truthful Conversations

Finally, there will be times when a coach will need to have a tough and truthful conversation with a leader. These conversations need to be handled with the greatest of care but can also result in tremendous growth for that leader. In Ephesians 4:15, Paul talks about his desire to see all of us "grow up into him who is the Head, that is, Christ." How does that happen? Well, in the same verse, Paul tells us that growing up in Christ requires "speaking the truth in love." Personal growth often requires honest conversations.

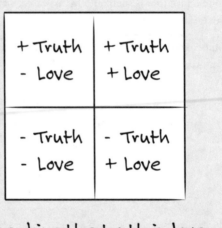

"...speaking the truth in love..."
Eph. 4:15

When we find ourselves in a situation that requires us to have a truthful conversation with a leader, we have four options:

Option 1: Neither loving nor truthful. I can have a tough conversation that is neither loving nor true. It won't do anything positive for the relationship with a leader, but it can be done. And it has been done. It's really more of an attack than a conversation. If you've ever been the victim of a tough conversation that was neither loving nor true, chances are you were left feeling like you got hit over the head with a two-by-four.

Option 2: Loving but not truthful. One way we often avoid a truthful conversation is by choosing to say things that are loving, but we never get around to speaking the truth. If I fall into this trap as a coach, I tend to avoid tough conversations at any cost. I will tell you you're okay when you're not okay. I'll encourage you and affirm you, but we'll never have an honest conversation where truths are told and real development occurs. If I avoid honest conversations and fall into this option, what happens to my credibility as a coach? It's lost. People will like me, but will they respect me? Probably not.

Option 3: Truthful but not loving. Have you ever had somebody ask you, "You know what your problem is?" They're not really asking you a question, are they? You know that whatever is coming next might be accurate, but it's sure not gonna leave you with any warm fuzzy feelings. If we fall into this option of speaking the truth in a not-so-loving way, what loses credibility? Sadly, the truth. Why? Because of how it was delivered. The leader will have a hard time listening, will be quick to justify their actions, and may not even hear what is said because they don't think you care about them.

Option 4: Both truthful and loving. This is the goal. We need coaches who understand how to develop relationships in which speaking the truth in love is normal and expected. It may mean that you have to communicate to a leader a particular growth area that needs to be addressed, because you believe it could cripple their ability to effectively lead. Why do you say this to them? Because as a coach, you care about that leader, and you care about the mission of helping people find their way back to God. Our goal, when we share the tough truth that needs to be heard, is this: speak the truth in love so that all of us will grow up in Christ.

I have a hunch that at this point coaching may seem overwhelming and you don't feel equipped to do it. Relax. Take a deep breath. What follows may be the simplest and yet most effective tool I have ever used. We simply call it the "Six Coaching Questions."

SIX COACHING QUESTIONS

Jon remembers that evening when we were first taught these questions: "We asked Carl George to spend some time with our volunteer coaches. We had some pretty big expectations of Carl that night. I envisioned him casting some grand vision to our coaches and challenging them to be the best of the best leaders! But to our momentary disappointment, Carl took a Sharpie and Post-it and wrote out six simple questions:

1. How are you?
 2. What are you celebrating?
3. What challenges are you experiencing?
4. What do you plan to do about those challenges?
5. How can I help you?
6. How can I pray for you?

"Then he said, 'Now I want you to break into pairs and spend the next thirty minutes asking and answering these questions.' That was it—that's all he did! But in retrospect, that night he shared with us the essence of coaching and how to really do it well. He taught us to ask people about their lives and to get good at listening, and perhaps most important, he taught us to give people the space to solve their own challenges."

Though they seem simple, let me briefly explain the hidden brilliance behind each of these questions.

1. *How are you?* Remember, at the heart of effective coaching is a relational investment. We begin every coaching conversation by checking in to see how the person we are coaching is really doing.

2. *What are you celebrating?* Every meeting at our church begins with some form of this question. Often it's stated like this: "Where are you/we winning?" Moving from "How are you?" to "What are you celebrating?" keeps the tone of the meeting relational and positive. It's tempting to quickly focus on what's not working or what is broken. This question keeps the conversation focused on where the leader is feeling successful.

3. *What challenges are you facing?* You might be thinking, "Finally, we get to something productive." Yes, the previous questions are very relational, but if it helps any, remember that when it comes to coaching, the relationship really is the task. This question gives your leader an opportunity to talk openly about the things that may need development in his group or team.

4. *How will you tackle those challenges?* Once a leader has disclosed some areas where he is experiencing some challenges with his life, group, or team, it is tempting to quickly move into fix-it mode and try to offer advice or solve the problem for him. Don't solve his problem for him. The best way you can serve a leader is to help him tap into the wisdom and insight that God has already given him to deal with whatever situation he is facing. It is the coach's role to draw those answers or solutions out of the leader.

5. *How can I help you?* Finally, the question we've been wanting to ask. This is an important question, but if you never get to this question because the leader has already come up with an action plan as you walked through the previous questions, consider yourself an extremely effective coach! There are times when a coach does need to step in and offer whatever assistance is necessary to help a leader in need.

6. *How can I pray for you?* The best way to wrap up a coaching conversation is to ask the leader how you can be praying for him. It is also a

great opportunity for you, as a coach, to ask the leader to be praying for you. This is one way a coach can help the leader know that this relationship is mutually beneficial. After the leader has had a chance to express some areas where he is in need of prayer, take a few moments to pray for the leader and reassure him that you will be praying for him regularly.

God's dream is not for the church to be led by a one-man weekly show but for it to be a team led by great coaches. Our staff at Community recognizes that our primary role is to equip and empower the people of the church to do the work of ministry. Our staff knows that when the game is on the line and the final point needs to be scored, the ball will be in the hands of our leaders, and those leaders need to be coached and prepared to take the winning shot. Behind the scenes, our staff works to prepare coaches to train and empower leaders who will do the work of helping people find their way back to God.

John Ciesniewski has shown remarkable consistency in his ability to develop leaders to not only lead people but also *lead and coach* other leaders. As you read his story, take note of the important role that coaching conversations have played as he moved through the leadership path.

JOHN CIESNIEWSKI'S STORY

I remember the first time we attended a celebration service at Community. While I had only been to church as an adult a handful of times before, I'd recently committed my life to Christ. What I experienced at Community was so out of the ordinary, I was inclined to stick with the familiar church experience I had known, even though I felt no real connection to it. But that night, I had what I can only describe as a Spirit-filled dream. I had never had a dream like this prior to that night—and I've never had one since. But it changed my life.

In my dream, the time was short—the world was falling apart, and my wife, Amy, and I knew we had to reach as many people as we could. We had to invite them to Community so that they could find their way back to God. And what's really odd is, I don't ever recall hearing that phrase "helping people find their way back to God." However, that was the unmistakable theme of my dream. I woke up in the middle of the night and wrote it all down. And even though we'd been there only once, the next morning I told Amy that we would be going back to Community.

A few weeks later we attended what we thought was a reception for new attenders at this new church. That's where our spiritual journey really

 Geeeez. It took all the way till chapter 8 for me to finally get some credit. God bless you, John Ciesniewski. —Jon

kicked into high gear — not at the class with Dave teaching but in the lobby, where his brother, Jon, invited us to attend his small group.✱

✗ (Small group was an answer to our prayers — we finally had some people to partner with us on our spiritual journey.) We found a place where we could ask questions and get real answers! We had a leader who took the time to continue what had begun the night we committed our lives to Christ. We had someone explain the significance of baptism to us, someone who would even challenge us with truth, spoken in love, when we didn't think we needed to be baptized.

In small group we were invited to put our spiritual gifts to work. We didn't even know we had gifts until small group. Amy started singing, and I actually led a small group of children! And I loved it! Within our first month, Amy and I were celebrating, connecting, and contributing.

With a year under my belt in small group, I was approached by our new small group director, Sue Natiello. Sue invited me out for lunch, where in so many words she said to me, "John, I see in you …" (I-C-N-U). And she identified the leadership gifts and potential that she saw in me to make a difference for God's kingdom. Then she proceeded to invite me to be her apprentice leader in a brand-new small group.

Sue met with me every week for an hour to prepare for group! She was super intentional about meeting and investing in me. Together, Sue and her husband, Tom, took Amy and me under their wing, and because of their coaching we experienced incredible growth relationally and spiritually. one-on-one

Along the way, I continued to grow in my leadership — I went from leading children to coaching adults who led children. Sue Natiello reproduced her adult small group, and I became a leader and followed in her footsteps. I met with as many as three apprentice leaders every week! I reproduced my group several times and actually began coaching leaders of adult groups myself.

Three years after Jon initially invited me to join his small group, I could sense the Holy Spirit opening another door for me. Many people—all on their own initiative—encouraged me to consider joining the staff at Community. People would say, "Have you ever thought about working for the church?" Others would say, "You know, you'd make a great small group director."

The amount of conversation around this decision was more than coincidental, and so Amy and I started talking very seriously about making the leap. Five months later I joined the staff as Community's adult ministry director, and since then I have led the launch of a new campus and served as a campus pastor, and now I serve as a regional campus pastor. As I reflect on my leadership journey, I am grateful for the people who have coached me along the way and for the opportunity to fulfill the dream I had to help people find their way back to God.

PART THREE

REPRODUCING COMMUNITIES OF 100–1,000

A missional church movement is accelerated by reproducing communities of one hundred to one thousand people. With the launch of every new venue, site, and church, the momentum of the movement increases. As these communities reproduce into their second, third, and fourth generations, the Jesus mission is being fulfilled. For a Reproducing Church Assessment, go to *www.reproducingchurch.org.*

REPRODUCING VENUES AND SITES

Seven Moves to Multisite

> **BIG IDEA** Launching new venues and sites accelerate the spread of a missional movement.
>
> ✗ Multisite Movement
> ✗ How the Multisite Story Began
> ✗ Reproducing Venues
> ✗ Seven Moves to Multisite

MULTISITE MOVEMENT

There was a time when you could say, "I'm going to the bank," and everyone knew that you meant a specific bank at a particular place in town. But now if you say, "I'm going to the bank," it could mean one of several branches! Some of us can remember the days when a hospital meant a specific facility. You could tell people, "I'm having some tests done at the hospital," and everyone knew that you meant a particular hospital facility downtown. But now one hospital may have multiple locations. And it wasn't too long ago that most colleges had only one campus. If you told someone, "I'm taking classes at State College," they not only knew the college but also knew what town you were talking about. Now that could mean one of many campuses in several different communities.

Right now I live in Naperville, a medium-sized city (population 165,000) just outside of Chicago, but I could never say to someone, "I'll meet you at Starbucks." The last time I counted, there were around ten Starbucks in Naperville alone, not to mention the ones in nearby communities. And I couldn't agree to meet someone at McDonald's without specifying which of the four McDonald's I meant—and that's just in my medium-sized suburban city! Well, now we can add to the list of businesses, schools, and other institutions with multiple locations the church. No longer does a church *necessarily* have only one site, one location, or one campus.*

✖ My top three places for coffee (in order): (1) Ground Level Café at the Yellow Box, (2) Dunkin' Donuts, (3) Starbucks. —Jon

While we certainly didn't start Community Christian Church with a franchising concept or the intention of being a multisite church, from what I've learned, McDonald's and Starbucks didn't start that way either. Obviously, though, the idea caught on rather quickly. Today these businesses are everywhere in our communities.

Over the past ten years, we have witnessed an explosive, exponential multisite movement among churches in the United States.

* In 1990 there were ten multisite churches in the U.S.
* In 1998 there were one hundred multisite churches in the U.S.
* In 2004 there were more than fifteen hundred multisite churches in the U.S.

Today ...

* Thirty-seven percent of all megachurches are multisite.[14]
* Seven of the ten fastest-growing churches in the U.S. are multisite.[15]
* Nine of the ten largest churches in the U.S. are multisite.[16]
* New sites are the common denominator among the one hundred fastest-growing churches, and they average 2.4 sites per church.[17]

Over the last several years, Community has had the opportunity to train thousands of pastors and church leaders to launch new locations. Multisite is no longer limited to the most innovative or even the fastest-growing churches. Multisite has become an option for any church seeking to start a missional movement and help more and more people find their way back to God.

Several years ago church consultant Bill Easum predicted, "The multisite movement will explode over the next few decades. Why? It is how the early church grew in the early centuries, and it is how the church is exploding in other parts of the world in cell and house churches."[18] What Bill predicted years ago is what we're now witnessing firsthand.

HOW THE MULTISITE STORY BEGAN

After a small group meeting one night, Nick and Bruno cornered me and asked, "How can we get this kind of genuine community into the properties we develop and manage?" It was one of the most surprising questions I've ever been asked. Nick and Bruno were successful real estate developers who were just beginning to find their way back to God. Bruno would say it this way: "We've built beautiful places, but we have yet to see people live in those places in a beautiful way." He was convinced that if he could give people what he was experiencing in small group, they would find it so much more valuable than if he just gave them a nice place to live.

A few months before this conversation, we had been discussing the gospel of John in our small group. We were reading the story of Nicodemus in John 3. We'd just read the part where Jesus tells Nicodemus, "No one can see the kingdom of God unless he is born again" (v. 3). Bruno's wife, Judy, looked down at her Bible, looked up at the rest of the group, looked down again, and then looked back up at us and said, "Born again? Born again? I think that's what is happening to me. I'm being born again!" And it was true. She was being born again. Right after that, Judy, Bruno, Nick and his wife, Terry, all became Christ followers and were baptized. Their story reminds me of something we like to say about including nonbelievers in our small groups: "Treat 'em like they are Christians till they realize they are not."

I think that Bruno and Nick's question, "How can we get this kind of genuine community into the properties we develop and manage?" indicates that when they became followers of Jesus at Community, they knew they weren't just joining a church where they could have all their spiritual needs met. They understood that they were joining a community of friends determined to spread the missional movement of Jesus. And they wanted to be a part of that.

Over the course of the next several months, Nick, Bruno, Jon, and I began to dream about how we could get this kind of genuine community from our small group into a brand-new real estate development. It seemed logical that since the church was only six years old and still meeting at Naperville North High School, we would begin to look for potential locations within Naperville. But over the next year, as we explored various locations, none of them seemed to work out: the cost was prohibitive, the acreage was too little, or the owner wasn't willing to sell.

Then Bruno asked me, "Why don't we move the whole church to Romeoville? My company has plans for a new development on a couple hundred acres there, and we could build a community center/church right in the middle of that brand-new community." We were always up for a new adventure ... but moving our whole church to an entirely new community twenty-five minutes south of our current location didn't make any sense. Then it hit me: "We started a brand-new church in Naperville; why can't we just do the same thing all over again in

Romeoville? We could use a similar strategy, but instead of it being a brand-new church, it will be a brand-new site that is a part of Community."

REPRODUCING VENUES

At about the same time that our church began reproducing *campuses*, North Coast Church in Vista, California, started reproducing *video venues*. The church was out of space and had used all the good time slots for their services. Lead pastor Larry Osborne says, "Our mindset was to have an overflow room that would be a reward and not a punishment. Most overflow rooms are a punishment for people who come late." Larry and his team ended up creating something called the Video Café. It was a new venue that gave people an opportunity to experience what they loved about North Coast in a more casual environment where they could sit at round tables and enjoy a cup of coffee, a pastry, and music with a slightly different style.

The staff at North Coast had no idea that they were starting something that would change the way church is done across the country. Today North Coast offers eleven distinct worship styles each weekend at their Vista campus, with a total of twenty-four unique weekend options. As a result, they've been able to significantly broaden their demographic makeup by reaching out in all directions. Larry says, "We've become younger, older, hipper, and more traditional—all at the same time."

Venue versus Multisite

The biggest difference between a video venue and a multisite campus is found in the target audience. Whereas multisite campuses generally aim to expand *geographical* outreach, video venues generally aim to expand *demographic* outreach. In addition, on-site video venues can be much easier to start than an off-site campus. Larry will tell you, "All you need is a room, a time slot, and a venue pastor." And because on-site video venues can share children's and youth programming as well as other support ministries, they can be launched much more quickly than a new off-site campus.

The staff at North Coast believes wholeheartedly that churches and pastors can reach a far broader demographic than they are currently reaching if they will offer the same message in a different cultural package. Larry says that truth presented authentically has broad appeal. It can reach a multitude of demographics as long as the message is surrounded by a cultural package with which people can identify.

Reward Element

Part of that cultural packaging includes what they call the "reward element." For instance, their Early Bird venue targets those who want to start the day at the crack of dawn. Getting an early start overshadows everything else; it's the reward element that draws them and keeps them. In Traditions, it's the hymns that draw traditionalists. And they will tell you this venue is not just for old people, as traditionalists come from all age groups. In the Last Call, it's the extended worship and hip feel that make the venue distinct. In the Message, it's the absence of singing.

For North Coast, the impetus for starting a new venue has been one of two things: a shortage of space or an identifiable group of people who love North Coast but wish it were (fill in the blank). The blank typically reflects a style or preference of that particular demographic. For instance, North Coast's Traditions was started because they had a large group who loved the messages and values of North Coast but hated the music and volume in the sanctuary. The Edge was started because they had a large constituency of eighteen- to twenty-four-year-olds who loved the church but wished the music and ambience were a lot hipper and louder. Larry says, "Each of these venues (and all of our other video venues) have turned potential critics into raving fans who bring large numbers of saved and unsaved friends with them."

We've learned a lot from North Coast and have added two video venues and nine more campuses since we launched our Romeoville campus. With each launch, we've followed a pattern that we've shared with thousands of church leaders all over the world. We call it the "Seven Moves to Multisite."

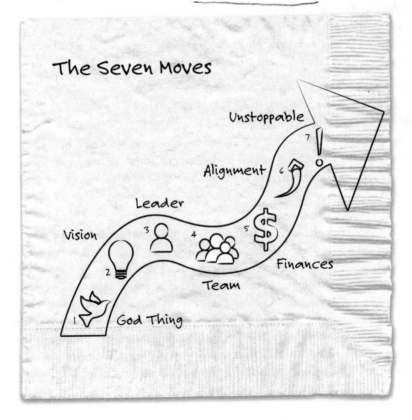

The Seven Moves

Unstoppable
7
Alignment 6
Leader
Vision 3
4
5 $
2
Finances
Team
1 God Thing

SEVEN MOVES TO MULTISITE

Do you use MapQuest? How about Google Maps? Or GPS? Whatever service you depend on to get you where you're going, they all will give you a specific route to get from point A to point B. You can take the route they give you, you can make up your own, or you can improvise based on what you're given. Regardless of how you use the service, there are usually a few streets you'll absolutely have to drive down and a number of intersections you'll have to cross no matter what path you take to get to your destination.

We've found the same to be true with multisite churches: there are many different ways to get from point A to point B — from one site to two, or from two to three — but there are a few roads you *always* have to travel and a number of inter-sections you *must* cross to successfully reproduce your

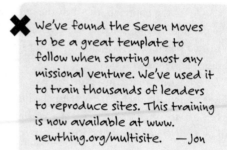

We've found the Seven Moves to be a great template to follow when starting most any missional venture. We've used it to train thousands of leaders to reproduce sites. This training is now available at www. newthing.org/multisite. —Jon

sites. What follows is something of a glance over our shoulder, looking back at the path we've taken. We call it the Seven Moves to Multisite.✶

Move 1: God Thing

We have learned to live by the words of Peter Drucker: "Decisions are not so much made as they become apparent." If you would have asked us a few years back what the first step for adding new locations was, we would have said, "It starts with a vision." But experience has taught us that spiritual entrepreneurs look for God things first — the vision develops out of those signs of God at work.

Romeoville Campus

When we made the move to start our Romeoville campus, it was so clear to us that God was at work. The decision was easy. The vision was clear. Put yourself in our situation: you have a couple of real estate developers who want to build a twenty-seven-thousand-square-foot community center with the direction for design coming from focus groups from your church leadership. They want to partner to establish a nonprofit to provide programming and services to the community (this resulted in the Institute for Community — *www.instituteforcommunity.org*). Not only that, they want to provide significant funding to support the start-up. What do you say? Isn't the answer apparent? "Yes!" God is at work!✶

Montgomery Campus

We didn't really *decide* to start our Montgomery campus either. Again, it was just so apparent to us that God was at work. The leadership of an existing but underresourced small church came to us and offered to give us their five acres of land and a nine-thousand-square-foot facility. It was a million-dollar asset they just wanted to hand over to us. Glenn Beiritz, who

 The IFC has expanded its vision to include a Community Life division that places Community Life Architects in apartment communities across the country in partnership with local churches and church plants. For more information, contact Bill Barton, Lead Architect of Community Life, at www.communitylife.info. —Jon

represented the small church in these conversations, had only one request—that somehow the building be used to further the mission of "helping people find their way back to God." The rest we could figure out in time. You might think, "Well, that's a no-brainer!" The answer seemed pretty apparent to us too! But there were actually three other churches and even one parachurch organization that they had approached before coming to us. We were the first to say yes.

Three Questions for Discovering God Things

When we're looking for God things, we find ourselves asking three key questions over and over:

> *Question 1: Where is God at work?* Henry Blackaby, in his book *Experiencing God*, encourages us to always be asking the question, "Where is God at work?" We have found that question to be particularly helpful in considering new sites or campuses. So we're constantly looking at the world around us, trying to discover where God may be at work, so that we can join him.

> *Question 2: Where is God dreaming?* In his book *An Unstoppable Force,* Erwin McManus says there is a second question we also need to be asking: "Where is God dreaming?" This question keeps us from being passive and waiting for God to reveal his work to us. Instead it challenges us to anticipate where God might be about to do something that only he can do.

> *Question 3: How is God confirming that he is at work?* The last question is a follow-up to the previous two questions. We also ask, "How is God confirming that he is at work?" This is a crucial question that holds us accountable to continuing to seek God through his Word, the Holy

Spirit, prayer, and the community of Christ followers so that we are certain that we are joining God in his work and not simply asking him to join us in our work.

Move 2: Vision

Our experience has been that the God thing is what makes the vision compelling. When we were first contacted by the Bieritz family about the Montgomery campus, we were excited about the possibility of using this church building on Montgomery Road in Montgomery, Illinois, as a new site. This elderly patriarch was ready to give away the building that had been his home church for his entire adult life. Initially we kept this possibility very quiet so that our lead team could pray and process through the decision. We'll never forget the day we told our staff about this God thing. No one outside of our lead team knew about the possibility of a new campus in Montgomery. After we finished the meeting where we announced the opportunity, I went back to my desk and found this email already in my inbox from a key leader on our staff, Sherry Gossman:*

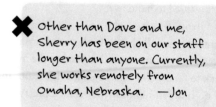

Other than Dave and me, Sherry has been on our staff longer than anyone. Currently, she works remotely from Omaha, Nebraska. —Jon

> Dave,
>
> Weird thing—I had a dream last night. It was weird, but what stood out to me was this little old lady standing there telling me that I needed to go and find this church in Montgomery. I kept asking her how to get there, and she told me to go down Montgomery Road. She said I would see the signs and they would tell me where to go. She assured me that I couldn't miss it, but is was important that I check it out.
>
> Then I hear about this church thing today with this property that someone wants to give us in Montgomery? On Montgomery Road? Weird, isn't it?
>
> Sherry

We believe that dream was God confirming that he indeed was giving us a vision to launch this new campus. God spoke in that dream to Sherry (and to all of us at Community) to make sure that we didn't miss his vision. Whenever we had the opportunity to vision cast for our new Montgomery campus, we always started with the God things: a gift of a million-dollar asset and the confirmation through a dream of a trusted leader. Our experience has shown that identifying and communicating the God thing is what makes this second move—the vision—so compelling!

Move 3: Leader

Lyle Schaller offered us some wise counsel when he coached us as we were getting started with multisite. He said, "When newcomers arrive at your new campus, they will have two questions that they will want answered: (1) Who is in charge? (2) Who can answer my questions?" With that advice and the growing realization that I could only be in one place at a time, we invented the role of the campus pastor.

For us, the third move has always been to identify the leader whom we now call the campus pastor. The campus pastor, who is the "face with the place," serves as the primary point person for that location. Once the campus pastor is identified, you can begin your countdown to launch. During the countdown phase, this leader will focus on three things: (1) praying like crazy, (2) casting vision for the new launch, and (3) developing the launch team. These are huge jobs, and they require a special leader.*

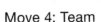 The Countdown to Launch resource is available for free at www.newthing.org. —Jon

Whatever you do, do not compromise or settle for second best when it comes to this leadership role. This person needs to have the same skill sets as a successful church planter. For the past several years, we have insisted that our campus pastors be assessed in the same way we assess our lead church planters. Once the campus pastor is identified, the focus of the launch now turns toward the development of the team of people who will work alongside him to launch the campus. That's the next move—team development.

Move 4: Team

Paid Staff Team

One part of the team that will launch this new campus is those who will be paid staff. Often a church-planting team will include a lead pastor, a creative arts/worship pastor, and a children's pastor. But when most churches are ready to start a new campus, they usually have those people on staff. So you may not want to duplicate those full-time positions, especially with your first or second launch.

Take a look at the whole church and decide what paid roles you need in order to make all locations and the entire church more effective. When we launched our Romeoville campus, one of the staff positions we hired was a full-time media person. Our single-campus church could not support a full-time media person.

However, with the growth and additional income that a new location provided, we were able to hire a full-time media person whose work impacted both locations. While a new campus might enable a church to hire specialists to serve the entire church, a new campus will still likely need a campus pastor and some part-time staff in the arts, possibly even a children's ministry director or another specialized ministry position, depending on the targeted demographic.

Unpaid Staff Team

Certainly, the most important part of the launch team is the unpaid staff. One of the tools that we have used to communicate vision and strategy for developing this unpaid team of volunteers is a "Launch Team Matrix." After we had been using this matrix for some time, we heard the story of how Wayne Cordeiro started New Hope Community Church in Honolulu, and we found it was remarkably similar.

Wayne said that once they had found a place to celebrate, he would walk through the facility and try to envision what it was going to look like that first weekend when God would pack that place with people finding their way back to him. Wayne would walk through the hospitality area and imagine how many people he would need serving there to accommodate the people God would send. He would walk into the auditorium and try to envision how many vocalists, instrumentalists, ushers, and greeters would be necessary. Then he would walk through the children's and student ministry areas and picture in his mind the same things, again and again for each and every area of ministry. He would then compile a complete list of all the ministry areas and the people he would need to lead and serve in those areas. At every launch team gathering, he would reference that list so they could clearly see where additional help was needed in order for them to launch successfully.

Each blank in the launch team matrix represents a leader or significant contributor who is needed before this campus is ready to launch. We draw this matrix on big pieces of foam core board and keep it in front of our staff and leadership team for ten months prior to launch. We pray over this matrix and ask God to send us the number of leaders, artists, and contributors we need to start this new location. As people step up to serve and lead, we write their names in the blanks and celebrate that we are that much closer to being ready to launch. We have found that when our matrix is about 80 percent full, we are ready to launch.✱

> The simplest and most valuable tool we've used to launch new celebration services, campuses, or churches is this Launch Team Matrix. Go get it for free at www.newthing.org. —Jon

Move 5: Finances

When we started Community, we were young, naive, and broke. Jon lived with me and Sue. He stayed in a vacant bedroom in our little apartment.* Our teammates

 Dave uses the term vacant very loosely. Most of the floor was occupied by moving boxes stacked two or three high. —Jon

Darren and Scott shared a small apartment. And the fifth member of our young staff, Georgia, had an apartment that doubled as a student ministry center, where we held our initial weekly youth gatherings. None of us were compensated well. We all agreed to take a salary of twenty thousand dollars a year.*

I tell you this because a primary goal was for the church to be self-supporting, and so we made choices that would help us achieve that goal quickly. We were fully self-supporting in just over one year. We began like missionaries, and we've continued to behave that way. We can do a lot with very little. When it comes to finances, we've made plenty of mistakes, but as I look

 Here's some kudos to Tim Sutherland. He was the top individual financial contributor to the start-up of Community and now is the leader of our teaching team. —Jon

over my shoulder to see how God's Spirit has led us down the path toward multisite, I know that finances are a step that can make or break you!

Here are a few suggestions we have regarding finances:

1. *Don't be afraid to ask for outside funding.* You need to approach launching a new location much like you would a new church plant. When we first started Community, we raised money from individuals, existing churches, parachurch groups, and church-planting organizations. One of the more encouraging developments over the past several years is the increase in church-planting organizations and other churches providing financial support for new campuses. Launching a new campus is a great opportunity to help more people find their way back to God, and you should offer as many people as possible the chance to be a part of it.

2. *Ask your new staff to raise part or all of their own support.* With the launch of the new campus, you will bring on additional staff who can be expected to raise at least part of their salary as well as start-up funds for this new launch. One litmus test for campus pastors is their ability to raise money for a project. New staff are in a unique position, with a

special opportunity to ask people to support them in this new venture for the next one to three years. The staff of your new location are connected to friends, family, coworkers, and churches who would love to be part of this new mission. Even as a larger church with multiple locations, we continue to ask new staff to raise part of their own salary.

3. *Ask your launch team to raise money.* Not only can you ask your staff to raise funds for their salaries and start-up costs; be sure to ask your launch team as well. When we launched our Shorewood campus, it was the first time that we made it an expectation of our launch team that if they were going to join this mission with their time and talents, they would also need to bring their treasures. (We reasoned that people who take mission trips overseas raise money to support that mission, and this mission was no less worthy.) So we set an expected amount that we hoped each family would give and asked them to make pledges to this mission.

4. *Make sure you have enough money in enough time.* Without the funding you need to give birth to a healthy new campus, you will start without the right equipment, you will cut corners in marketing, or you will not add the staff who are needed. One way or another, with each of our campus launches, we came up with enough money, but on several occasions our funding came in later than we intended, and it resulted in tremendous amounts of added stress. Our staff spent a lot of extra time waiting to get approval to purchase the equipment and supplies we needed. And when they finally got what they needed, they had to burn the midnight oil to get everything in place and installed in time before launch. A certain level of chaos is expected in any start-up venture, but inadequate or late

> ✖ When we launched our Montgomery campus, several of our staff maxed out their credit cards to make last-minute purchases. While I don't recommend that, I love the "whatever it takes" approach. —Jon

funding can take a heavy toll on your staff and launch team. So make sure you have enough money in enough time!*

Move 6: Alignment

As we've trained pastors and leaders in multisite, one question that surfaces more than any other is this: "How do we reproduce and still maintain quality and alignment?" It's the same question any rapidly growing company asks when it expands or adds new locations. And it is a great question. As our church reproduced new campuses, two things were particularly significant for us to maintain alignment.

Leadership Community

Since the first days of Community, we have had our monthly Leadership Community gathering, where we bring together all of our leaders from all our locations (see chapter 4 for more details on this). This coming together provides great momentum, keeping our campuses and leaders all focused on the same vision and giving us the opportunity to celebrate what God is doing at all of our locations. Our monthly Leadership Community gathering is a key strategy for us in achieving alignment as a multisite church.

The Big Idea

One of the most significant decisions we had to make with regard to alignment was how we would approach topics and themes for celebration services. We had all kinds of questions:

- ✻ Should we have all of our campuses on the same theme?
- ✻ Do we have one campus a week behind another campus and rotate the bands, worship leaders, and other creative teams?
- ✻ Does each campus develop its own themes and artists?
- ✻ Do small groups as well as Kids' City (our children's ministry) continue to develop their own themes?

In response to these questions and ideas, we implemented what we call "the Big Idea." Every week at Community we focus on one theme — the Big Idea. The Big Idea is being taught and experienced in all of our large groups and small groups, and

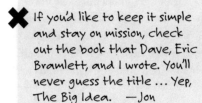

If you'd like to keep it simple and stay on mission, check out the book that Dave, Eric Bramlett, and I wrote. You'll never guess the title ... Yep, The Big Idea. —Jon

as a result it is also being discussed around the dinner table in the homes of our attenders. Having a single, common theme across all of our campuses and groups has been a significant key to church alignment.✻

Move 7: Unstoppable!

While running the Chicago Marathon, I distinctly remember "hitting the wall" at mile twenty-one. I felt like I had nothing left in me. Every muscle and bone in my body was screaming, "Give up!" Three guys from Community actually ran alongside me for those last few miles to make sure I didn't stop. Thanks to them, I finished the race.

There will come a time in the process of starting a new campus when it will be easy to give up, give in, or just stop what you are doing. Honestly, I haven't had enough experience to know if this is a matter of spiritual warfare or if it is just something that is true of any entrepreneurial endeavor. I don't know … maybe it's both! But I do know this: how you as a leader respond in that moment is absolutely critical. Don't stop or give up!

In Jim Collins' bestseller *Good to Great*, he describes the leader who is able to take a good organization and turn it into a truly great organization. He calls these individuals level-five leaders. Level-five leaders demonstrate two characteristics. First, they are *other centered* and show tremendous personal humility, and second, they show an unwavering *resolve* to do whatever needs to be done. Collins describes these level-five leaders with a single word—*unstoppable*.

As we were starting our Romeoville campus, we planned to meet in the community center, but it was five months behind schedule and under construction. So we had to find another place to meet for those five months. It would have been easy to say, "Let's just wait," or, "Let's postpone this for now." But instead we hustled and found a local elementary school that in retrospect was the best place for us to start. How did we find it? The people on our team were *unstoppable*!

While we were launching our Montgomery campus, the money was late coming in and we were way behind on renovating the donated church building. Our team was literally painting walls and testing equipment past midnight on the evening before our grand opening. We never would have pulled it off had we not decided beforehand that we would be *unstoppable*!

When you hit the wall and you feel like giving up or quitting altogether, in that moment you'll need that level-five leadership. You and your team must be resolved and focused on doing what needs to be done; you must be *unstoppable*!

✶ ✶ ✶

We have taught these seven moves to hundreds of churches and thousands of leaders around the world who have gone on to start new venues and sites. I hope this basic understanding of how to reproduce venues and sites will encourage you to believe that you too can do it. In the next chapter, we dare you to dream beyond just two or three sites by exploring the benefits and the how-to's of going to four sites or more.

REPRODUCING MULTIPLE SITES

Four or More: Reaching a Region

> **BIG IDEA** Continual reproduction of sites increases the momentum of a missional movement.
> * Prank-Calling Bill Hybels
> * Benefits of Multisite versus Church Planting
> * Benefits of Multisite versus Large Church
> * Pain at Three Sites and Crisis at Four!
> * The Eight Most Important Questions for Four Sites or More

PRANK-CALLING BILL HYBELS

It was one of the strangest experiences of my life. We were still six months from going to multiple sites, and I was at our Quincy Avenue office on a Saturday morning when something totally bizarre happened. Something inside of me said, "Call Bill Hybels and tell him about multisite." I'd never spoken with Bill. I didn't know him at all. And I wasn't meditating, praying, or doing anything spiritual, but suddenly I had this prompting I was supposed to pick up my phone and tell the pastor of the largest church in North America about how our little church was going to add a second site in Romeoville. Lots of people have ideas that they think people in influential positions should know about. So I didn't take it too seriously, but I did start flipping through my Rolodex to see if I had Willow Creek's phone number.

And what happened next I can explain only as a billion-to-one long shot or a prompting from God. Suddenly a ten-digit phone number just popped into my head.

First came the number 1 and then an area code and then a seven-digit phone number. To this day I can't fully explain it, but a phone number suddenly came to mind.

So I reached over and picked up the phone and dialed the ten-digit number. I wasn't prepared for what I heard next: "Hello, this is Bill Hybels' office." I didn't know what to say. So I said nothing. Again I heard, "Hello, this is Bill Hybels' office." Finally I said, "Hi, this is Dave Ferguson." Then the lady said, "I'm sorry, but this is Bill's private line . . . How did you get this number?" I didn't know what to say . . . so finally I said it. "Well, I think God told me the number." Now she was silent. I tried to explain: "I know this sounds crazy, but I was just sitting here and a ten-digit phone number popped into my head, and something inside told me that Bill needed to hear about how we were getting ready to go to multiple locations." Even *I* thought I sounded crazy.

Eventually Bill's assistant did what she was supposed to do with crazy people who call his private line without permission; she took my number and promised to get back to me. A couple of days later I got a phone call and was told to call Dr. Bilezikian, a founding elder at Willow Creek, and he would listen to what I was supposed to tell Bill. I knew I was getting the runaround, but by now I was absolutely convinced that God had given me this phone number and that this new expression of a church with multiple sites was something that had to be shared with others. So I called Dr. Bilezikian, and after I explained what had happened, he laughed and said to me, "Oh, so you are the crazy charismatic pastor that they wanted me to follow up with." He suggested, "Perhaps subliminally you knew Bill's phone number and forgot that you once knew it." I never did get through to Bill.✶

Four years after "accidentally" calling Hybels' private line, I got a call from Willow asking if our lead team could meet with their executive team and provide some coaching regarding their new multisite regional strategy. That was fun. After we finished the coaching session, I was walk-

> ✗ If you want Hybels' private number, drop me a note, and for one hundred dollars it is yours. First five hundred requests only. —Jon

> ✗ What we fail to mention is that immediately after his conversation with Hybels, Dave was swept away by security and spent the rest of the night in the Lake County Jail on stalking charges. —Jon

ing out with Bill, and for the first time I told him the story. Even then I felt kind of foolish, but I remember him listening and saying, "I take that kind of stuff seriously."✶

That crazy experience confirmed for me that God was doing something special at Community. He was spreading this missional movement through reproducing sites. This was something he wanted other church leaders to know about, and I would do my best to share it. Over the next several years, through New-Thing, Leadership Network, Exponential, and other platforms, we have been able to train and influence thousands of church leaders in the multisite model.

Here are just six of the many benefits that demonstrate what multisite offers that you don't get in a church plant or in a single-site large church. Many of these are based on Jim Collins' "genius of the and" principle—"the ferocious insistence that you can and must have both at once."

check out

BENEFITS OF MULTISITE VERSUS CHURCH PLANTING

Resources: Less Cost and Greater Outreach

We have had the opportunity to start both new churches *and* new campuses, and we believe that every church should be involved in both of these endeavors! However, during the past several years, we have found that starting a new campus both costs less *and* reaches more people than starting a new church.

The cost comparison I'm making is with regard to high-impact church plants and campuses that launch with an intention of averaging more than two hundred people from the beginning. Using that as our baseline parameter, we figure that we will spend approximately $250,000 on a new campus, and in a similar setting a new church would cost about $400,000 to launch. The difference in the cost is not about staffing, facilities, or marketing. The cost differential is in the *amount of time* it takes for the church to become self-supporting versus the amount of time it takes a new campus to become self-supporting. While campuses will typically be self-supporting in eighteen to twenty-four months, a church plant will often take at least thirty-six months.

That said, the biggest difference isn't in the cost but in the number of lives you impact for every dollar you spend. The following graph will help explain what we mean.

	Launch Attendance	First Quarter Attendance/Retention	First Year Attendance/Retention
Church Plant	465	226/48%	228/49%
Campus Plant	501	323/63%	285/57%

When we launched Community, we had 465 people attend our first celebration service, and our average attendance for the first three months was 226, a 48 percent retention rate. We have never since launched a campus that had a retention rate that low. The average campus at Community now launches with 501 people in attendance and an average of 323 people for the first quarter, a 63 percent retention rate. That difference between 226 and 323 is 97 people—that's an increase of 31 percent. That is huge! Bottom line: what we discovered in this process was that our new campuses cost us less money to start, resulted in greater retention, and reached more people.

Excellence: New-Church Vibe and Big-Church Punch

I remember Lyle Schaller telling me when we first transitioned to multiple sites, "Dave, the most important thing you offer to this new site is your large-church culture." At first I wasn't sure what he was talking about, but I eventually realized that he meant expectations and excellence. We were able to launch the second site with the same level of excellence that it took us eight years to achieve at our original church plant. We believe that the reason we see higher retention rates with a new campus versus a new church has a lot to do with the level of excellence and the quality of a newcomer's experience. The new site has all of the benefits of a new-church vibe but also has the big-church punch when it comes to excellence.

When we launched Community, we didn't have a complete band for our celebration service. The Kids' City consisted of volunteers from other churches and students from a nearby Bible college. We only had thirty-five adults involved in small groups, all led by people on staff. But when we started our second site, we had a full band, multimedia, drama, hospitality teams, and a full Kids' City volunteer staff. We also had ten volunteer leaders waiting to start small groups with a capacity for more than one hundred unconnected people. So the first-time attender got to experience the best of both worlds!

Marketing: Brand New and Trusted Brand

My adrenaline is still pumping. Why? I just heard that we are getting a Chick-fil-A in Chicago! Better yet, it is within a ten-minute drive of my house. Some of you take this for granted because you have one on every corner where you live. But in Chicago there is no other fast-food restaurant like Chick-fil-A, where you get real chicken, sweet tea, waffle fries, and people who say, "My pleasure," to your every request. Chick-fil-A is a brand that I trust, and now they have a brand-new store near me! I will never go to Wendy's again.✗

 What about the milk shakes at Chick-fil-A? The "hand-spun" milk shakes alone are worth the drive. —Jon

We all have brands that we trust: Nike, Starbucks, Honda ... you fill in the blank. That is the idea behind marketing— the development of a trust relationship between the product and the customer. We've found that a similar dynamic is true with the launch of a multisite church. In the past, people had a brand loyalty to a particular denomination; now much of that brand loyalty lies with individual churches. When a church opens a brand-new location in a nearby neighborhood or city, people respond because it is already a trusted brand. From a marketing perspective, a church plant is brand new, but it has not been around long enough to become a *trusted* brand.

At Community we have experienced this phenomenon. People who were inactive and didn't attend church became active when we moved to their neighborhood. People who had heard about us but did not attend because it was too far away now gave us a visit. People who loved the church told their neighbors when we located nearby. Multisite churches have the marketing benefit of being *both* brand new and a trusted brand.

BENEFITS OF MULTISITE VERSUS LARGE CHURCH

While there are benefits to a multisite church over a church plant, there are also benefits to a multisite church over a large church.

Diversity: Homogeneous and Heterogeneous

While 95 percent of churches in the United States are homogeneous (made up of one major ethnic or socioeconomic group), this is not typically the case with multisite churches. Leadership Network surveyed more than one thousand churches with multiple sites and found that 48 percent had significant racial diversity and 72 percent had significant socioeconomic diversity. In addition, we were recently part of an extensive study of a dozen hand-selected megachurches, and Community was found to be much more diverse than any of the other eleven churches.

Of our eleven sites, four of the locations have a much different demographic than our first site in Naperville, where the average age is thirty-two and 80 percent of the people are Anglo-American. If you were to visit our Pilsen campus, located in Chicago's largest Hispanic community, you could go to a service in English or Spanish. Or you could go to our East Aurora campus, where more than 90 percent of the people are Hispanic, and be a part of a bilingual service. If you went to our Carillon campus, you would find that it has a much different look because everyone is over fifty-five — it's located in an active adult golf community for seniors.
* It would look even more

> Our dad and mom (Earl and Pat Ferguson) lead the Carillon campus, and they are making plans to reproduce more locations in other active adult communities around the country. — Jon

different if you were to visit our Romeoville campus, where it is truly a multicultural experience. The population is roughly an even split into thirds of African-American, Hispanic, and Anglo backgrounds. All four of these sites are growing and seeing people from different cultures and of all different ages finding their way back to God!

Geography: Local and Regional

Another benefit of the multisite church over a single-site large church is *geography*. Paul and Carol first heard about Community from their son, who was a regular attender and leader at the church. Paul and Carol would attend every once in a while, but didn't come every week because they lived over forty minutes away from our first location. When they heard from their son that we would be starting a new location within ten minutes of their home, Paul and Carol became regular attenders at the new site. They are a great example of how the multisite church is both local *and* regional.

As we got ready to start our Montgomery campus, word got out in the months leading up to the grand opening. I remember getting a call from Mike and Sue, a couple who used to go to Community but moved thirty minutes west of our first site. I hadn't seen them in two or three years. As I talked with them, they were very excited about this new campus we were planning to launch near them. They ended the phone conversation with, "Well, we have canceled our trip to see family at Easter so we can be at Community! We'll see you at Easter, when the new site opens." Even though we were only thirty minutes away, somehow that seemed too far for them. But once we opened a new site in their community, they became 3C Christ followers and eventually key leaders on that campus.

This advantage is mostly about geography. It may seem obvious to some, but it still needs to be said: *people are more inclined to be a part of a church that is closer to where they live.* In addition, they are much more likely to invite their neighbors when the church is close. The advantage of a multisite church is that you can be both local *and* regional.

Impact: More Outreach and More Maturity

While the growth of the average single-site church will often reach a plateau, the typical multisite church will, on average, see its outreach increase by 13 percent annually and will grow by 33 percent after becoming a multisite church. We experienced similar results at our church. While we have seen growth every year since we started, the years that we have experienced only single-digit growth are those years when we did not start a new site. The years when we did start a new site have seen double-digit growth ranging from 15 percent to 39 percent.

It may not come as a surprise that multisite churches are experiencing greater outreach than your typical single-site church, but what may surprise you is that they are also seeing more depth and spiritual maturity among members. At Community, we challenge people to become 3C Christ followers. What we have discovered is that while people will drive long distances to join the weekly celebration service at a large church, if they live more than thirty minutes away, their ability to connect and contribute is diminished. Jay and Ruthie are a good example of a couple who were nominally involved, falling far short of being 3C Christ followers. They would show up twice a month at a celebration service, were not connected in a small group, and were not contributing their time or their treasures. But when we started a new site within walking distance of their house, everything seemed to change for them. Today Jay and Ruthie not only make our celebration services a regular part of their week; they are both leading groups. Additionally, they are contributing financially and evangelistically in ways they never had before.

Our experience is teaching us that a church that reproduces sites will also experience the benefit of getting more people connected with the community and involved in difference-making ministry. We saw this benefit in a dramatic way when we started our Shorewood campus. Our Romeoville campus sent 150 of its very best people to help launch this new campus. At that time, 54 percent of the people at our Romeoville campus were connected to a small group and were serving. So when Romeoville sent all those people to launch the Shorewood campus, we were concerned about the negative impact this might have on our Romeoville campus. One year later we saw the outreach of *both* sites increase from 800 weekly to more than 1,100 weekly, with 74 percent of the people at both locations connected in a small group and involved in serving. Wow! More outreach leads to growth and maturity.

PAIN AT THREE SITES AND CRISIS AT FOUR!

As we reproduced our second, third, and fourth sites, we were increasingly excited about helping more and more people find their way back to God, bringing transformation to these communities, and spreading this missional movement. However, at the same time, it became much more difficult to make things work organizationally. For example, when we went to three sites, it meant that some of our arts staff would have oversight of three different locations: that's ten adult celebration services and nine Kids' City celebration services! When you stop and think about recruiting all the musicians, vocalists, and tech support people and then rehearsing all of them for a total of eighteen services *every* week ... that is an overwhelming challenge! While it was painful, we somehow got it done. But when we added our fourth site, we reached a point of crisis. I remember Eric Bramlett, who oversees our arts ministries, coming to me and saying, "Dave, this is not working." And he was right. More and more people were coming to all four of our Community sites, but we did not have the systems, infrastructure, or organizational design to make it all work. We were in crisis!

I was visiting with Lyle Schaller, looking for some answers when I heard him say, "Dave, in the coming years there will be hundreds if not thousands of multi-site churches. The majority of these will be two sites, very few will be three sites, but a surprisingly large number will be four sites or more." Confused, I asked Lyle, "Why?" He explained, "You can stumble to two sites, but you have to plan, think, and restructure to get to three or more." Once again Schaller was correct.[*]

Our experience at Community and in coaching hundreds of other churches has taught us that you can go from one to two sites with little change in your structure or organizational design. And you might be able to stretch it to three sites with some added willpower. However, to go to four sites and beyond will take a more sophisticated organizational structure, greater intentionality about developing leaders and artists, and being very clear about the things that are non-negotiables.

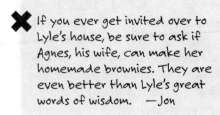

If you ever get invited over to Lyle's house, be sure to ask if Agnes, his wife, can make her homemade brownies. They are even better than Lyle's great words of wisdom. —Jon

As we began to make sense of our world with four sites (and then five sites and now eleven sites), we got more and more requests from churches to coach them and give advice on how to move beyond two or three sites. In our coaching of these churches, eight important questions seem to come up over and over again, questions that *must* be answered before you can make the transition to four or more sites.

THE EIGHT MOST IMPORTANT QUESTIONS FOR FOUR SITES OR MORE

1. The Dream Question: What Is the Dream?

One of the first questions I ask people when they tell me they want to go to multiple sites is, "How many sites?" or "How big is your dream?" If they say, "We'd like to be a church of two or three sites," then their challenges are not necessarily easy, but they are pretty simple and straightforward. I often tell churches wanting to go from one site to two sites that it is just like adding another celebration service. The only difference is that instead of adding another celebration service at your current location, you are going to add one at a different location. If you think of it in those terms, it dramatically reduces the complexity.

Now, if a church leader answers the dream question by saying, "We want to be a church of four or more sites," then the challenges ahead are both significant and increasingly complex. These challenges will include deciding what will be decentralized to each location and what will be centralized. The question of centralized ver-

1. What is the dream?

2. What is essential to your brand?

3. What is your organizational design?

4. Will you use video teaching, a team of teachers, or both?

5. Do you have a leadership farm system?

6. Do you have a plan for artist development?

7. Will you have enough money in enough time?

8. How are you going to keep the mission on target?

sus decentralized will include issues such as decision-making processes, curriculum creation and content, finances, and so on. This is a great example of how dreaming big will change your questions, as we talked about in chapter 3. In this case, bigger dreams naturally result in more-challenging questions. So before you can address any of those issues, start by prayerfully answering the question, what is the dream?

2. The Brand Question: What Is Essential to Your Brand?

When McDonald's opens a new location, they may or may not have a playground area, but you know they will have hamburgers. When Starbucks opens a new store, they may or may not have a drive-thru, but you know they will have coffee. Some things are *essential* to a brand, and other things are *optional*. One of the tough decisions every church has to make when reproducing more than two or three sites is determining which ministries are essential and which ministries are optional.

When Community starts a new site, we know that a celebration service, adult small groups, Kids' City, ministry to underresourced communities, and an emphasis on hospitality are *essential*. At some of our larger sites, we will also have a support and recovery ministry and a School for the Arts. Now, I love our support and recovery ministry and our School for the Arts, but we cannot afford to reproduce everything at our brand-new sites. So we must honestly answer the question, what is essential to our brand?*

 Disclaimer! Disclaimer! Most of our campuses have been started in communities with young families. Brand isn't as important as mission. What is essential to your brand may need to be adjusted based on the context. —Jon

3. The Organization Question: What Is Your Organizational Design?

If you answered the dream question by saying two or three sites, then I would recommend an organizational design that takes your existing vertical ministry silos and adds the horizontal influence of campus pastors across these ministries. In this organizational design, the authority resides in the vertical silos, and influence resides with the campus pastor horizontally. The organizational design looks like this:

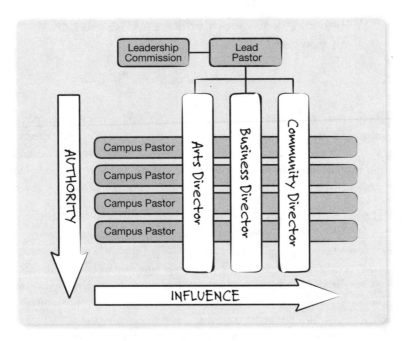

If you answered the dream question by saying four or more sites, then I would recommend that you take the previous organizational design and turn it on its

side.* The biggest change is that the authority now resides with the campus pastor, and the influence resides with the ministries. This shift is necessary in order to make sure that excellent and effective ministry is happening at every location. The organizational design for four or more sites now looks like this:

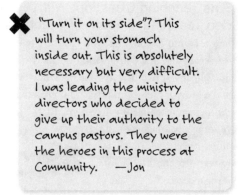

"Turn it on its side"? This will turn your stomach inside out. This is absolutely necessary but very difficult. I was leading the ministry directors who decided to give up their authority to the campus pastors. They were the heroes in this process at Community. —Jon

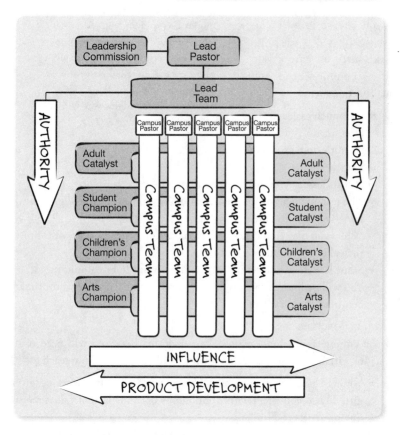

Resolving this question of organizational design is critical for churches that dream of more than four sites. If you don't answer this question, it's likely that you will not realize your dream.

4. The Teaching Question: Will You Use Video Teaching, a Team of Teachers, or Both?

When it comes to teaching, you basically have three choices: video teaching, in-person teaching, or a combination of the two. I am convinced that as long as it is done well, any of the three approaches will work. Research backs this up and shows that the growth rates of multisite churches that use video teaching and those that use in-person teaching are almost exactly the same. However, the different options have some advantages (**+**) and disadvantages (**–**) that you may want to consider before making a choice.*

Video Teaching

If you choose to go exclusively with video teaching, make sure you have a very gifted communicator and quality equipment.

 Gotta give a shout-out from one younger brother to another. Geoff Surratt (younger brother of Greg Surratt) teamed up with Greg Ligon and Warren Bird to write two great books on the topic of multisite, with lots of additional detail and information: The Multi-Site Church Revolution and A Multi-Site Church Road Trip.   —Jon

- **+** It is much easier to reproduce a video than it is to reproduce a teacher.
- **+** It costs less to reproduce a video than it does to reproduce a teacher.
- **+** The teaching will have a consistent quality and will be in alignment with the vision of the church.
- **–** While you may find other venues to develop teachers, it does diminish the value of reproducing teachers.
- **–** Some leaders with teaching gifts will not want to be campus pastors.
- **–** You will be limited to reproducing sites in contexts where your primary communicator is effective.

Team of Teachers

If you choose to develop a team of in-person teachers, you will need to use a teaching gift assessment for deciding who should and should not teach.

- **+** You will be developing more and better teachers to use their God-given gift. This is consistent with a philosophy of ministry that values reproducing artists and leaders.
- **+** In our previous book, *The Big Idea*, we explain how a collaborative approach with a teaching team can create a better message in much less time.
- **+** You will be able to attract high-capacity leaders who also have teaching gifts to be campus pastors.

- The number of teaching pastors is not one teacher per campus. To give your teaching pastors time off or allow for the unexpected, you will need at least three teachers for every two campuses.
- Hiring three teaching pastors for every two campuses will be expensive.
- It will require great intentionality as well as time and energy to develop more and better teachers.

Combo of Video and In-Person

Of the three options, this is my preference. I believe that by both using video teaching and developing a team of teachers, you get the best of both worlds.

+ You will be able to use both high-capacity leaders who don't want to teach and leaders with the gift of teaching as campus pastors.
+ You get the benefit of collaboration that creates a better message in less time, but you are still able to use video teaching effectively.
+ You will be able to start a new campus in any context, because you can match it with video teaching or an in-person teacher who will be effective in that setting.
- It is likely that some campus pastors will want to teach who are not gifted. The use of a teaching team assessment will mean that you will have to tell some people no to teaching.
- It is harder to explain why you use a combo rather than just video teaching ("We value high-quality teaching") or in-person teaching ("We value the development of teaching gifts").

5. The Leadership Question: Do You Have a Leadership Farm System?

Churches that dream of having four or more sites are like baseball teams. Baseball teams need a good farm system that is developing new and young players who can take the field to improve their team and replace retiring players. New players will come to a team in two ways: via free agency and through a team's farm system. The more expensive way is to pay big bucks and sign a free agent from another team. The more efficient means is to create a farm system that is constantly developing talent from within your organization. Since a multisite church's dream is to spread a missional movement through reproducing new sites, it needs a farm system of new and young leaders. Yes, a church can go the free agent route and recruit leaders from other churches, but churches with big dreams will never see them fulfilled if they are dependent on other churches and organizations to do their leadership development for them.

At Community most all of our campus pastors and many of our church planters in our NewThing Network have come up through the farm system. In chapter 2 you read about the leadership path and how Troy McMahon went from being an apprentice leader to a campus pastor to a network leader. The following leadership path is essential for developing a farm system.

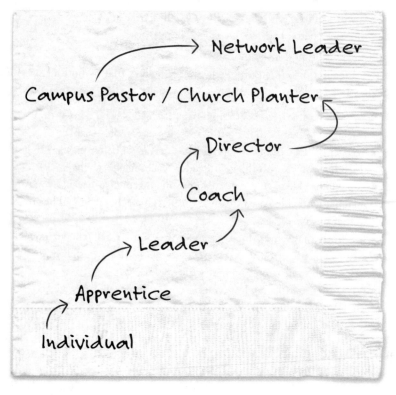

Do you have a farm system that is growing new campus pastors? If not, where are you going to find the leaders and staff for those future sites that are part of your dream?

6. The Artist Question: Do You Have a Plan for Artist Development?

Of all the multisite questions on this list, the one that most often gets overlooked is the artist question. In the same way that you need a leadership development strategy, you also need an artist development strategy. A church that wants to reproduce beyond four sites must be intentional about developing artists. All your large group events require artists who will facilitate and lead the celebration services. These artists include those whom we see up front — the musicians, vocalists, actors, and dancers — as well as those who are behind the scenes — the sound technicians and videographers.

Because of the size of our dreams at Community, we have an informal and a formal process for developing artists. Our informal process is through apprenticeships. We encourage our actors to have an understudy, our musicians to have a second chair, and our technicians to have people shadow them. Our formal process is through our School for the Arts, where we have more than four hundred artists enrolled in classes and workshops, developing and growing in their art.

If you are planning on reproducing more sites, what is your formal and informal process for developing more (and better) artists?

7. The Funding Question: Will You Have Enough Money in Enough Time?

Our two greatest resources are money and time. It's no different when it comes to reproducing your fourth site and beyond. You not only need money; you will need it at the right time. So as you make plans to launch your fourth site and beyond, make sure you have a well-developed pro forma, do the number crunching, and know for sure that you have the necessary funds.

The amount you will need to fund future sites will be different based on your expectations and your context. Some megachurches expect a new site to have more than a thousand people in attendance at the launch and to continue growing from there. These new sites may have budgets well over one million dollars. Other churches will start new sites with a single volunteer leader and will do it all on a shoestring budget. Chances are, your church is somewhere in between these two possibilities, and the best way to answer the funding question is to do the following:

1. Have a portion of your ongoing budget that goes to new sites. We currently set aside at least 10 percent of our budget for reproducing both new sites and new churches.
2. Know and communicate the date you expect the site to be self-supporting.
3. Insist that every campus pastor prepare a pro forma for the new site that shows how it will become self-supporting.
4. Put in place accountability by requiring that the needed funding is secured before finalizing the launch of a new campus.
5. Create a financial model that provides support for your central services as well as funding for new campus launches.

Make sure you answer the funding question. Failure to answer this question will not only negatively impact each new site you launch but also affect the existing church and your overall dream.

8. The Alignment Question: How Are You Going to Keep the Mission on Target?

The alignment question asks how you are going to keep all the sites moving toward the same vision with the same values. If there is vision and value drift by any of the locations, it will slow down the whole church. Even worse, it could result in veering off course and missing the target altogether. But if you get all locations moving toward the same vision with the same values, you will exponentially increase the impact of your church! Some churches with a big dream have stopped at two locations because they didn't answer the alignment question. Other churches are seeing their big dream realized as all their sites are on mission and moving forward.

At Community, our strategic team and our campus pastors developed what we call the "Campus Constants" that keep us in alignment:

- ✳ *Mission.* Helping people find their way back to God.
- ✳ *Strategic vision.* To grow a movement of reproducing churches committed to "the sixty-seven and the twenty" (67 percent of the world's population lives outside of a relationship with Christ; 20 percent of people worldwide live in extreme poverty both locally and globally).
- ✳ *3 Cs.* Celebrate, connect, and contribute will serve as the foundation for spiritual growth.
- ✳ *Big Idea.* One Big Idea for adults, students, and children will be implemented weekly.
- ✳ *Teaching team.* The teaching team will set the teaching schedule and will serve as the primary communicators, either in person or by video-cast.
- ✳ *Leadership structure.* One leadership structure with coach, leader, and apprentice leader.
- ✳ *Leadership community.* Monthly gathering of leaders for Vision, Skill, and Huddle times will take place at a central location.
- ✳ *Financial model.* 70/20/10, with each campus operating on 70 percent or less of its offerings within three years of a launch. Twenty percent or less of campus offerings will be used to support the catalyst (what we call our central services), and 10 percent will be used for new churchwide endeavors.
- ✳ *Web.* One centralized website for the church, representing all locations. One centralized web-based database (3CMS) for people, groups, events, and finances will be used to measure our 3C status.
- ✳ *Central services.* One centralized process or system for business services: banking, staffing, payroll, benefits, capital expenditures, lease agreements, etc.

If your dream is to move beyond three locations and continually reproduce sites, spending time with your team prayerfully answering these eight questions is absolutely critical. Our experience is that once you start reproducing more and more sites, you will also begin to reproduce churches, which is the topic of our next chapter.

CHAPTER
11

REPRODUCING CHURCHES

Impacting the World

BIG IDEA Launching new churches is foundational to spreading a missional movement.

- Hope in Church Planting
- Four Lessons to Save You Four Years
- How to Send Well: Lessons for the Lead Pastor
- How to Leave Well: Lessons for the Church-Planter-to-Be

HOPE IN CHURCH PLANTING

In the introduction to this book, I painted a rather disheartening picture highlighting the ineffectiveness of the church in America. It is my hope that the chapters that have followed have sparked within you a glimmer of hope and a vision for how God can use you and your friends to start a missional movement, a movement that not only changes the lives of people you know for eternity but also impacts neighborhoods, cities, countries ... possibly the world.

I am encouraged by what I see developing in the church today. There is a new Jesus-fueled spirit of adventure and entrepreneurialism among some of the brightest leaders you'll find anywhere. These are men and women who are not willing to stand by and follow the status quo of apathy that lulls many Christians to be indifferent to the Jesus mission. These emerging leaders are launching new churches in a variety of forms, but they all believe that the Acts 1:8 mission of Jesus was meant to be fulfilled, and they believe that God has commissioned them to be a part of fulfilling that mission.*

Dave Olson, director of the American Church Research Project and author of *The American Church in Crisis*, conducted groundbreaking research from more than two hundred thousand churches in the United States. His research compared the impact of new

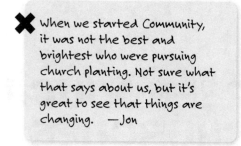

When we started Community, it was not the best and brightest who were pursuing church planting. Not sure what that says about us, but it's great to see that things are changing. —Jon

churches with that of existing churches. The graph below shows the percentage of yearly growth based on the decade in which a church was started. His data goes back more than two hundred years.[19]

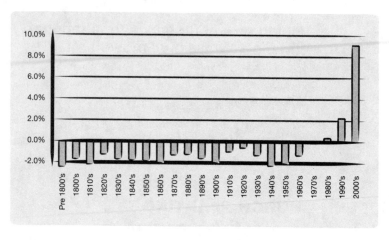

Of the decades represented by the graph:

* Eighteen out of twenty-two decades show negative growth.
* Two out of twenty-two decades indicate less than 1 percent growth or a plateau.
* Only two decades indicate a significant positive growth rate.
* The first positive indicator is among churches started in the last ten to twenty years, at a 2.2 percent growth rate.
* However, new churches started in the last ten years grew on average by 9 percent.

If that's not enough evidence for you, there's more. New churches have three to four times the number of people finding their way back to God per person as do established churches.[20] This means that if an established church of two hundred and fifty people helped ten people find their way back to God, in that same time frame a new church of two hundred and fifty would likely help thirty to forty people find their way back to him. And in the first ten years, new churches grow twenty-three times faster than churches over ten years old.[21] All of this seems to clearly suggest that *new* churches are the most effective at helping people find their way back to God.

Let me share with you four stories from Community's first four years of church planting. Each of these stories illustrates a specific church-planting lesson we learned, a lesson that is sure to save you *at least* four years!

FOUR LESSONS TO SAVE YOU FOUR YEARS
Dave Richa and Jacob's Well, Denver

"Why would you want to do that?" That was my gut-level and even audible response when Dave Richa, our student ministry director at the time, first approached me about planting a new church. I couldn't imagine that anyone would ever want to leave Community. We'd gained a reputation as having a strong staff team and being a great environment in which to work. Occasionally at conferences or workshops I would boast about how our staff had such long tenures. I'd say, "Nobody ever wants to leave our staff."

So when Dave first told me he wanted to leave to plant a new church, all I heard him say was that he wanted to leave. I'm not even sure it registered with me that he wanted to plant a church. To me, it was all about the leaving. And I'm sure that not only was it a blow to my ego, but also I couldn't imagine Community without Dave Richa. He had become a great friend and a tremendous leader on our staff. I just figured we'd always be working together.

We continued to dialogue about Dave's dream to plant a church in the Denver area. It became obvious that this wasn't some "idea of the week" for Dave. This was something he believed God wanted him to do, and to be obedient to God, he simply couldn't ignore it. After wrestling with this vision and having some conversations with Jon and others on our team, we finally decided that this idea had to be from God. We'd been talking about reproducing leaders, small groups, celebration services, and new campuses, but we had never really considered church planting. To be honest, this was taking us out of our comfort zone.✱

Dave quickly began to develop a strategy for this new vision. He identified a specific location just outside of Denver. The community he selected

> ✖ We were convinced it wasn't Richa's "idea of the week," but I wasn't. Richa had a new name for our student ministry every six months. —Jon

was experiencing tremendous growth—new people were moving in every day. Together we mapped out a three-year financial and fundraising strategy. We contacted various people and organizations we hoped would support this new mission. And we were amazed at the enthusiastic response we received. Both Rocky Mountain Church and Church Planters of the Rockies supported the project financially, and Community agreed to continue paying Dave's salary for three years after the launch of the church.

When we finally went public at Community with this dream to plant a new church in Denver, we were just blown away at the response. At one of our Leadership Community gatherings, we shared the news about Dave and our plan to launch this new church. I said to our leadership, "We need to pray for Dave. We need to encourage him and support him financially. And some of you in this room need to seriously consider moving to Denver and joining Dave in launching this new church." I believed that I was saying what God wanted me to say, but still I was amazed when thirty-five people signed on to leave their current jobs, sell their homes, and relocate from Chicago to Denver to be part of this new thing that God was doing. Eighteen months later Jacob's Well Community Church launched and ushered our church into the great adventure of church planting.

Church-Planting Lesson 1: Ask People to Move Where God Is Moving

Since Dave Richa was the first leader we had released to launch a new church, this was also the first time we had ever asked people to leave their jobs, sell their homes, transfer schools, and move to be part of the launch team for a new church. When I stood before our Leadership Community and asked them not only to pray for Dave and his team but also to consider moving to Denver with them, I had no idea what kind of response I would receive.

Now every chance I get to stand before our church and our leaders with a new church planter, I ask them to pray for the planter and I ask them to consider moving as well. (We've not only seen people move to Denver; we've seen people move to other cities, like Boston, Detroit, New York, and Kansas City. Don't be afraid to ask people to move. People will move where God is moving!)

Brian Moll and Forefront Church, New York City

Sometime during the year that followed the tragic events of September 11, 2001, I received a letter from Paul Williams, the president of the Orchard Group, a church-planting organization focused on major metro areas of the northeastern region of the United States. In the letter, Paul shared his conviction that God was at work in a new way in New York City. People seemed to be increasingly receptive to the love of Jesus. In light of that, he asked if I would be interested in leading a church plant in New York myself. I was intrigued by the idea, but

I didn't feel God was leading me in that direction. I declined but let him know that we would like to partner with them to launch a new church in Manhattan.

What followed was months of searching for the right person to lead this new church. We interviewed several strong candidates who would have been great church planters. With several of them, it was clear that New York was a place they were willing to go, should God call them to go there, but it wasn't a place they loved or longed to be. That wasn't good enough for us. We wanted to find someone whose lifelong dream was to plant a church in New York City. So we waited until we finally received a call from Brian Moll.*

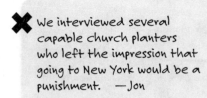

We interviewed several capable church planters who left the impression that going to New York would be a punishment. —Jon

In some ways, Brian was the least likely candidate for a church plant in New York City. Brian grew up in rural Oklahoma, and he was currently on staff at Northside Christian Church in New Albany, Indiana. However, Brian had a strong track record of developing leaders at Northside and was an outstanding communicator. He had long been dreaming of planting a church in New York. He loved the city and was undeniably drawn to be about God's work in a major urban center.*

Brian loved New York so much, he named his first child Brooklyn before he ever moved there. —Jon

We put all of our church planters and campus pastors through CPAC—Church Planters Assessment Center (see www.churchplanting4me.org). —Jon

After several phone calls, interviews, and a three-day church-planting assessment, Brian was hired to launch the new church.* This plant was a partnership between Community, Orchard Group, Stadia, Northside Christian Church, and several other organizations. Brian agreed to come to Community to serve a leadership residency for seven months to be immersed in a reproducing church culture. He and his wife, Alison, and their three children moved to Chicago in May and by December were moving to Manhattan to launch the new church. After raising the necessary money, starting small groups, and developing a launch team, Forefront

Community Church opened its doors the following September. Today Forefront has two locations and reaches more than four hundred people every weekend.

Church-Planting Lesson 2: Don't Skip a Leadership Residency

A leadership residency is an invaluable experience for a leader preparing to launch a new church. The opportunity to remove yourself from your current context and immerse yourself in a reproducing church culture is priceless. Many of our residents have significant ministry experience and have families with children, and yet they will be the first to tell you that this costly and time-consuming step on their journey to planting a church is more than worthwhile.✱

✕ We're looking for one leadership resident for every NewThing church or site. If you're interested, go to www.newthing.org. —Jon

Brian will tell you that he initially questioned the value of the time he would spend at Community. "At first I thought of it more as 'detox' before I jumped on the church-planting bandwagon," says Brian. "But soon after landing at Community, I discovered that the next seven months were going to be critical for the success of a healthy church in New York."

Brian describes one of the lessons he learned from his residency this way: "I learned the priority of reproduction. Leaders reproduce — they reproduce Christ followers, artists, leaders, small groups, celebration services, campuses, and churches throughout their city and around the world. Without strong leadership and a firm grasp of the value of reproduction, churches begin to grow stale and get desperate or die (or in most cases, both). One of the most critical values I took with me as I journeyed east to New York was that the health of our church was dependent on our ability to reproduce at all levels."

Dave Dummitt and 242 Community Church in Detroit

While we were in dialogue with Brian Moll about launching a church in New York City, we received a phone call from Dave Dummitt. Dave was on staff at First Church of Christ in Burlington, Kentucky. He had started and led a young adult ministry, overseeing the growth from zero to five hundred people in just a few years. Dave had been sensing that perhaps God was calling him to plant a church. He was going to be traveling in our area, so we asked him to stop by the Yellow Box's Ground Level Café for coffee.

I still remember that day as we were sitting in the café talking with Dave about his future. Having worked together as long as we have, Jon and I know each other's thoughts without saying a word. With a couple of glances in Jon's direction, I knew we were in full agreement that Dave would make an outstanding church planter. But when we talked about the residency aspect of his journey, I remember Dave having some doubts: "You mean I have to move my family from Kentucky to Chicago for this leadership residency?" I simply told him, "You don't have to; you have to *want* to."

While Dave Dummitt was still trying to uncover God's plan for his future and praying through this possibility, Bob Smith, a police officer in Brighton, Michigan, just west of Detroit, was praying that God would bring the right leader to plant a church in his community. Bob had not only been dreaming and praying about a new church in his community; he'd also begun to gather a launch team, build a partnership with the owner of a local fitness club, and even raise funds to get this church started.

Eventually Dave decided that church planting was indeed the direction God was leading, so he, his wife, Rachel, and their two children spent the summer with us at Community, where Dave served as a leadership resident. Then Dave moved with his family to Brighton to launch 242 Community Church. Remarkably, close to twenty people moved with Dave and Rachel from Kentucky to Brighton, including several members of the band from his young adult minis-

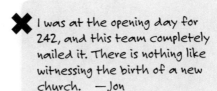

I was at the opening day for 242, and this team completely nailed it. There is nothing like witnessing the birth of a new church. —Jon

try. Today 242 Community Church has two locations, one in Brighton and one in Ann Arbor, and they are reaching more than thirteen hundred people every weekend.*

Church-Planting Lesson 3: Start with a Winning Team

Most of us know the value of starting a new church with a team. However, there's a huge difference between starting with a team and starting with a *winning* team. A winning team is a group of people with a proven track record. Dave Dummitt and his friend Bob Smith started 242 Community Church with a *winning* team.

The launch of 242 Community Church was the convergence of two distinct teams: the launch team being developed by Bob Smith in Brighton as well as the team of people that Dave brought with him from Kentucky. The team from Kentucky included a number of incredibly talented artists and leaders who had been expanding their leadership capacity under Dave's leadership in the young adult ministry. This team's experience in the young adult ministry served as an incubator for what would later become 242 Community Church. When this group combined with the group coalescing in Brighton, it formed an incredible team that was able to jump-start the success of this church on day one.

While it's unusual to be able to start a church with a team as well developed as the one that came together to launch 242 Community Church, Dave's experience demonstrates the importance of starting with a winning team. A strong team of leaders provides you with the ability to launch larger, and it gives added stability and sustainability that can last for months after the launch. Certainly, many factors have contributed to the rapid growth of 242 Community Church. But there is little doubt that the size and quality of the launch team were two of the most significant factors.

Hank Wilson and Reunion Church, Boston

During that same summer when Dave Dummitt and Brian Moll were residents at Community, Hank Wilson, our Montgomery campus pastor, was sensing God calling him to plant a church in Boston. I love Hank's story. It was fall of 2004. Hank was in Boston with some friends from Community who were also considering being part of the church plant. The Yankees were in Boston playing the Red Sox in the American League Championship Series. If you remember that series, the Red Sox were down three games to none. No team in baseball history had ever come back from a 3–0 deficit, and it was a pretty safe bet that the Red Sox had no hope of coming back. So at the time, Hank made a comment to his buddy Mike: "If the Red Sox come back from a 3–0 deficit, we'll know for sure that God wants us to move to Boston." Both seemed to be pretty unlikely possibilities.

Now, if you know anything about the 2004 American League Championship Series, you know that the Red Sox accomplished the most remarkable comeback in major-league baseball history. That incredible feat, combined with lots of prayer and affirmation from friends and church leaders, eventually led Hank and about twenty-five others to move from the Midwest to launch a new church in Boston.

A few years later, more than three hundred people gather every Sunday at the Back Bay Hilton to celebrate what God is doing at Reunion Church. And Reunion is making plans to launch a new campus next year. Incidentally, Reunion's offices are in the shadow of Fenway Park—where the Red Sox engineered their amazing comeback and won the series.★

 As a Cubs fan, 2004 became a bitter year for me when the Red Sox won the World Series. Prior to that, I felt like Boston could feel my pain. And then when the White Sox won it in 2005 ... Need I say more? —Jon

Church-Planting Lesson 4: Plant with Multiple Partners

Who ever would have guessed that a multisite church in Chicago would partner with two different church-planting organizations in the eastern part of the

United States and three large megachurches (one in Dallas, one in St. Louis, and another in Lexington) to plant a church in one of the most unchurched cities in the country? Well, that's exactly how Reunion Church was launched. Reunion was a unique partnership with Restoration House Ministries; Stadia; Compass Church in Dallas; Crossroads Christian Church in Lexington, Kentucky; and Harvester Church in St. Louis.

If you've ever watched NASCAR, you've probably noticed that almost every car is sponsored by multiple companies and products. Every square inch of a car's surface is covered with a corporate logo or decal. I doubt that you could find a car with just a single corporate sponsor. Financing a successful NASCAR team takes multiple corporate sponsors, and each one of those sponsors will claim that team as its own. In the same way, we've found that it takes multiple partners to successfully launch a church plant. And best of all, everyone involved gets the credit!

Launching in major metropolitan areas is very demanding. It requires strategic partners who bring together church-planting experience, an understanding of the local culture, and resources to do what no single entity could do on its own. One of the partners in this plant, Restoration House, brought knowledge of church development in New England. Stadia brought resources and coaching. The three church partners brought the resources of large churches and the support and passionate energy it takes to reach a major city. All of this combined to plant a growing, innovative church that helps people in Boston find their way back to God.

Hank's story is similar to Dave Richa's in some ways. Hank was part of our staff at Community before he went on to launch a new church. In addition to Hank and Dave, we've also released staff members Troy McMahon (Troy was a campus pastor) and Jim Semradek (also a campus pastor) to launch new churches. Through the process of releasing several of our staff to launch new churches, I've learned a few things about how to "send well." So for just a minute, let me speak to the lead pastors reading this book. If you're not a lead pastor, you can probably skip this section (but if you've made it this far, you probably won't).

HOW TO SEND WELL: LESSONS FOR THE LEAD PASTOR

Lesson 1: Let Go

Many lead pastors will likely have the same response I did when Dave Richa came to me saying he wanted to leave our church to start a *new* church in Colorado: feelings of being abandoned. It's almost impossible not to take someone's choosing to leave personally. Let me challenge you to indeed take it *personally*, but in a different way than you might think. Chances are, this person who is telling you he wants to leave and start a new church never would have developed to the place where he has the confidence to do what he's wanting to do now if you hadn't given him the freedom and the opportunities to fully develop his gifts and calling in his current role. When you find yourself in a place where you need to respond to someone leaving to plant a new church, you've got three basic options:

1. You can bless him and get behind it.
2. You can fight it and try to get him to stay. (It won't work; he's gonna go.)
3. You can kick him to the curb and say, "Good luck."

There may be times when you need to fight it a little, especially if you genuinely don't think it's in his best interest. Let me caution you, though. With every one of the staff we have released to plant a church, there were times early on in the conversation when I was convinced it wasn't the right time. But I've found that if you wait for the "right time," you'll never plant any churches. If I had pushed back too hard, it might even have led to a significant strain on our relationship.[*]

> ✘ Not only did Dave think it wasn't the right time almost every time; so did I. Don't listen too closely to your first response. It's probably wrong or selfish. —Jon

I have found that once a leader gets to the place where he is talking to you about it, he's already decided he's ready to leave. The best thing you can do is bless him, challenge him in areas where he still needs development, and get behind this new vision.

Lesson 2: Be Available

While the church-planter-to-be needs to assert himself to communicate and keep you updated on the progress he is making toward launching a new church, you will also have to work hard at being available to provide sufficient coaching and direction. Be warned! The closer you get to the time of his departure, the more difficult it will be to make yourself available to him. It's almost inevitable that there even will be times when you see his plans for this new church as a distraction. In those moments, make the extra effort to schedule regular times for getting together with him and continue to stay current on the progress he is making in developing this new mission.

Lesson 3: Celebrate Publicly

When you finally agree and accept that this staff member is going to leave and start a new church (and there is no turning back), it's time to go public with the news and celebrate this new venture as often as possible. With every one of the people who have left Community to plant a new church, we have had a public celebration and an anointing service during one of our Leadership Community gatherings. This is a great opportunity for you, as the lead pastor, to take your private blessing public, letting the entire church know that you believe in this person's leadership and vision and that you are behind their new mission one hundred percent. It's also a great opportunity for you to look your leaders in the eye and challenge them to consider supporting this new church plant through their prayers, through their generosity, or even by moving with the team to be part of the new plant.

Lesson 4: Stay Connected

It can be difficult to maintain good communication while the future church planter is still around prior to leaving, but it is *increasingly* difficult to keep those lines of communication open *after* he has moved to start the new church. Yet continued communication is important for both of you: the church planter and the lead pastor. Church planting can be incredibly lonely. The person you have sent to launch this new church will relate to you in ways he may never have before. This is a great opportunity for your relationship to transition to the next level. Your church planter will discover, perhaps for the first time, what it is like to be the point person for something as daunting as starting a new church. Set up regular times to connect via the phone or videoconferencing. There may be times when it seems like your calls don't accomplish much, but that relational connection, encouragement, and prayer support will mean a lot to the new church planter.

✗ ✗ ✗

While we've made plenty of mistakes, we've also learned some valuable lessons about how a church-planter-to-be can leave well. So if you're thinking about gathering your friends together to spread this missional movement and you're currently on staff at a church, consider learning from our experience.

HOW TO LEAVE WELL: LESSONS FOR THE CHURCH-PLANTER-TO-BE

Lesson 1: Talk Early

Troy McMahon began talking to me about the possibility of launching a new church while his vision was still in its infancy. I knew that Troy had been thinking and praying about planting a new church for quite some time, but by engaging me in dialogue early on, he gave me time to process his plan. Even though I was resistant at times, knowing what he was thinking helped me to get behind his vision and communicate it to our church. One of the biggest mistakes church planters make is to wait too long before they share their dream with senior leadership. Senior leaders may be surprised by the news and may even feel like they're being *told* what's going to happen rather than having the opportunity to be a part of God's unfolding dream for this new ministry.

Lesson 2: Give Credit

Mark Nelson, lead pastor at Crossings Church in Knoxville, Tennessee, had been in ministry leadership for twenty years prior to coming to Community for his leadership residency. The campus ministry he led at Purdue University was one of the largest in the United States, serving more than a thousand students. Mark had as much experience in ministry as Jon or me. However, Mark repeatedly went out of his way to express appreciation for the investment we made in him before, during, and following his leadership residency. This is not only important for the senior leadership; it is also important for the sending church to feel affirmed in their mission, even as they mourn the loss of someone they have grown to love.

Lesson 3: Keep Communicating

Before Hank Wilson left to launch Reunion Church in Boston, he and I continued to meet regularly to discuss his plans and map a strategy for a successful launch. Hank also did an excellent job of communicating to me who was planning to move to Boston to be part of this new mission. I realize that at times it was difficult for Hank to get my attention, because I still had some significant initiatives and other opportunities that needed my time and focus at our church. However, Hank's persistent dialogue proved invaluable as we walked this path together.

Lesson 4: Identify a Successor

Working with senior leadership to identify and develop a successor gives a strong indication that you are as interested in the future health of the sending church as you are in the future development of the new church plant. Ideally, you will have already been developing an apprentice. As Hank Wilson was making plans to launch a new church in Boston, he also identified Carter Moss as his apprentice campus pastor. This made for an extremely smooth transition when Hank finally left. Sure, we still missed Hank, but we also knew that the Montgomery campus would be left in good hands. Under Carter's leadership, the Montgomery campus has continued to grow and has helped launch three more campuses.*

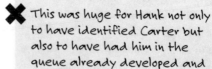

This was huge for Hank not only to have identified Carter but also to have had him in the queue already developed and ready to take over. —Jon

NEWTHING

Dave Richa, Dave Dummitt, and Brian Moll—that initial trio of church planters became the foundation for our NewThing Network. The vision for NewThing is "to be a catalyst for a movement of reproducing churches." And what you've just read are a few examples, stories of what God is doing through NewThing to accomplish the mission of Jesus. It is our dream that in the years ahead there will be thousands of stories like these, stories of people who faithfully answered God's call, gathered their friends, and went where God said to go.

PART FOUR

REPRODUCING MOVEMENTS OF 10,000s

A missional church movement is realized as it impacts ten thousand people and more. This occurs as apostolic leaders are moved by God's Spirit to empower other leaders through an infrastructure of reproducing networks.

REPRODUCING NETWORKS

The Infrastructure of Movements

BIG IDEA Every missional movement has a reproducing infrastructure.

✗ The Power of Networks
✗ Reproducing Church Networks
✗ Collaborative Church Networks
✗ What Makes a Reproducing Network Work?

THE POWER OF NETWORKS

As we near the close of this book, I want to say to you once again what I said at the start: "You can do it." Though it can seem overwhelming and impossible, you, your friends, and your church *can* start a missional movement. Don't read this chapter as though it applies to someone else or as an inspirational devotion on the heroic tales of other Christ followers. This chapter really is meant for you! And I believe that, not just because I'm writing this book but also because I am seeing it happen before my very eyes. At our church, what started as a bunch of college friends with a vision to reach Chicago is now a missional movement of reproducing churches all over the world, helping thousands and thousands of people find their way back to God. We haven't seen a full-blown exponential movement yet, but I'm convinced that we are getting a glimpse of what is yet to come. I believe that God is going to use NewThing and other church-planting networks like ours to catalyze a movement that will actually accomplish the mission of Jesus.

As we've seen throughout this book, before you can start a movement, you need to understand what it takes to make a movement move! It has been my observation over the past several years that within every movement is an *infrastructure* of reproduction. Let me give you a few examples of what I mean.

The Alcoholics Anonymous movement was originally based on the message of the gospel and has brought hope and sobriety to millions of people. Alcoholics Anonymous was started by Bill Wilson and his friend Dr. Bob Smith in 1935, and after two years they had helped forty alcoholics to get sober. Two years later that number had more than doubled to over one hundred people. Today Bill W.'s friends are estimated at between two million and three million people worldwide. What is the secret that makes AA *move*? It has a simple reproducible infrastructure of twelve-step groups.

On the other end of the spectrum, what is it that makes al-Qaeda the most infamous terrorist organization on the planet? In case you didn't know, it's not just Osama bin Laden. While his name is virtually synonymous with al-Qaeda, he didn't start this movement on his own. It was also started by Dr. Ayman al-Zawahiri, al-Qaeda's theological leader and advisor, the man who oversees the infrastructure of small, mobile, decentralized cells that are now in more than one hundred countries around the world. What is it that makes al-Qaeda *move*? It is the loosely organized, reproducing network of well-trained terrorist cells.

How did the internet collect more information in my lifetime than had been accumulated in all of human history? The origins of the internet go back to the 1960s, when the United States funded some research projects through the military to build robust, fault-tolerant, and distributed computer networks.∗ Then in the early '90s, it became accessible to the public through the invention of the World Wide Web. Since then, it's grown by more than 100 percent annually, with explosive growth beyond that in some

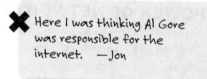

Here I was thinking Al Gore was responsible for the internet. —Jon

years. Today more than one-fourth of the world's total population regularly uses the internet. What makes the internet *move*? Its infrastructure is made up of reproducing networks that consist of millions of private, public, academic, business, and government networks.

Alcoholics Anonymous, al-Qaeda, and the internet all have seen rapid reproduction in the last century. How? Through an infrastructure that reproduces. If you can understand the rapid reproduction of Alcoholics Anonymous, al-Qaeda, and the internet, then you can understand how we will one day see an exponential movement of the Jesus mission. Whenever that day comes, it will require an infrastructure of reproducing church networks!

REPRODUCING CHURCH NETWORKS

So what exactly is a reproducing church network? Simply defined, a reproducing church network is *a group of churches in partnership that reproduces new churches and new sites.* In recent years, there has been an incredible rise in the number of new networks formed with a vision of rapid reproduction. In addition to NewThing (*www.newthing.org*), some of the most influential networks currently are:✱

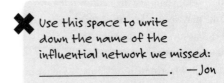

> Use this space to write down the name of the influential network we missed: _____. —Jon

* ✱ Acts 29 (*www.a29.org*)
* ✱ Association of Related Churches (*www.relatedchurches.com*)
* ✱ Church Multiplication Associates (*www.cmaresources.org*)
* ✱ Emerging Leadership Initiative (*www.elichurchplanting.com*)
* ✱ Infinity Alliance (*www.infinityalliance.com*)
* ✱ Forge (*www.forge.org.au*)
* ✱ Missio (*www.missio.us*)
* ✱ Orchard Group (*www.orchardgroup.org*)
* ✱ Redeemer Church Planting Center (*www.redeemer.com*)
* ✱ Stadia (*www.stadia.cc*)
* ✱ Vision360 (*www.vision360.com*)

Most of these networks are part of an alliance of networks working together called the Exponential Network.✱

While the phenomenon of rapid church planting is new to many of us, it is not a new idea, especially when you study church history. Today there are 41,826 Methodist congregations around the world and more than 12 million members worldwide. Chances are, there is probably a Methodist church near you. While the Methodist denomination is now in decline, it experienced tremendous growth for over a century. Do you know what one of the keys was to their explosive growth? They didn't start out as a denomination; they started as

> The Exponential Network sponsors the annual Exponential Conference (www.exponential. org). It is the largest and fastest-growing church-planting conference in the world. If you haven't been, you gotta go. —Jon

a simple network of churches and church planters. Methodism began with John Wesley, who had a dream of a movement of reproducing churches that would accomplish the mission of Jesus. Does that sound familiar? Wesley, who was a part of the Anglican Church of his day, began to enroll others in what they called "the method." Together they catalyzed a movement. So while reproducing church networks may seem like a new thing in our day, from a historical perspective they have been around for centuries.

It's important to remember that *networks* are not to be confused with *denominations*. Bob Harrington of Church Coaching Solutions writes, "Although they share similar characteristics, networks are not denominations; denominations represent the centralized means of organizing relationships and mission among like-minded Christians, while networks represent de-centralized relational circles."

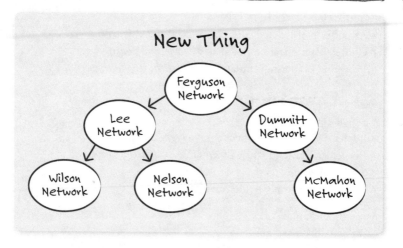

As we've shared before, it was out of a dream to see a movement of reproducing churches that we started the NewThing Network. Our goal wasn't to have a centralized organizational leadership. At first the network was just a simple partnership between Community and Jacob's Well Community Church. Soon we reproduced a third, fourth, and fifth church. Very quickly the number of churches that we were starting and affiliating with was too many for a single network. So we began to reproduce not only churches but also networks of churches, and we began referring to ourselves as NewThing because we were now more than a single network. As the networks themselves reproduced, we began to refer to each network by the last name of the network leader. The first two churches within NewThing to reproduce both churches and sites were 242 Community, under the leadership of Dave Dummitt, and Suncrest Christian Church, led by Greg Lee. Each of these reproducing churches launched a new network. Soon afterward, the Lee Network sent out Mark Nelson of Crossings to start a network focused on reproducing churches in university cities, and Hank Wilson from Boston's Reunion Church was sent out to reproduce churches in urban centers. The Dummitt network saw the potential in Troy McMahon from Restore Church in Kansas City, and they launched their own reproducing network. Each of these networks now has four to six reproducing churches in them and has plans for doubling every year for the next two years, bringing our total number of networks to twenty-four.

NewThing is just one of an exploding number of new reproducing church networks. More and more leaders and churches are catching the Acts 1:8 vision of a movement of people living as sold-out Christ followers. At the same time that many are catching this vision, however, we are witnessing a significant decline in every single mainline denomination. The combination of these two factors has contributed to the frenetic pace at which these new networks are forming. While most of these networks are still quite small, Ed Stetzer, the president of Lifeway Research, refers to them as "midgets with levers" because their influence is so significant. These networks (like NewThing) are focused on a big dream, and they are passionately committed to accomplishing it together.

COLLABORATIVE CHURCH NETWORKS

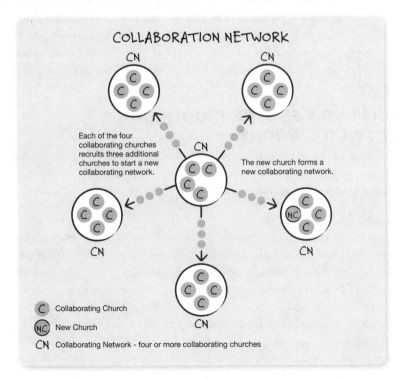

COLLABORATION NETWORK

Each of the four collaborating churches recruits three additional churches to start a new collaborating network.

The new church forms a new collaborating network.

C Collaborating Church

(NC) New Church

CN Collaborating Network - four or more collaborating churches

In addition to *reproducing* networks, there are also *collaborative* networks where individuals, organizations, and church-planting churches come together in partnership to plant more churches together than they could alone. Stadia, in particular, has put much of their effort into developing these types of collaborative networks. The focus of a collaborative network is more on a short-term affiliation rather than on a long-term, ongoing relationship (as we see with the reproducing networks). In addition, the focus tends to be more on planting a single new church or site and then forming a collaboration with other networks to do it again. Though these collaborative networks have a common vision and ideology and are often willing to partner with reproducing networks, there are some slight differences.* Most of these collaborative networks have as their goal launching a

 NewThing has partnered with Stadia on several new church plants. We're big fans of what they do. —Jon

X high-impact church/site with more than two hundred people from the start. They know that this will require at least two hundred thousand dollars. This approach allows virtually any church to be involved in planting a healthy, high-impact church—regardless of the size of its budget. For example, four churches partnering together and each committing seventeen thousand dollars per year for three years gives you a total of two hundred thousand dollars, the amount typically needed to plant a church. When more than four churches partner to form a network, the yearly financial commitment is even less.

WHAT MAKES A REPRODUCING NETWORK WORK?

So if reproducing networks are what make movements move, then what makes a network work? Great question! Here is a diagram that shows the infrastructure of a missional movement and the five working pieces that make a network work:

Apostolic Leadership

When you hear the phrase *apostolic leader*, who comes to mind? Perhaps the names that come to mind are pastors who write bestselling books and lead megachurches. We think of guys like John Wimber, who back in the 1980s started the Vineyard Church movement, a movement which now has more than six hundred churches in the United States and eighteen hundred churches worldwide. Apostolic leaders are to the church what Michael Jordan is to basketball or Babe Ruth is to baseball. These guys are the Hall of Famers, right? Well, while it's true that many of these "popular" spiritual leaders likely have the gift of apostolic leader-

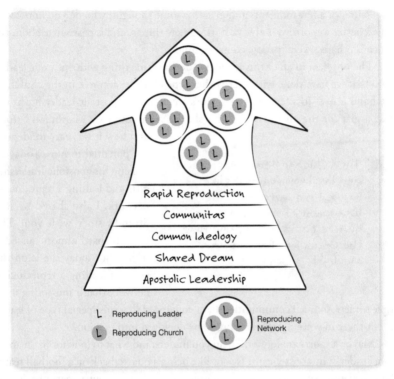

ship, we want to suggest that some of you reading this have it as well. And so do some of the people around you, such as your friends and colleagues.

When Jesus wanted to catalyze his movement, his first priority was choosing twelve apostolic leaders. Not to be too obvious, but we would do well to do the same. These apostolic leaders are the people who can lead reproducing networks and help others lead reproducing churches, small groups, and missional teams. Apostolic leaders have three unique qualities:

- ✱ *Apostolic leaders see the future clearly.* They see a better tomorrow and vision cast in such a way that others want to give their energy and resources to make that new tomorrow become a reality—today!
- ✱ *Apostolic leaders start new things.* They are entrepreneurial, able to start something from nothing and empower others to do the same. Wherever life takes them, they leave in their path new small groups, missional communities, campuses, and churches full of Christ followers.
- ✱ *Apostolic leaders embed and guard truth.* They are able to instill the ideology and values of the gospel into these new communities of Christ followers. When necessary, they will also reprimand and defend when the truth of the gospel is not upheld.

Pause for a few moments and give this some thought: who do you know who sees a better tomorrow, is always starting new things, and is passionate about the truth? Perhaps several people come to mind.

The problem in all of this is that we do the same thing with apostolic leadership that we have done with every other type of leadership role in the church — we hand it over to a few all-stars. Here's a newsflash: apostolic leadership is not just a gift for the all-stars. Earlier I shared with you Troy McMahon's story, and how it was easy to identify the potential in him. Today he is using his apostolic leadership gifts and leading a reproducing network. I also shared Kirsten Strand's story with you. The truth is that I almost missed it in her, but today she is on the verge of leading a reproducing network that is impacting multiple underresourced communities. I am convinced that this special type of leader is out there in your church, waiting to be deployed into mission.

✖ I'm a Chicago Bears fan, and I've known what it's like to need a quarterback. We had twenty-four starting quarterbacks in the same time the Green Bay Packers had one. Ugh! —Jon

Maybe a sports analogy will help you understand what to look for in an apostolic leader. The apostolic gift is a lot like being a quarterback on a football team. You need every position to make a complete team, but without a quarterback, you have no chance of being a winning team. The quarterback is a special position, make no mistake. Still, consider that every year there are ninety quarterbacks who play on NFL teams, and every year there are fifteen to thirty players who get drafted. In addition, there are six hundred who play on Division I college football teams, and another two hundred thousand high school quarterbacks. My point is this: quarterback is an important position, but there are a lot of them out there. And we must identify them and let them lead our huddles.✶

In his book *The Forgotten Ways*, Alan Hirsh says, "I can find no situation where the church has significantly extended the mission of God, let alone when the church achieved rapid metabolic growth, where apostolic leadership cannot be found in some form or another. In fact, the more significant the mission impact, the easier it is to discern this mode of leadership."[22]

Before we finish our discussion of apostolic leadership, I want to bring up two great tests that are ahead for the church if we are going to move forward and develop reproducing networks:

1. *We must restore and acknowledge the role of apostolic leadership.* There was no doubt about apostleship in Paul's mind when he wrote, "It was

he who gave some to be apostles, some to be prophets, some to be evangelists, and some to be pastors and teachers, to prepare God's people for works of service" (Eph. 4:11). We must acknowledge the gift and restore the role of apostolic leadership with the kind of enthusiasm with which a football team welcomes a quarterback. You know that without that position, you will not win!

2. *We must develop an apprenticeship model for emerging apostolic leaders.*
I remember sitting in a room at the Yellow Box with other NewThing pastors discussing the rapid growth of our networks and wondering how we should organize ourselves as a movement. I already knew that all movements have an infrastructure of reproduction and that we needed to reproduce more and more networks to catalyze a larger movement. As I was sitting there thinking about all of this, I suddenly looked up at Dave Dummitt and Greg Lee and said to them, "You guys need to lead your own networks." It sounded like a good idea to them, and in that moment we gave birth to two more networks.

As I study the Scriptures, I see the very same thing in the relationship between the apostle Paul and Timothy. In 2 Timothy 1, Paul wrote, "For this reason I remind you to fan into flame the gift of God, which is in you through the laying on of my hands. For God did not give us a spirit of timidity, but a spirit of power, of love and of self-discipline.... And of this gospel I was appointed a herald and an apostle and a teacher" (vv. 6–7, 11). Paul recognized that Timothy was someone who could be an apostolic leader, and he encouraged him: "Use that gift, Timothy; we need a quarterback."

Shared Dream

If you watch the video of Martin Luther King Jr. giving his "I Have a Dream" speech on the steps of the Lincoln Memorial, you will see him leave his notes, look to the sky, and begin speaking from the heart. "I have a dream.... I have a dream that my four little children will one day live in a nation where they will not be judged by the color of their skin but by the content of their character." The dream of this one man catalyzed an entire movement that united diverse people from different backgrounds, and it is a dream that is still inspiring people decades later.

Apostolic leadership provides that kind of dream to people, a dream that inspires and motivates people to action. Those are the kinds of dreams that are needed to catalyze a movement of reproducing churches. Movements depend on the cooperation and collaboration of believers with diverse giftings, passions, ethnicities, and theological perspectives. Yet the dream of accomplishing the mission of Jesus is the one thing powerful enough to hold them all together!

John Basham, a new-church strategy coordinator in England, has an exercise he uses to help young leaders understand what a reproducing network looks like. Every morning for several days these young leaders study the twenty-eight chapters of Acts and think about how church planting was done in the first century. At the close of the training, Basham has each of them write out an additional chapter to the book of Acts that explains how a church-planting movement will reach the people to whom God has sent them. Exercises like this help to flesh out the dream that God has placed inside an apostolic leader.

There is something profoundly spiritual that occurs when an apostolic leader shares his dream, writes down his manifesto, and communicates his intention to change the world. That dream, when communicated to others, awakens something latent in the human spirit. The dream focuses the energy of divergent leaders, artists, small groups, teams, churches, and networks and brings alignment. It motivates others to be on mission and gives them a glimpse of what that new tomorrow will be like.

Common Ideology

Once the dream is articulated clearly, the reproducing networks need a common ideology. These shared foundational beliefs and goals become the DNA of the network and have the potential to transform casual friendships into relationships between brothers and sisters in Christ.

Ori Brafman and Rod Beckstrom, in their book *The Starfish and the Spider*, state that "ideology is the fuel that drives the decentralized organization.... Take away the ideology, and the organization will crumble."[23] I'm using the term *ideology* because it includes both theology and philosophy. Ideology includes the important biblical and doctrinal commitments as well as the unique ways of doing and being. Both are essential elements that hold a network or a movement together.

At NewThing we are unapologetically evangelical, transdenominational, and relentlessly committed to helping people find their way back to God. While our vision is for NewThing to be the catalyst for a movement of reproducing churches, if you want a good sense of what makes us unique from other similar organizations, I would point you to these four Rs:

✳ *Reproducing.* We're all about reproducing leaders, artists, small groups, teams, campuses, churches, and networks in order to fuel a movement of reproducing churches.

✳ *Relationships.* Almost every NewThing pastor is part of our network because he had a relational connection with someone who was already in our network. One of the highlights of our semiannual gatherings is the opportunity to reconnect with each other face-to-face.

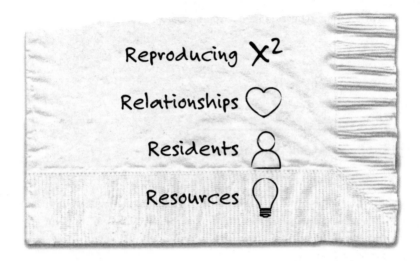

* *Residents.* We ask every one of our churches and sites to have at least one leadership resident on their team. The leadership resident is a future church planter, campus pastor, or creative arts director in training.
* *Resources.* One of the benefits of being part of NewThing is the opportunity to share in the collective knowledge and experience of all the pastors in our networks. From message transcripts to videos to training ideas, our resources help our churches reproduce faster and more effectively.

Communitas

Network leaders know that being in a community doesn't necessarily create a cause, but the experience of working toward a common cause can create community. I've often seen leaders pull together people, small groups, and even churches in an effort to create unity, with the hope that this newfound unity will coalesce into a cause. Sadly, it does not work. On the other hand, when leaders or churches are working shoulder to shoulder for a cause, they find commonality in the shared dream and become a band of brothers and sisters. The shared cause leads to genuine community.

Cause-created community is very different from the ways that we use the word *community* in other contexts (as in a "gated golf community" or "the financial community"). Alan Hirsh refers to this cause-created community, the type of community that you find in a missional movement, as *communitas.* He explains, "I have come to believe that *communitas* is thoroughly biblical and inextricably linked to Apostolic Genius.... [It is] normative for the pilgrim people of God."[24]

Here is a simple equation for developing *communitas*:*

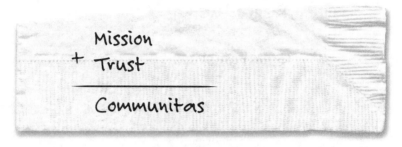

$$\frac{\text{Mission} + \text{Trust}}{\text{Communitas}}$$

Bill is one of the guys in the Wednesday night parenting small group that Sue and I attend. It seems like almost every week, Bill will tell us of the time when he and a few of his buddies all boarded a chartered bus right after Hurricane Katrina and headed to New Orleans to do whatever they could to help. He describes the next few days working side by side with other brothers as fulfilling and exhausting—but it was also a defining moment for him as a follower of Jesus. Why? For the first time in his life, Bill experienced communitas—a cause-created community advancing the mission of Jesus.

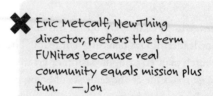

Eric Metcalf, NewThing director, prefers the term FUNitas because real community equals mission plus fun. —Jon

I remember my first short-term mission trip to Haiti with about twenty teens from the student ministry I was leading. For two weeks we spent every day loving and being loved by little orphan kids living in the poorest country in the western hemisphere. When I got home from that trip, I literally did not have the words to describe what we had experienced together. Now I know what it was, and I have the word to describe it—*communitas*.

Communitas is one of the five pieces that make a reproducing church network work. Whenever a group of friends come together for the cause of Christ, leave behind the consumeristic thinking that "the community exists for me," and move together toward "I exist for the community and the community exists for the world," you have *communitas*.

The second part of the *communitas* equation is something a bit more subtle, something that never gets talked about—trust. Without trust, the *communitas* of your network or movement will be broken. *Communitas* is found in networks where leaders and churches take great risks (emotional, relational, spiritual, and financial) to accomplish a shared dream. The shared risk deepens friendships and develops trust.

Stephen Covey's book *The Speed of Trust* describes how "trust is the one thing that changes everything . . . and that trust affects the trajectory and outcomes of our lives—both personally and professionally." Covey says that trust is made up of four core credibilities:

1. *Integrity.* You know their character.
2. *Intent.* You know their agenda.
3. *Capabilities.* You know their gifts/talents.
4. *Results.* You know their performance.[25]

When you are on mission together, you learn to trust these core credibilities. That sort of trust doesn't happen when you are just holding hands; it happens as you are risking and working together in shared mission. *best place to find a mate*

To reinforce and build that trust within a network, we encourage three relational connections within NewThing.

1. *Monthly one-on-one.* A monthly coaching conversation on the phone, via videoconferencing or in person, with each of the pastors in our network. Again, I recommend using the six coaching questions (see chap. 8).
2. *Monthly network calls.* In addition to a monthly one-on-one, we pull together all the pastors in the network to celebrate wins, troubleshoot challenges, and do skills training.
3. *Semiannual gatherings.* Two times a year we get everyone together for an overnight. This can be with other networks within our movement or at an event or conference. The relational connection that happens at these gatherings is invaluable. Within NewThing we schedule these the first week of December and toward the end of spring.

Without trust, you have only a static organization. With a common mission and trust, you have that wonderful experience of *communitas*, and *communitas* is one of the keys to a reproducing network.

Rapid Reproduction

I just read David Garrison's book *Church Planting Movements*. I confess that it messed me up pretty good! It also confirmed for me the last piece that I believe contributes to a successful reproducing network—rapid reproduction! In his book, Garrison cites example after example of places where church-planting movements are taking shape as churches reproduce at a remarkable rate.

He tells the story of Jan and David Watson, who were sent to work with an unreached people group in 1989. At the time, fewer than thirty churches existed among more than ninety million impoverished people speaking the Bhojpuri language.

The task of reaching all ninety million people seemed nearly impossible — except the Watsons believed in a God who specializes in doing the impossible. Their early efforts at outreach seemed to confirm the dismal prospects for reaching this people group. Six evangelists were sent by the Watsons to Bhojpuri villages, and they were brutally murdered within a year. At that point, David wanted to give up and leave, but God wouldn't release him to return home.

That time of soul-searching and turmoil led the couple to adopt a new strategy for rapid reproduction. It was a simple strategy that focused on three things: finding a person of peace, discipling him into the Christian faith, and making him the pastor of a brand-new church.

Almost immediately they began to see results. In 1993 the number of churches among this people group jumped from 28 to 36. The following year, there were 78 churches. And the year after that, the number had jumped exponentially to 220. In 1998 cautious estimates placed the number of Christ-following Bhojpuri at more than 55,000. By the year 2000 there were more than 3,200 churches and 250,000 believers. Today there are close to 1,000,000 Bhojpuri believers.

Rapid reproduction is one of the essential working pieces in a network. As a leader, you will lead the way forward by modeling it for others. You will pave the way for them by giving them permission to do it too. And you will accelerate the growth by holding others accountable for it.

My friend Neil Cole knows as much about rapid reproduction as anyone in North America. In *Organic Church*, Neil tells the story of rapid reproduction in the network he leads, Church Multiplication Associates (CMA): "In our first year, we began ten new churches. In our second year, CMA started 18 new churches. The next year, we added 52 new starts. The momentum was beyond our expectation. In 2002, we averaged two churches a week being started and had 106 starts. The following year we saw around 200 starts in a single year. We estimate that close to 400 churches were started in 2004, but counting the churches has become a daunting task. At the time of this writing there have been close to 800 churches started, in thirty-two states and twenty-three nations around the world, in only six years."[26] That is rapid reproduction!

If you neglect this last working piece, I can tell you that you will never have a true reproducing network. At best you might end up with a cluster of networks or a hub, or perhaps even a denomination. But if you want to see a reproducing network turn into a movement, you will need to have rapid reproduction occurring at every level: leader, artist, campus, church, and yes, even the network itself!

A REPRODUCING MOVEMENT

Accomplishing Jesus' Mission

BIG IDEA A missional movement has a momentum empowered by God's Spirit.

* The Mystery of Movement
* The Power of Movement
* Movement Accomplishes the Mission of Jesus
* Movement Is Easier Than You Think
* Leading a Movement
* Time to Get Movin'!

THE MYSTERY OF MOVEMENT

I had just finished a videoconference call with A.J. Lall, who knows firsthand what rapid reproduction looks like — A.J. is responsible for planting nearly one thousand churches in India! I asked A.J., "What is it that you have done that led to this rapid reproduction?" He paused and gave this explanation: "Dave, we really believe in evangelism, we really believe in prayer, and we make training our leaders a priority." I confess, I was waiting for something more. "And ... what else?" But that was it. I didn't say it out loud, but inside I was thinking, "I know lots and lots of churches that believe in evangelism, prayer, and training their leaders. That *can't* be the real difference. There must be something else that he's just not telling me!" *

On another occasion I was having lunch with Pastor Ha of Onnuri Church in Seoul, South Korea, during a leadership conference. I asked Pastor Ha the same question I had asked A.J., about how the church he had started twenty-five years ago had grown to more than sixty thousand followers and had sent out more than one thousand missionaries around the world. I just knew his response was going to be really good! After all, the guy is a brilliant leader. Pastor Ha took another bite of his lunch and began to talk about three

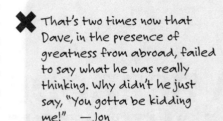

That's two times now that Dave, in the presence of greatness from abroad, failed to say what he was really thinking. Why didn't he just say, "You gotta be kidding me!" —Jon

priorities: early morning prayer, evangelism, and training their leaders. I knew he was telling me the truth, but I couldn't help but think once again, "You gotta be kidding me. You can do better than that! I could get that same answer from the church down the street with fourteen people that has never sent anyone anywhere except to the next church down the street!"

Now, don't misunderstand my reactions to these answers. I'm not against training leaders. After all, much of this book is about that very idea. I'm certainly not against prayer. How can you be against prayer? And I'm definitely not against evangelism. I believe in it wholeheartedly. I just knew there had to be *another* dynamic at work.

THE POWER OF MOVEMENT

I got a clue to solving the mystery of the missing element in rapid reproduction while I was standing in a baseball field helping to coach my son's Little League team. Every year, I coach my kids' teams, but last year my friend Red was the head coach and I served as his assistant coach.✶ Red loves coaching baseball, and he does a great job. He's been doing it for over twenty years. Even after his own boys quit playing, he kept coaching because he loved it so much. But Red has another love in addition to baseball. Birds.

Dave and I can explain pretty much everything with a sports story. —Jon

Oftentimes he will stop a practice and say, "Hey, boys, do you see that bird over there? It's a common grackle." Or he will point out a flock of Canada geese, make us all listen to them, and then tell us some interesting fact. I've learned quite a bit about birds from my friend Red.

One interesting fact I learned that day, standing in the baseball field while coaching my son's team, was why geese fly in a V-formation. Have you ever noticed that geese that are migrating always fly together in the shape of a V? God had a good reason for including that as part of their instinctual behavior. As each bird flaps its wings, it creates uplift for the other birds that are following behind. Scientists tell us that by flying in a V-formation, the whole flock is able to fly much farther than they ever could on their own. They estimate that flying in this V-formation adds at least 71 percent more flying range compared with that of a single bird flying alone. I think that's amazing!

What Coach Red was describing at that moment was the power of a movement. Just like geese, when people, churches, or networks all come together and move in a common direction, they can get there more quickly and with less work than if they go it alone. That's the power of movement. If you were to ask one of these geese flying south in a V-formation, "What is it that you are doing that has led you to fly so fast with such ease?" The goose (if it could talk) would probably say, "I just flap my wings." And that would certainly be true. But what the goose might not be aware of is the invisible dynamic at work among the larger flock — the hidden power that allows him to fly farther as he travels with other geese in a unified formation.

As I began to reflect on my conversations with A.J. and Pastor Ha, I had a hunch that one of the reasons why they were able to reproduce more easily than others was the existence of an invisible dynamic at work, something of which they weren't fully aware. I was beginning to unlock the mystery surrounding my question. These leaders, like geese flying in a V-formation, were experiencing the added blessing of a larger movement. Being a part of a larger movement was allowing them to get where God was leading more quickly and easily than they could on their own. As I thought further, I recognized two unseen benefits that always come when you are part of a movement.*

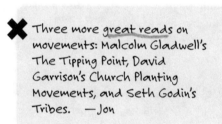

❌ Three more great reads on movements: Malcolm Gladwell's The Tipping Point, David Garrison's Church Planting Movements, and Seth Godin's Tribes. —Jon

Benefit 1: Movement Increases Influence

Sociologists don't agree on the exact percentages, but they do know one thing: when the *minority* of any group reaches somewhere between 8 percent and 17 percent, it has a profound influence on the *majority*. For example, Prison Fellowship has learned that if they can reach just *10 percent* of the inmates in a prison, they can have a huge influence on the culture of the entire prison.

I once had a late-night discussion with Tim Keller, senior pastor of Redeemer

Presbyterian Church in Manhattan, in which he told me that if the churches of New York City could reach and mobilize *8 percent or 9 percent* of the population of the city to be genuine Christ

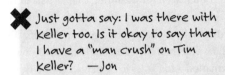

Just gotta say: I was there with Keller too. Is it okay to say that I have a "man crush" on Tim Keller? —Jon

followers, that would be the tipping point for influencing the entire city.✱

When Jon and I think about the long-term vision of NewThing, we often use *17 percent*, a percentage most sociologists believe is a tipping point of influence. We strategize and think about what it would take to see one billion people become apprentices of Jesus. Why? Because one billion is approximately 17 percent of the world population. And because a missional movement of just 17 percent of the world population has the power to influence the remaining 83 percent of the globe for Jesus.

Benefit 2: Movement Decreases Resistance

Movement has the power to increase your influence, but it can also decrease the resistance you face. Do you remember the term *drafting*, which we mentioned in chapter 2? It's a term used in competitive biking, running, and even Olympic swimming. NASCAR fans are also probably quite familiar with the concept. Drafting is when you get behind the lead car or the lead pack, and the momentum of others actually decreases the resistance and allows you to move with greater velocity while exerting less energy.✱

Truth is, we know nothing about NASCAR. We had to Google it just to figure out what the letters even represent. —Jon

Junior Johnson is credited with discovering drafting at the 1960 Daytona 500. Stuck with an inferior car, Johnson had little to no chance of winning the race. He found something that allowed him to overcome the great odds: the high-speed, aerodynamic draft at Daytona International Speedway. In the draft, the car in front breaks the air and creates a vacuum behind it. Any car that is close to the rear bumper of the lead vehicle is caught in the vacuum and "pulled" around the track, which allows it to keep pace.

When the rear car pulls out to pass, it's able to make a quick "slingshot" pass. If you have seen the movie *Talladega Nights*, just think, "Shake 'n' bake, baby!" When Junior Johnson figured this out, it gave him a tremendous advantage. He won the race despite driving ten miles an hour slower than his competition.

I think it is appropriate that Johnson's nickname is Junior. In NewThing we have seen the same kind of drafting effect that younger reproducing churches have as they follow after more-established churches. In this case, the established church in front breaks the resistance and creates a vacuum behind it. When the new church is planted, it is able to make a quick slingshot move and pass the existing church. Take a look at this table and notice that while it took Community nine years to reproduce its first site/church, each of the subsequent church plants were able to move forward or slingshot past Community with even greater momentum.

Church	Age When Reproduced First Site
Community	9 years
242 Community	4 years
LifePointe Church	4 years
Forefront Church	3.5 years
Restore Community Church	2 years

MOVEMENT ACCOMPLISHES THE MISSION OF JESUS

Jesus understood the importance of this invisible dynamic when he challenged his closest friends to start his missional movement in Jerusalem and spread it to Judea and Samaria to the ends of the earth (Acts 1:8). He knew that a *movement* was the only way to accomplish his mission of bringing good news to all people for all of eternity. This small band of friends accepted the challenge that Jesus gave them. The movement got a great start, building up speed and velocity on the day of Pentecost (Acts 2:1–4), when "about three thousand were added to their number" (2:41).

The momentum of the Jesus mission continued to increase and pick up speed, and soon the early church was adding "to their number daily those who were being saved" (Acts 2:47). Soon the apprentices to Jesus numbered so many that they could no longer be counted. The Bible describes it this way: "Multitudes of men and women were constantly added to their number" (Acts 5:14 NASB). This group of friends had grown quite large and could no longer be ignored. Some people loved these followers of Jesus, while others were threatened by their popularity and persecuted them. The mass of the Jesus movement continued to grow as the church was "scattered throughout Judea and Samaria" (Acts 8:1). The mission of Jesus was now in full force—and it possesses a forward momentum that continues to this day.

As someone willing to trade my life for this mission, I look back on those early church days and ask, "What was the difference? What made that movement succeed?" It's basically the same question I asked A.J. Lall and Pastor Ha. It's the same question I ask when I hear how God is at work in China—thirty-nine thousand new converts every day joining the mission of Jesus! What is the missing element that makes the difference?

(Here is what I've concluded. The missing element is massive numbers of people obeying the leading of God's Spirit all moving together in the same direction on the same mission. That is a movement. A movement has spiritual dynamics that allow you to get where God is leading you more quickly and more easily than you ever could on your own.)

A MOVEMENT IS EASIER THAN YOU THINK

As we near the end of the book, you might be thinking, "Dave, this is all very inspiring, but a movement feels very daunting to me—almost impossible." At the risk of underselling everything I've said, let me explain why a missional movement might be a lot easier than you would think. Sociologist Rodney Stark, in his book *The Rise of Christianity*, offers some of the very best research I've seen on the topic of movements and dispels the myth that the church of the first few centuries grew at miraculous rates that are not possible today.

He writes, "[Most] studies of the rise of Christianity all stress the movement's rapid growth, but rarely are any figures offered.... [It is assumed that] in order for Christianity to have achieved success in the time allowed, it must have grown at rates that seem incredible in light of modern experiences."[27] Stark goes on to show how the early church grew from about one thousand (he chooses a very conservative starting point) in AD 40 to more than thirty-three million by AD 350. Stark explains, "Hence, 40 percent per decade or 3.42 percent per year seems the most plausible estimate of the rate at which Christianity actually grew during the first several centuries."[28]

What Stark is saying is that the early church didn't grow at a pace that is unimaginable. No, the math reveals that the early church grew exponentially at a rate of about 3.5 percent every year. Do you think you and your friends can do that? I do!

LEADING A MOVEMENT

Because of what I've seen and what I believe lies ahead for us, I'm constantly thinking about how to lead a movement. As I've read and thought, I've found that there are three primary tasks a leader must fulfill to lead a movement.

1. Vivid Vision

The last session of a full day at the Exponential Conference was finished, and several of us from NewThing were sitting across the table from Mark and Monica Nel-

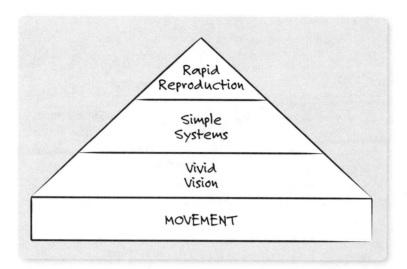

son. Mark had led a great campus ministry at Purdue University and is a very gifted leader and communicator. We were talking about the possibility of church planting. They were hesitating. They couldn't quite see it yet, but we could all see it in them.*

I remember saying to Mark and his wife, "You two can so do this!" As the conversation continued into the night, we shared with them a vivid vision for how we could do this together.

 I knew Mark was right for NewThing when I learned that he was an avid Cubs fan. Did I mention I love the Cubs? —Jon

Mark and Monica could see the vision, and they wanted to be a part of it. A year later Mark planted a church called Crossings in Knoxville, Tennessee, and now he is leading a network for NewThing. Here is how Mark tells his story:

MARK NELSON'S STORY

Being a Part of a Movement

The question isn't that profound. Especially not in the context in which I first read it. It was just one of about a dozen questions I browsed through in preparation to lead a small group one night a few months ago. The question was this: "Have you ever been part of a movement that was about bringing restoration to the world?"

See, nothing special. But the effect on me was pretty significant. I came to the realization that I *was* a part of a movement and didn't even know it.

Some Background

It was a conversation with Dave and Jon Ferguson and other staff from Community at the Exponential Conference in Orlando that rocked my world. After almost twenty years of ministry in churches and on a university campus, my wife, Monica, and I decided to join NewThing and plant a church in downtown Knoxville, Tennessee.

We moved our family to Chicago so I could be a leadership resident at Community. That was not the easiest thing for me to do at forty-two years old with a family of five, but the residency proved invaluable as we prepared to launch this new community in Knoxville.

It wasn't so much the practical ideas or the theological principles we learned during the residency that had the greatest impact. It was being able to immerse ourselves into a culture that had the DNA that we felt God was calling us to have in Knoxville. It's difficult to emphasize how important this time was as we prepared to launch a year later.

Once we moved to Knoxville, we spent another six months planning and praying, launching a half dozen small groups, and sharing the vision and values of this faith community. Finally, in February, we launched this mission we called Crossings, committed to helping people find their way back to God.*

 Crossings served free Eli's cheescake to all the attenders on opening day. The president of Eli's found out and now continues the tradition on the church's anniversary every year for free. —Jon

An email I received three hours after our first service read, "It has been eight years since I attended worship. I was empty. Tired. Scared. Ashamed. Today I actually prayed. I cried. I smiled. I thought. Even laughed. Growing up in the church, today I felt like I had taken my very first Communion. Today I shared a room with many yet felt like it was just God and me ... finally. I could cry and forgive myself. I felt like I had found a home where I can dust myself off and finally let God catch up to me."

Reproducing the Vision

We believe that part of God's vision for Crossings includes being a catalyst for a movement of reproducing churches by reproducing what God has brought to fruition in our community through the planting of new sites and churches around the country. With a specific vision of launching faith communities in the "downtowns of university towns," Crossings plans to launch its second site in just a few months and hopefully plant new sites every other year after that.

We have also begun a leadership residency program for leaders to come and be a part of our community, to immerse themselves into the life and culture of Crossings, and then to go from here to further this reproducing movement.

Back to that question: "Have you ever been part of a movement that was about bringing restoration to the world?" The answer (even though I felt like I was allowed to be a part of some pretty amazing ministry in the past twenty years) was no, I had never felt like I had been part of a movement that was about restoring all things ... until now.

Planting churches that change lives and communities, and training new leaders to do the same—I can't imagine answering God's call on my life in any other way, and I can't imagine not doing this in the context of a reproducing movement.

In *Tribes*, Seth Godin says that one of the key elements of a movement is "to publish a manifesto."[29] This does not mean you have to have it in print and on a bookshelf; a manifesto is the clearly articulated, preferred future of the vision for that movement. So one of the primary tasks for you, as a movement leader, is to constantly keep the vision vivid. The vision needs to be so vivid that people like Mark Nelson can clearly see it—and then decide they want to be a part of it.

2. Simple Systems

If the vision is vivid, then the next task of leading a movement is making sure the systems are simple and reproducible. By *simple*, I do not mean easy or watered

↑ reproduceable

> ✖ This is my favorite section in the entire book. Simple systems work! —Jon

down. I mean <u>understandable</u> and easily <u>communicated</u>. The systems in a missional movement should be few and so simple that you can reproduce them on the back of a napkin by memory. Here are some of the simple systems we have introduced to you in this book:*

Celebrate Connect contribute

A Simple Way to Follow Jesus: The Three Cs (page 93)

When we look at Acts 2, we see three key experiences and relationships that every Christ follower must continue to grow in: celebrate, connect, and contribute. As followers of Jesus, we must continue to grow with all that we are in our love for God (celebrate), his church (connect), and the world (contribute). The three Cs are a very challenging but simple expectation for every Christ follower.

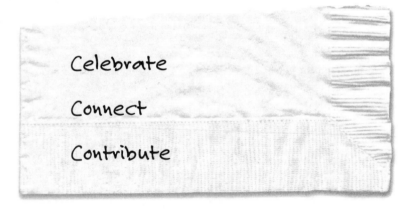

Celebrate

Connect

Contribute

 ## A Simple Way to Develop Leaders: Leadership Path (page 32)

We base the leadership path on 2 Timothy 2:2, where Paul writes to his apprentice Timothy, "The things you have heard me say in the presence of many witnesses entrust to reliable men who will also be qualified to teach others." Paul describes four generations of leadership development:

Paul ➔ Timothy ➔ Reliable Men ➔ Others

Here is what that leadership path looks like for us:

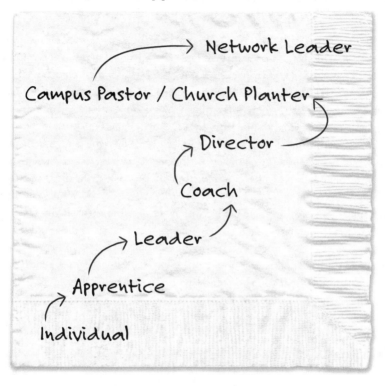

Network Leader

Campus Pastor / Church Planter

Director

Coach

Leader

Apprentice

Individual

A Simple Way to Train an Apprentice: Five Steps (page 63)

Paul's training of his young apprentice Timothy is described by Luke in Acts 16:3: "Paul wanted to take [Timothy] along on the journey." Here is our interpretation of what it might have looked like for Paul to take Timothy along for the journey:

1. I do. You watch. We talk.
2. I do. You help. We talk.
3. You do. I help. We talk.
4. You do. I watch. We talk.
5. You do. Someone else watches.

(As complexity increases, reproducibility decreases.) If you want to lead a movement, make sure that the systems are simple and reproducible.

3. Rapid Reproduction

The most remarkable contemporary example of a missional movement is the one that is taking place in China. In the last sixty years, the Chinese church has rapidly reproduced from about 2 million followers of Jesus to more than 130 million. To give some perspective, those 130 million Christ followers soon will outnumber the members of the Communist Party by a two to one margin.

This growth came during a time of persecution, when the church grew primarily through small house churches. As the persecution increased, these house churches seemed to reproduce even more rapidly. Why? Perhaps the best explanation for this is found in the book *The Starfish and the Spider*. While a starfish and a spider look similar, there is a big difference between them. If you take off a spider's head, you pretty much take out that spider. The spider dies. And if you cut off a spider's leg, it might survive, but it will be crippled. If you cut off two or three of the spider's legs, it is not likely to live at all. But what happens if you cut a starfish in half? If you chop off a leg of a starfish, what does it do? Amazingly, the starfish grows another leg, and the chopped-off leg grows into another starfish. Chop the starfish into ten pieces, and it produces ten starfish. That's what has been happening in China over the last six decades. As opponents have tried to divide and destroy the Chinese church, they have simply responded to the challenge by reproducing.

TIME TO GET MOVIN'!

Once again, let me tell you: you *can* do it. The missional movement that Jesus dreamed of was meant to be spread by you and your friends. It will mean some huge shifts in your life, your ministry, your time, your future. You will have to love going more than staying. You will need to have a bias for risk, living on the edge rather than staying in the safety of the center. You will soon develop a burden for the lost that you just don't have for the found. If you are ready and willing to make these shifts, you are ready to start moving!

There is just one more thing. On the next page is an empty napkin. And it's waiting for a dream. Your dream. Use it as the simple canvas to reveal the dream God has for your life.

So what is your dream? If you don't know what it is, let me challenge you to stop right now and pray. Ask God, "Lord, let me see the dream you have for my life." Give it some time. If you need to bookmark this page and come back to it again someday, that's okay. Just make sure that you come back.

And if you know your dream, I dare you to put it on that napkin right now.

Oh, and I have one more thing to say.

Ready?

Here it is.

"You can do it."

Don't look around like I'm talking to somebody else. I'm talking to you. Yes, you—the one holding this book in your hand, the one reading the words on this page. Please hear this: as sure as you were born, God has birthed within you a dream for your life.

And you *can* do it.

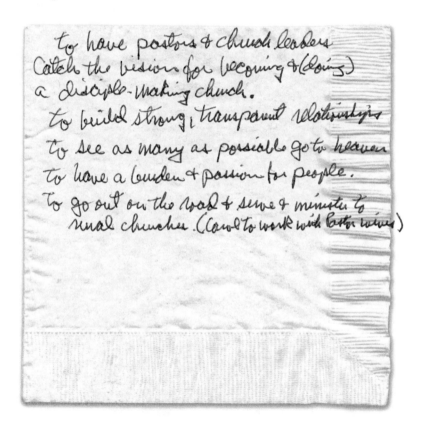

to have pastors & church leaders
catch the vision for becoming & (doing)
a disciple-making church.
to build strong, transparent relationships
to see as many as possible go to heaven
to have a burden & passion for people.
to go out on the road & serve & minister to
rural churches. (Carol to work with pastor wives)

ACKNOWLEDGMENTS

Books, like movements, begin with one or two people, and they require lots of friends to create the momentum necessary to see it have a significant impact. We are grateful for the collaborative work of many friends whose lives and work have influenced every page of this book. Thank you for your friendship. Thank you for your partnership. Thank you for your commitment to the mission of helping people find their way back to God.

Thank you to all our friends on the team at Community. You are the greatest team on the planet!

Andrew Partain; Anne Prunty; Becky Stevenson; Bernie Vollmann; Beth Kolar; Bob Lowe; Brad Prunty; Bret Koontz; Brian Prunty; Brian Zehr; Brooke Bright; BT Norman; Carrie Larson; Carter Moss; Cathy Cuny; Chris Heller; Christi Neill; Christine Tuck; Cynthia Wallbruch; Dani Seaton; David Girdwood; Debbie Benjamin; Dennis Taylor; Derick Thompson; Diane Dassing; Donna Winter; Doug White; Earl Ferguson; Eli Orozco; Elic Bramlett; Eric Bramlett; Eric Metcalf; Erin Metcalf; Genea Browne; Ginger Koontz; Israel Ruiz; Jack Arellano; Jake Kirchner; James Finley; Janet Miller; Julie Bullock; Jeff Ekblad; Jen Weibye; Jenn Moss; Jennifer Barrett; John Ciesniewski; Julie Girdwood; Karen Hess; Kerry Marshall; Kevin Lewis; Kevin MacDonald; Kevin Moore; Kim DiPadova; Kim Hammond; Kirsten Strand; Lee Messersmith; Lupe Kalter; Mark Dwyer; Mary Partee; Mick Marshall; Mike Tjaarda; Nick Fiddick; Nick Plassman; Obe Arellano; Pam Haines; Pat Ferguson; Pat Masek; Paul Warner; Perry Martin; Pillara Smith; Randy Wheeler; Rick Guzman; Robbin Grigsby; Robin Hautz; Ron Kelso; Sam Menesses; Sara Bills-Thwing; Scott Knollenberg; Sean Bublitz; Shannon Gutierrez; Shawn Williams; Sher Sheets; Sherry Gossman; Stephanie Mack; Steve Caballero; Steve Kerby; Sue Ferguson; Suzie Reeves; Tammy Melchien;

Tim Bakker; Tim Raad; Tim Sutherland; Tina Caceres; T.J. Friesen; Tom Greever; Tony Germann; Yolanda Pena; Zach Goforth.

Thank you to all our friends in NewThing. Together we are catalyzing a movement of reproducing churches.

Donnie Williams and the team at Lifepointe Church
Dave Richa and the team at Jacob's Well Church
Nate Ferguson and the team at The Village Christian Church
Dave Dummitt and the team at 2|42 Community Church
Brian Moll and the team at Forefront Church
Joe Sutherland and the team at Community Christian Church at High Vista
Mark Weigt and the team at The Ridge Community Church
Greg Lee and the team at Suncrest Christian Church
Hank Wilson and the team at Reunion Christian Church
Mark Nelson and the team at Crossings
Matt Payne and the team at Church! At Bethany
Troy McMahon and the team at Restore Community Church
Jeff Pessina and the team at Philippine Frontline Missions
Matt Mehaffey and the team at The Pursuit Christian Church
Bret Kays and the team at Southpoint Community Christian Church
Greg Hunt and the team at Paseo Christian Church
Chris Hornbrook and the team at Momentum Christian Church
Jim Semradek and the team at Waterfront Christian Church
Aaron Monts and the team at IKON Christian Community
Sean Spoelstra and the team at Encounter Church
Matt Larson and the team at Anthem Church
Bill Carroll and the team with The France Project
Mark Michael and the team at Crossbridge Christian Church
Ben Davis and the team at River Glen Christian Church
Troy Jackson and the team at University Christian Church
Nate Bush and the team at New City Christian Church

Thank you to Leadership Network for allowing us to use your platform of influence. We do not take that for granted. Thank you Greg Ligon, Stephanie Plagens, Mark Sweeney, Dave Travis, and Bob Buford.

Thank you to the great people at Zondervan. You made this journey fun and collaborative every step of the way. Thank you Chris Fann, Ryan Pazdur, Brian Phipps, and Paul Engle.

Thank you to our good friend and covisionary Todd Wilson for including us in all of your amazing and creative missional endeavors. Our partnership with the

Exponential Conference and Exponential Alliance continues to have an impact beyond what we ever would have dreamed up.

Thank you to Sherry Gossman for her creative genius, Carter Moss for his outstanding work on the discussion questions, Cynthia Wallbruch for her excellent editing work, and Doug Leddon for his helpful critique ... seriously!

Thank you to the amazing and absolutely unstoppable Pat Masek! While you didn't write any of the words in this book, every sentence is punctuated with your ambition to see it finished. Shew! We're done. And we genuinely could not have done it without you.

Dave: Thank you, Sue, for encouraging us and for critiquing and proofing this book. I love you. And thank you to three amazing kids: Amy, Josh, and Caleb. Your uncle Jon and I wrote this book with you and your cousins in mind. Our hope is it will inspire emerging leaders like you to use their God-given gifts to start and spread missional movements of their own.

Jon: Thank you, Lisa. Your steadfast prayers, encouragement, and faith have been a consistent source of strength for this journey—beginning to now. Thank you to Graham. I'm amazed by your youthful wisdom and leadership. And thank you to my girl, Chloe; you are so full of fun and discernment. You three motivate me to dream, lead, and write with an optimistic hope for the future of the Jesus mission.

DISCUSSION QUESTIONS

Visit *www.exponentialseries.com* for video introductions to each chapter and for discussion questions in digital format.

CHAPTER 1: YOU

Big Idea: A missional movement can start with you.

Open

Think back to your childhood years. What is the craziest or funniest goal you set for yourself ("When I grow up, I'm gonna ...")? Which of your childhood dreams came true? *a ranch for wayward kids*

didn't happen

Explore

The beginning of a God-inspired movement starts with you. Check out just a few of the promises in God's Word that show us how much he is committed to carrying out his mission through us:

> *You will receive power* when the Holy Spirit comes *on you*; and *you will be my witnesses* in Jerusalem, and in all Judea and Samaria, and to the ends of the earth.
>
> —Acts 1:8

X
> The LORD will *fulfill his purpose for me*; your love, O LORD, endures forever—do not abandon the works of your hands.
>
> —Psalm 138:8

X
> With this in mind, we constantly pray for you, that our God may count you worthy of his calling, and that by his power he may *fulfill* every good purpose of yours and every act prompted by your faith.
>
> —2 Thessalonians 1:11

Delight yourself in the LORD *and he will give you the desires of your heart. Commit your way to the* LORD*; trust in him and he will do this.*

—Psalm 37:4–5

1. Which of the above promises of God is most empowering to you?
2. Have you ever had someone say to you, "You can do it," and it truly empowered you to accomplish something? What was that like?
3. Have you ever looked someone in the eye and said, "You can do it"? How could these promises of God help you affirm and empower someone to pursue their God-given dream?
4. What is your "napkin dream"? Who else knows about it?
5. What steps can you take to ensure that your dream doesn't simply end with you but reproduces and has a lasting impact for many years to come?
6. What is the biggest obstacle currently holding you back from carrying out the next mission God has for you? What will it take to overcome that obstacle?

Move

Here's your assignment: If you have never written out your napkin dream, grab your journal (or a napkin!) and write or draw it out right now. (Remember, be as grandiose as you want.) If you haven't shared it with someone yet, go share it with a trusted friend. If you haven't talked to God about it yet, share it with him. Then figure out the *first step* to making it happen, and do it. Because you can!

CHAPTER 2: THE LEADERSHIP PATH

Big Idea: The leadership path is a life-on-life process for developing leaders in a missional movement.

Open

What is one project you took on alone (either by choice or not) in which, in retrospect, you definitely needed the help of others to be successful?

Explore

The leadership path is a process for reproducing leaders to start and spread a missional church movement. In order to see a movement, you need yourself and a mass of people led by the Spirit, moving in the right direction at the right speed.

So how do you create movement? Movement is created when you influence others en masse to join you in living your lives together with spiritual velocity.

Jesus went up on a mountainside and called to him those he wanted, and they came to him. He appointed twelve—designating them apostles— that they might be with him and that he might send them out to preach and to have authority to drive out demons.

—Mark 3:13–15

After this the Lord appointed seventy-two others and sent them two by two ahead of him to every town and place where he was about to go. He told them, "The harvest is plentiful, but the workers are few. Ask the Lord of the harvest, therefore, to send out workers into his harvest field. Go! I am sending you out like lambs among wolves." ... The seventy-two returned with joy and said, "Lord, even the demons submit to us in your name."

—Luke 10:1–3, 17

Since we live by the Spirit, let us keep in step with the Spirit.

—Galatians 5:25

1. Why do you think God chose to rely on people to carry out his mission, when he is fully capable of doing it himself?
2. What is one example of a time in your life when you were able to have significant influence or make a real impact because you were moving in the right direction with a group of people?
3. What are the greatest advantages of doing ministry alongside other people rather than alone? What are the challenges of doing ministry alongside other people?
4. What does it mean to you to "keep in step with the Spirit" (Gal. 5:25)? What can that practically look like? How can a group of people on mission together best help one another "keep in step with the Spirit"?

Move

Review the leadership path. Where would you put yourself on that path? What is keeping you from moving to the next step? What is the next practical step you can take to get there?

CHAPTER 3: APPRENTICE

Big Idea: Missional movement begins by becoming an apprentice of Jesus.

Open

If you could follow anyone in the world around for a week (anyone living or historical, but *not* someone from the Bible), who would it be? What would you hope to gain from the experience?

Explore

One person cannot start a movement. Just like Jesus, we simply *must* do it with other people. So the key to both starting and spreading a movement is *apprenticeship*—selecting people to pour ourselves into so they can become the next generation of leadership.

> As Jesus was walking beside the Sea of Galilee, he saw two brothers, Simon called Peter and his brother Andrew. They were casting a net into the lake, for they were fishermen. *"Come, follow me,"* Jesus said, "and I will make you fishers of men." At once they *left their nets and followed him.*
>
> —Matthew 4:18–20

> As Jesus went on from there, he saw a man named Matthew sitting at the tax collector's booth. *"Follow me,"* he told him, and Matthew got up and *followed him.*
>
> —Matthew 9:9

> Then Jesus said to his disciples, "If anyone would *come after me*, he must *deny himself* and take up his cross and *follow me."*
>
> —Matthew 16:24

> When they saw the courage of Peter and John and realized that they were unschooled, ordinary men, they were astonished and they took note that these men *had been with Jesus.*
>
> —Acts 4:13

1. What do you think Jesus' first disciples had to leave behind in order to follow him? What have you left behind to follow Jesus?
2. How do you think you are doing right now at following Jesus? Where has he led you that you've followed? Where is he leading that you are resisting?
3. Can you share an example of someone whom you apprenticed or discipled? If not, what would you say has kept you from doing that?
4. Whose investment into you has been the most impactful? What is the main reason why he or she had such a tremendous impact on you?
5. Jesus was very intentional about who he chose as his apprentices. We examined three characteristics that Jesus highly valued for his apprentices: *Spirit-led*, *missional*, and *reproducing*. Which of these three characteristics do you need to see more of in your life? What can you do to develop that in your life?

6. In addition to these three, what do you think are the most critical qualities to look for in an apprentice?

Move

Write down the names of three different people in your life whom you would consider inviting into apprenticeship. Stop and pray over these three names, and ask God to empower you to ask them, and to move in their hearts to prepare them to be asked.

Now write down one more name: the name of someone who may seem like a long shot, but in whom you would love to see God do a powerful work so they would someday step into apprenticeship.

CHAPTER 4: REPRODUCING LEADERS

Big Idea: A leader must develop four key relationships to start a missional movement.

Open

Think about a child or some children you hope to influence. What is one quality or value that you most hope will get passed on to them, and then on to their children?

Explore

The only way we can accomplish the Jesus mission is for our leaders to catch the vision of investing themselves in someone else who can also lead. Everything rises and falls on leadership. When we talk about the idea of apprenticeship, we're not talking about finding people who can help us do tasks more effectively. And we're not talking about preparing people to simply replace us so we can move on to something else. We are talking about reproducing our leadership so that our part in the mission won't stop with us; it will carry on to future generations.

> The things you have heard me say in the presence of many witnesses entrust to reliable men who will also be qualified to teach others.
>
> —2 Timothy 2:2

> [Paul] came to Derbe and then to Lystra, where a disciple named Timothy lived.... Paul wanted to take him along on the journey.... As they traveled from town to town, they delivered the decisions reached by the apostles and elders in Jerusalem for the people to obey. So the churches were strengthened in the faith and grew daily in numbers.
>
> —Acts 16:1, 3–5

1. Which of the twelve indicators of a lack of leadership on page 000 is most convicting to you right now in your leadership?
2. In 2 Timothy 2 and Acts 16 we get a glimpse of what it may have looked like for Paul to invest in Timothy. What do you think gave Paul such urgency about investing in future generations of leaders?
3. What is your leadership track record? Can people look at your life and see evidence that people have followed you? Have you ever apprenticed and released a new leader? What was that experience like?
4. How are you doing in developing the following four key relationships of a reproducing leader? What can you do to move forward in each of those relationships?
   a. followers
   b. apprentices
   c. peers
   d. a coach
5. What do you think are the biggest barriers that prevent leaders from intentionally developing apprentices? What could you do to help leaders buy into the vision and importance of apprentices?

Move

As we examined, Paul paints a beautiful picture of four generations' worth of reproduction in his simple command to Timothy. Try drawing out a "reproduction tree" that includes you. Start with whoever invested in you (there's two generations), then try to fill in as much as you know of who invested into him or her, and then include those you've developed and who they've gone on to impact. Reflect on this tree and let Jesus' strategy sink in — hopefully you find it both encouraging and challenging! Then pray over it, thanking God for those who have gone before you, and praying for God to continue extending it through you and beyond you for many generations to come.

CHAPTER 5: REPRODUCING ARTISTS

Big Idea: Attracting and reproducing artists is essential to starting a missional movement.

Open

What art form speaks to you and moves you the most: Music? Movies? Theater? Dance? Something else? What is one of your favorite examples of how that art form has impacted you?

Explore

We need leaders who grow people up in Christ, mobilize them for the mission of Jesus, and apprentice the next generation. We also need artists who lead and facilitate the large group gatherings of worship and celebration of our God. Artists and creatives will be the ones to lead the way and catalyze the creation of new faith communities.

1. Evaluate your current church/ministry: On a scale of 1 to 10, how are you doing when it comes to "excellence" in the arts ministry? On that same scale, how are you doing with "reproducing" in your arts ministry?
2. What is one artistic risk that you are glad your church or ministry has taken? Why are you thankful that risk was taken?
3. What is one practical step your church/ministry can take right now to start attracting more and better artists?
4. At which of the five factors for reproducing artists given in this chapter would you say your church or ministry is currently best? Which one do you think needs the most work?
5. Music and celebration certainly played an important part in God's story in the Old Testament, as musicians often led the way into battle. But it doesn't stop there. Look at the vital role the arts must continue to play in the life of a Christ follower, as discussed by the New Testament writers as well:

   "About midnight Paul and Silas were praying and singing hymns to God, and the other prisoners were listening to them. Suddenly there was such a violent earthquake that the foundations of the prison were shaken. At once all the prison doors flew open, and everybody's chains came loose" (Acts 16:25–26).

   "Be filled with the Spirit. Speak to one another with psalms, hymns and spiritual songs. Sing and make music in your heart to the Lord, always giving thanks to God the Father for everything, in the name of our Lord Jesus Christ" (Eph. 5:18–20).

   "Let the word of Christ dwell in you richly as you teach and admonish one another with all wisdom, and as you sing psalms, hymns and spiritual songs with gratitude in your hearts to God" (Col. 3:16).

6. What do these verses say to you about the importance of the arts in our lives as Christ followers?

Move

Write down a number: the number of artists you feel your current church/ministry needs in order to fulfill its vision for the next 18–24 months. Now write down the first three steps you can take to achieve that goal. (Review your answers to questions 3 and 4 for ideas!)

CHAPTER 6: REPRODUCING GROUPS

Big Idea: Reproducing small groups connect the unconnected and spread a missional movement.

Open

Tell about a small group or team you were a part of that personally impacted you most. What made it so impactful?

Explore

Loneliness and desperation are not God's dream. God never intended for us to do life by ourselves, on our own. One answer to loneliness and isolation is for every person to be connected to a life-changing community of people who can get you through anything life brings your way. These communities are far from perfect, because they're composed of messed-up, broken people just like you and your friends. They work because in these groups are people who seek to do life together and encourage each other to grow in their relationship with God, each other, and the world.

Let's examine again the beautiful picture of biblical community that Luke paints for us in Acts 2:42–47:

> They devoted themselves to the apostles' teaching and to the fellowship, to the breaking of bread and to prayer. Everyone was filled with awe, and many wonders and miraculous signs were done by the apostles. All the believers were together and had everything in common. Selling their possessions and goods, they gave to anyone as he had need. Every day they continued to meet together in the temple courts. They broke bread in their homes and ate together with glad and sincere hearts, praising God and enjoying the favor of all the people. And the Lord added to their number daily those who were being saved.

1. What specifically was it about this community that so impacted the people of that day and caused so many of them to become Christ followers and join the community?
2. If nonbelievers today were to witness this type of community, how do you think they would respond?
3. What are the biggest barriers to people (Christ followers or not) experiencing this deep, authentic type of community?

4. Paul later reminds the church about the importance of staying connected to community: "Let us not give up meeting together, as some are in the habit of doing, but let us encourage one another—and all the more as you see the Day approaching" (Heb. 10:25). Why are small groups so critical to creating a missional movement?

5. What can be difficult about reproducing small groups? Why is it crucial that small groups keep focus on reproducing?

Move

First, examine how you are doing at staying connected into community. Are you a part of a community of Christ followers that is encouraging/challenging you in your walk with God?

Second, examine how you are going to help create opportunities for others to connect into community. Who do you know who is craving and needing this type of community? What can you do to help connect them?

CHAPTER 7: REPRODUCING MISSIONAL TEAMS

Big Idea: Missional teams ensure that movement is always going and sending.

Open

Which mission-oriented movie is the most inspiring to you (e.g., *Braveheart, The Bourne Identity, Hoosiers, Mission Impossible*, etc.)? Why?

Explore

A missional movement is always going and sending. Following Jesus implies movement, and as we move, we are called to keep in step with the Holy Spirit.

1. What is your response to the statement, "At least one-third to one-half of the American population will never come to churches like we have now"? Do you find it challenging, scary, convicting, inspiring, all of the above, or something else? Why?

2. What similarities or differences do you see between how the early believers approached church as we read in Acts and how we approach church today?

3. Read the following verses:

"Go and make disciples of all nations" (Matt. 28:19).
"Ask the Lord of the harvest, therefore, to *send* out workers into his harvest field. *Go!* I am *sending* you" (Luke 10:2–3).
"The angel said to the women, 'Do not be afraid, for I know that you

are looking for Jesus, who was crucified. He is not here; he has risen, just as he said. Come and see the place where he lay. Then *go* quickly and tell ...'" (Matt. 28:5–7).

"How, then, can they call on the one they have not believed in? And how can they believe in the one of whom they have not heard? And how can they hear without someone preaching to them? And how can they preach unless they are *sent*? As it is written, 'How beautiful are the feet of those who *bring* good news!'" (Rom. 10:14–15).

Why do you think God put such an emphasis on sending/going? What are some examples of how your church/ministry is effectively doing that? How can you take steps forward in sending/going?

4. "But you will receive power when the Holy Spirit comes on you; and you will be my witnesses in Jerusalem, and in all Judea and Samaria, and to the ends of the earth" (Acts 1:8). Do you believe Jesus meant for this mission to be accomplished in your lifetime? Why or why not?

5. Here's a great one-sentence summary of how the early believers approached the Jesus mission: "Day after day, in the temple courts and from house to house, they never stopped teaching and proclaiming the good news that Jesus is the Christ" (Acts 5:42). How does this verse challenge you when it comes to being on mission?

6. What groups of people in your community would likely never enter a church building? What would it take to reach them?

Move

Who is someone you could empower, inspire, and release so that God could use them where they're most influential to lead a missional team or 3C Community? Where might God be calling *you* to lead a missional team or 3C Community?

CHAPTER 8: REPRODUCING COACHES

Big Idea: The coach-leader relationship is crucial to sustaining a missional movement.

Open

When you think of someone who has been a great coach to you, who comes to mind? What made that person so impactful to you?

Explore

A coach is a leader of leaders whose intentional investment in the lives of other leaders encourages them, challenges them, and holds them accountable to grow in their skills as leaders and in their journeys as Christ followers. When the relationship is best, both the leader and the coach benefit by becoming more and more like Jesus, as well as by becoming more and more effective in fulfilling their God-given leadership responsibilities. Paul modeled this well with his leaders — he cared for them deeply, he encouraged and inspired them, and he was not afraid to challenge them with a high standard:

> Follow my example, as I follow the example of Christ. I praise you for remembering me in everything and for holding to the teachings, just as I passed them on to you.
>
> — 1 Corinthians 11:1–2

> I thank God, whom I serve, as my forefathers did, with a clear conscience, as night and day I constantly remember you in my prayers. Recalling your tears, I long to see you, so that I may be filled with joy. I have been reminded of your sincere faith, which first lived in your grandmother Lois and in your mother Eunice and, I am persuaded, now lives in you also.... But join with me in suffering for the gospel, by the power of God, who has saved us and called us to a holy life.... What you heard from me, keep as the pattern of sound teaching, with faith and love in Christ Jesus.
>
> — 2 Timothy 1:3–5, 8–9, 13

1. From the preceding Scripture verses, what impresses you most about Paul's relationship with those he was "coaching"? How can Paul's example impact how coaches are trained and developed in your church or ministry?
2. What are the biggest advantages of relying on volunteer coaches instead of paid staff? What are the challenges of this approach?
3. Why do you think relationship has to be at the center of the coaching model? What happens if it's not?
4. How can you help your leaders understand the value of and the vision behind coaching, rather than seeing it as "micromanaging" or "keeping an eye on"?
5. Share one story of a time when someone had an I-C-N-U conversation with you. How did it make you feel? How did you respond? When have you had an I-C-N-U conversation with someone else? How did it turn out?

Move

Commit to having at least one of the following three conversations with someone in the next week. Or really challenge yourself and commit to having all three!

1. Have an I-C-N-U conversation to empower/inspire someone to a vision.
2. Make a big ask (no mini-asks!) of someone to call them to their next level of leadership.
3. Have a truth-in-love conversation, especially the one you've been putting off that you know God wants you to have.

CHAPTER 9: REPRODUCING VENUES AND SITES

Big Idea: Launching new venues and sites accelerates the spread of a missional movement.

Open

If you could start your own business, what would it be? What geographic area or particular people group would you target?

Explore

Multisite is no longer limited to the most innovative or even fastest-growing churches. Multisite has become an option for any church seeking to accomplish the Jesus mission.

> The multisite movement will explode over the next few decades. Why? It is how the early church grew in the early centuries, and it is how the church is exploding in other parts of the world in cell and house churches. Churches with limited land and a Great Commission mindset will find multisite the most economic way to be faithful and grow.
>
> —Bill Easum, *Beyond the Box*

> Be wise in the way you act toward outsiders; make the most of every opportunity.
>
> —Colossians 4:5

> [Jesus] said to them, "Go into all the world and preach the good news to all creation."
>
> —Mark 16:15

1. Jesus' words in Mark 16 and Paul's words in Colossians 4 have a significant level of urgency about helping people find their way back to God. On a scale from 1 to 10, what is your current level of urgency?
2. What is one "God thing" you have seen in your life—an instance when you knew God was at work, so you followed?
3. Where do you think God might be at work right now in the community where you live? What might God be dreaming about there?

4. Which of the seven moves to multisite are you most confident about right now for your church or ministry? Which one do you anticipate will be the most challenging?

5. What is one opportunity in your life right now where you need to "lead with a yes"?

Move

Write down the seven moves to multisite in your journal (leaving space under each one to write). Now go through each one:

1. If you're past that move, write down how it was accomplished.

2. If you're not there yet, write down what it will mean to accomplish it, and a few ideas for how you think it can be done.

CHAPTER 10: REPRODUCING MULTIPLE SITES

Big Idea: Continual reproduction of sites increases the momentum of a missional movement.

Open

What franchise or chain do you wish would open a new location in your neighborhood or community?

Explore

Notice how in Acts, Paul saw the value of releasing and relying on his apprentices to help reach other regions:

> Afterward Paul felt compelled by the Spirit to go over to Macedonia and Achaia before going to Jerusalem. "And after that," he said, "I must go on to Rome!" *He sent his two assistants,* Timothy and Erastus, ahead to Macedonia while he stayed a while longer in the province of Asia.
>
> —Acts 19:21 – 23 (our paraphrase)

Paul also knew the "genius of the *and*" when it came to how to do church — he would reach people publicly in large gatherings *and* through smaller house gatherings:

> You know that I have not hesitated to preach anything that would be helpful to you but have *taught you publicly and from house to house.* I have declared to both Jews and Greeks that they must turn to God in repentance and have faith in our Lord Jesus.
>
> —Acts 20:20 – 21

1. What are some ways that the missional church movement in Acts reflects a multisite approach to church?
2. What do you see as the greatest advantages to the multisite approach? What do you see as the greatest challenges?
3. What are some topics churches wrestle with that they normally approach as an either/or issue but could benefit from thinking about it in terms of both/and?
4. Which of the benefits of multisite church mentioned (resources, excellence, marketing, diversity, geography, impact) is most important to you in your current ministry context?

Move

Spend some time working through the eight questions presented in this chapter. Write down your response for each one, discuss them with your team, and then spend some time praying over them.

CHAPTER 11: REPRODUCING CHURCHES

Big Idea: Launching new churches is foundational to spreading a missional movement.

Open

The apostle Paul uses the human body as a metaphor for the church and how it should function. What metaphors can you come up with for what the church was meant to be? (Humorous ones are allowed!)

Explore

When we look at the effectiveness of the church, particularly in the United States, the indicators are not encouraging. However, if there is a bright spot, a glimmer of hope, it is in the starting of new churches and sites.

> What, after all, is Apollos? And what is Paul? Only servants, through whom you came to believe—as the Lord has assigned to each his task. I planted the seed, Apollos watered it, but God made it grow. So neither he who plants nor he who waters is anything, but only God, who makes things grow. The man who plants and the man who waters have one purpose, and each will be rewarded according to his own labor. For we are God's fellow workers; you are God's field, God's building.
>
> —1 Corinthians 3:5–9

1. How would you state the "Big Idea" of Paul's words in 1 Corinthians 3:5–9? What do these words have to say to us about how we start new churches?

2. What excites you most about the idea of planting a church? What scares you most about the idea?

3. Consider Alan Hirsch's prediction: "We risk the eventual demise of Christianity as a religious force in Western history—witness Europe in the last hundred years." What is your reaction to this statement? Skeptical? Anxious? Overwhelmed? Motivated? Convicted?

4. What are the things you believe must change in the church in the United States in order not only to avoid the church's "eventual demise" but also to see it thrive once again?

5. It has been said that "the local church is the hope of the world." Do you believe this statement? Why or why not?

6. Check out Jesus' words in Revelation to the church in Ephesus: "I know your deeds, your hard work and your perseverance. I know that you cannot tolerate wicked men, that you have tested those who claim to be apostles but are not, and have found them false. You have persevered and have endured hardships for my name, and have not grown weary. Yet I hold this against you: You have forsaken your first love. Remember the height from which you have fallen! Repent and do the things you did at first" (Rev. 2:2–5). Notice the areas in which Jesus affirms and challenges this church. What is your reaction to these affirmations and challenges to the church in Ephesus? Would Jesus have similar words to say to you, or different ones? Explain.

Move

Pretend you are talking to a skeptical person who doesn't believe in Christ or the church. Articulate (either verbally or written down) your view of the church:

1. why the church exists (why God designed it that way)
2. what the church's primary mission/focus should be
3. how the church will survive and thrive from generation to generation

CHAPTER 12: REPRODUCING NETWORKS

Big Idea: Every missional movement has a reproducing infrastructure.

Open

What people movement from history would you like to have experienced up close and personal? If you have experienced one firsthand, share that experience.

Explore

For this reason I remind you to fan into flame the gift of God, which is in you through the laying on of my hands. For God did not give us a spirit of timidity, but a spirit of power, of love and of self-discipline.... And of this gospel I was appointed a *herald* and an *apostle* and a *teacher*.

—2 Timothy 1:6–7, 11

It was he who gave some to be *apostles*, some to be *prophets*, some to be *evangelists*, and some to be *pastors* and *teachers*, to prepare God's people for works of service, so that the body of Christ may be built up until we all reach unity in the faith and in the knowledge of the Son of God and become mature, attaining to the whole measure of the fullness of Christ.

—Ephesians 4:11–13

Forget the former things; do not dwell on the past. See, I am doing a *new thing*! Now it springs up; do you not perceive it? I am *making a way* in the desert and streams in the wasteland.

—Isaiah 43:18–19

1. What do you think is the single most important factor for rapid, consistent reproduction of an idea or a mission?
2. What are the biggest advantages of decentralizing an organization or mission? What are the biggest challenges/risks in doing that?
3. In Ephesians 4 and 2 Timothy 1 Paul references apostles. Who are some people you would consider to be apostolic leaders? (It's okay to answer yourself!) Explain why you chose them.
4. If you could accomplish anything for God, and he told you ahead of time that it would succeed, what would you try?

Move

Pray about, think through, and then write down your responses to these two statements:

1. If God moves in the heart of (insert name here) to join me in this mission, I would welcome him/her to join me.
2. If God will just do (insert challenge here), that will be a sign to me that he is in this movement and wants me to move forward.

CHAPTER 13: A REPRODUCING MOVEMENT

Big Idea: A missional movement has a momentum empowered by God's Spirit.

Open

Share the story of a time when God accomplished something through you that you never would have thought was possible. (No answer is too small—it's all big!)

Explore

The challenge of leading a movement is great. But remember, you can do it! The missional movement that Jesus dreamed of was meant to be started and spread by people just like you and your friends. The opportunity to get distracted by the lesser good or tremendous evil will be there. But to lead a movement, you must make sure the vision is vivid, the systems are simple, and the reproduction is rapid. It will mean some huge shifts. You will have to love going more than staying. You will need to have a bias for the risk of being on the edge rather than for the safety of being in the center. You will have to have a burden for the lost that you don't have for the found. If you can make those shifts, you are ready to start moving!

> You will receive power when the Holy Spirit comes on you; and you will be my witnesses in Jerusalem, and in all Judea and Samaria, and to the ends of the earth.
>
> —Acts 1:8

> Then Jesus came to them and said, "All authority in heaven and on earth has been given to me. Therefore go and make disciples of all nations, baptizing them in the name of the Father and of the Son and of the Holy Spirit, and teaching them to obey everything I have commanded you. And surely I am with you always, to the very end of the age."
>
> —Matthew 28:18–20

> I thank my God every time I remember you. In all my prayers for all of you, I always pray with joy because of your partnership in the gospel from the first day until now, being confident of this, that he who began a good work in you will carry it on to completion until the day of Christ Jesus.
>
> —Philippians 1:3–6

> "I know the plans I have for you," declares the LORD, "plans to prosper you and not to harm you, plans to give you hope and a future. Then you will call upon me and come and pray to me, and I will listen to you. You will seek me and find me when you seek me with all your heart."
>
> —Jeremiah 29:11–13

1. Which of the above promises from God about his mission for you is most inspiring? Why?

2. Think about the first three major factors for rapid reproduction that we covered in this chapter: consistent prayer, evangelism, training leaders. Rate your current church/ministry on a scale of 1 ("we barely do this") to 10 ("we consistently do this really well").

3. Now rate yourself personally on the same 1 to 10 scale in each of those three areas

4. It's easy to think of reasons why we don't believe God could really start a movement through us. What do you think are the top two reasons people would most often cite? What do you think God would say to those reasons?

5. Deep in your gut, how do you think God wants to work through you to start and spread a missional church movement?

Move

If you haven't yet done the action step from chapter 1, do it now: grab your journal (or a napkin!), write down your God-inspired dream, and share it with someone.

Now commit to spending focused time every day for the next seven days praying about it. Consider fasting for a period of time as well. Ask God to confirm the dream, to clarify his vision for you, to give you all the courage and faith to carry it out, and to show you the next steps.

NOTES

1. Ram Charan, *Leaders at All Levels* (San Francisco: Jossey-Bass, 2007), 25.
2. A 3C Christ follower is someone who is growing in three experiences: Celebrate, which is primarily about our relationship with God; Connect, which is primarily about our relationship with the church; and Contribute, which is primarily about our relationship with the world.
3. Neil Cole, *Organic Leadership* (Grand Rapids: Baker, 2009), 259–60.
4. Charan, *Leaders at All Levels*, 2.
5. Richard Florida, *The Rise of the Creative Class* (New York: Basic, 2002), 218.
6. Ibid., 242.
7. George A. Kaplan, "Alameda County [California] Health and Ways of Living Study, 1974 Panel" (Berkeley, Calif.: Human Population Laboratory, California Dept. of Health Services [producer], 1974; Ann Arbor, Mich.: Inter-university Consortium for Political and Social Research [distributor], January 1, 2008). Computer file, ICPSR06838-v2. doi:10.3886/ICPSR06838.
8. Dallas Willard, *The Divine Conspiracy* (New York: HarperCollins, 1998), 386.
9. These questions were inspired by a talk I heard Andy Stanley give.
10. Joseph Myers, *Organic Community* (Grand Rapids: Baker, 2007), 41–48.
11. Nelson Searcy, *Activate* (Ventura, CA: Regal, 2008), 33.
12. Joel Comiskey, *Home Cell Group Explosion* (Houston: Touch Publications, 1998), 33–94.
13. Mike Krzyzewski, *Leading with the Heart* (New York: Warner Business Books, 2000), 161.
14. "Multi-Site Churches: A New Variety of Religious Experience," *USA Today*, December 16, 2009.
15. According to *Outreach* magazine.
16. "Multi-Site Churches," *USA Today*.
17. *Outreach* magazine.

18. Bill Easum, *Beyond the Box* (Loveland, CO: Group, 2003).
19. David Olson, *The American Church in Crisis* (Grand Rapids: Zondervan, 2008).
20. Ibid.
21. Ibid.
22. Alan Hirsh, *The Forgotten Ways* (Grand Rapids: Baker, 2006), 151.
23. Ori Brafman and Rod Beckstrom, *The Starfish and the Spider* (London: Penguin, 2006), 206.
24. Hirsh, *The Forgotten Ways*, 223.
25. Stephen Covey, *The Speed of Trust* (New York: Free Press, 2006), table of contents quote by Marcus Buckingham.
26. Neil Cole, *Organic Church* (San Francisco: Jossey-Bass, 2005), 26.
27. Rodney Stark, *The Rise of Christianity* (San Francisco: HarperSanFrancisco, 1996), 4.
28. Ibid.
29. Seth Godin, *Tribes* (London: Penguin, 2008), 103.

Dave Ferguson is a spiritual entrepreneur and the lead pastor of Community Christian Church, an innovative multisite missional church with eleven locations in Chicago. Dave is the movement leader for NewThing, an international network of reproducing churches. He is also the coauthor of *The Big Idea*. Check out the latest from Dave on his blog (*www.daveferguson.org*) or follow his everyday adventures on twitter *@daveferguson*.

Jon Ferguson is the cofounding pastor of Community Christian Church. He serves as teaching pastor and leads the team of executive staff champions for adult, student, children's, and creative arts ministries across all CCC locations. Jon is the cofounder and movement architect of NewThing (*www.newthing.org*). He also serves on the boards of the Exponential Network and Stadia East. Jon previously coauthored *The Big Idea* with Dave Ferguson.

About the Exponential Series

The interest in church planting has grown significantly in recent years. The need for new churches has never been greater. At the same time, the number of models and approaches are expanding. To address the unique opportunities of churches in this landscape, Exponential Network, in partnership with Leadership Network and Zondervan, presents the Exponential Series.

Books in this series:

- Tell the reproducing church story.
- Celebrate the diversity of models and approaches God is using to reproduce healthy congregations.
- Highlight the innovative and pioneering practices of healthy reproducing churches.
- Equip, inspire, and challenge kingdom-minded leaders with the tools they need in their journey of becoming reproducing church leaders.

Exponential (*www.exponentialnetwork.com*) exists to attract, inspire, and equip kingdom-minded leaders to engage in a movement of high-impact, reproducing churches. We provide a national voice for this movement through the Exponential Conference, the Exponential Initiative, Exponential Venture, and the Exponential Series.

Leadership Network (*www.leadnet.org*), an initiative of OneHundredX, exists to honor God and serve others by investing in innovative churches. Our goal is to help those leaders and organizations refine their strategies and accelerate their own innovations.

For more information about the Exponential Series, go to *www.exponential series.org*.

About Leadership Network

Since 1984, Leadership Network has fostered church innovation and growth by diligently pursuing its far-reaching mission statement: *To identify high-capacity Christian leaders, to connect them with other leaders, and to help them multiply their impact.*

While specific techniques may vary as the church faces new opportunities and challenges, Leadership Network consistently focuses on bringing together entrepreneurial leaders who are pursuing similar ministry initiatives. The resulting peer-to-peer interaction, dialogue, and collaboration — often across denominational lines — helps these leaders better refine their individual strategies and accelerate their own innovations.

To further enhance this process, Leadership Network develops and distributes highly targeted ministry tools and resources, including books, DVDs and videotapes, special reports, e-publications, and free downloads.

For additional information on the mission or activities of Leadership Network, please contact:

LEADERSHIP NETWORK®

800-765-5323 • www.leadnet.org • client.care@leadnet.org

Kind of like this

You've got a regular plant and then you've got NewThing. We're more than an individual thing; we're a conversation, a connection, a relationship, a culture... What we're doing is bigger than the original. It's more powerful, more messy, and a ton more fun. And you could be a part of it. Become a leadership resident and get everything you need to plant a church, develop artists or even lead a network. This isn't just any thing, **it's a new thing.**

Introducing Multi-Site Training On-Line

Designed for those who are currently a multi-site church or considering the multi-site option. Customize and select the training your team needs to reproduce leaders, artists and campuses.

new thing
www.newthing.org

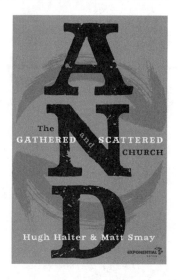

Share Your Thoughts

With the Author: Your comments will be forwarded to the author when you send them to *zauthor@zondervan.com*.

With Zondervan: Submit your review of this book by writing to *zreview@zondervan.com*.

Free Online Resources at
www.zondervan.com

Zondervan AuthorTracker: Be notified whenever your favorite authors publish new books, go on tour, or post an update about what's happening in their lives at www.zondervan.com/authortracker.

Daily Bible Verses and Devotions: Enrich your life with daily Bible verses or devotions that help you start every morning focused on God. Visit www.zondervan.com/newsletters.

Free Email Publications: Sign up for newsletters on Christian living, academic resources, church ministry, fiction, children's resources, and more. Visit www.zondervan.com/newsletters.

Zondervan Bible Search: Find and compare Bible passages in a variety of translations at www.zondervanbiblesearch.com.

Other Benefits: Register yourself to receive online benefits like coupons and special offers, or to participate in research.